TO MICHAEL –
THANK YOU FOR LEADING
THE WAY TO BETTER
HEALTH + NUTRITION TO
ALL IN TURKANA!

THE FIRST
1,000 DAYS

*A Crucial Time for Mothers
and Children—And the World*

Roger Thurow

THE CHICAGO COUNCIL
ON GLOBAL AFFAIRS

PUBLICAFFAIRS
New York

Published in the United States by PublicAffairs™, a Member of the Perseus Books Group
All rights reserved.
Printed in the United States of America.

PublicAffairs books are available at special discounts for bulk purchases in the U.S. by corporations, institutions, and other organizations. For more information, please contact the Special Markets Department at the Perseus Books Group, 2300 Chestnut Street, Suite 200, Philadelphia, PA 19103, call (800) 810-4145, ext. 5000, or e-mail special.markets@perseusbooks.com.

Book design by Linda Mark

Library of Congress Cataloging-in-Publication Data
Names: Thurow, Roger, author.
Title: The first 1,000 days : a crucial time for mothers and children—and the
    world / Roger Thurow.
Other titles: First thousand days
Description: First Edition. | New York : PublicAffairs, 2016.
Identifiers: LCCN 2015050285 (print) | LCCN 2016002750 (ebook) |
    ISBN 9781610395854 (hardback) | ISBN 9781610395861 (ebook)
Subjects: LCSH: Infants—Nutrition—Case studies. | Infants—Health and
    hygiene—Case studies. | BISAC: FAMILY & RELATIONSHIPS / Life Stages /
    Infants & Toddlers. | PSYCHOLOGY / Developmental / Child. | FAMILY &
    RELATIONSHIPS / Parenting / General.
Classification: LCC RJ216 .T48 2016 (print) | LCC RJ216 (ebook) | DDC
    618.92/02—dc23
First Edition

10 9 8 7 6 5 4 3 2 1

THE FIRST
1,000 DAYS

For Laura, Anne, May,
and Moms Everywhere

CONTENTS

PART FOUR | THE SECOND YEAR

Photographs follow page 152

THE FIRST
1,000 DAYS

INTRODUCTION TO A MOVEMENT

"YOUR CHILD CAN ACHIEVE GREAT THINGS."

Two young women on opposite sides of the world—one in northern Uganda, one on the South Side of Chicago—heard these words and dearly hoped they could be true. Both were pregnant, five months or so, and anxious about doing their best for their first child. But greatness? It was an audacious thought, given their surroundings. Esther Okwir, a tall, lithe twenty-year-old, was fresh from the fields of her family's small farm in the bush outside the Ugandan town of Lira, where mere survival was a lofty achievement in a harsh climate for both agriculture and peace. Jessica Saldana, an athletic, scholarly teenager, was preparing to begin her junior year at one of Chicago's lowest-achieving high schools in an impoverished, worn-out neighborhood that too often, for too many kids, had proved to be a dead-end for ambition.

Esther's imagination soared as she sat on the concrete floor of a veranda stretching beyond the maternity ward of the local health post. She was joined by three dozen other moms-to-be and new moms. They crowded together under a tin awning, seeking refuge from a relentless noonday sun that pushed the temperature toward 100. Esther, barefoot,

1

had walked a mile along the dirt road from her home to be there. She was grateful for the rest, the shade, the occasional puff of wind. Most of all, she was grateful for the lesson that began to unfold: a primer on maternal and infant health care.

"This time is very important to you as mothers and to your children," began Susan Ejang, the midwife at the clinic and a mom herself. Despite the heat, she had wrapped herself in a white lab coat, believing it added authority to her words. "The time of your pregnancy and the first two years of your child's life will determine the health of your child, the ability to learn in school, to perform at a future job. This is the time the brain grows most." This time, Susan told the moms, is precious and fleeting, "just 1,000 days from the beginning of your pregnancy to your child's second birthday."

Susan knew what was at stake, for it is in these 1,000 days when stunting, mentally or physically or both, begins. In the second decade of the twenty-first century, one of every four children under the age of five in the world was stunted—about 170 million children in total, according to the World Health Organization. That astonishing number included more than 2 million children in Uganda. A child who is severely stunted is sentenced to a life of underachievement: diminished performance in school, lower productivity and wages in the workplace, more health problems throughout life, and a greater propensity for chronic illnesses such as diabetes and heart disease as an adult. And that life sentence is most often rendered by the time a child is two. For stunting is largely the result of a debilitating mix of poor nutrition, unclean environments, and lack of caregiver stimulation during the 1,000 days.

So Susan hammered home her messages. Get good rest, she insisted. Don't stress. Get the required vaccinations for you and your child. Boil your drinking water. Wash your hands after every visit to the toilet. Cover your food to keep the flies away and to keep the parasites and bacteria out of your body. Sleep under mosquito bed nets to ward off malaria. Come to the clinic to deliver the baby. Breastfeed for at least six months. Don't even think about getting pregnant again for two years; you must focus on this child.

Esther and the women savored every morsel of advice—new and profound for them—and murmured agreement. "Yes, yes," they promised.

They had grown up during the murderous madness of warlord Joseph Kony and his Lord's Resistance Army—years of terror when it was folly to think of potential greatness. But Kony was gone now and these moms wanted to believe that they could make a difference in the healthy, successful development of their children. They were eager listeners.

"Now," Susan continued, "this is most important. You must learn to eat a balanced diet and cook properly." She disappeared momentarily into the maternity ward, a cinder-block room sparsely furnished with several metal-frame beds covered by flimsy mattresses and threadbare sheets. It was here, in this clinic with no running water, no lights in the middle of the night, no modern medical equipment, where most of the women now gathered on the veranda would give birth. Susan returned carrying a stack of colorful posters featuring luscious foods and lists of the nutrients within them.

"Vegetables, fruits, proteins, carbohydrates. Eggs, green vegetables, pumpkin, bananas. Do you have these things at home?" Susan asked, pointing to the pictures of the foods. "Yes, you have these things at home. They are all around us. You and your children need a mix of everything. Proper nutrition helps the body and the brain grow. It prevents stunting."

Zinc, folate, iodine, iron—she rattled off the vital nutrients, strange words to many of the mothers. A, B, C, D, E—she recited an alphabet of essential vitamins, foreign letters to those moms who couldn't read.

Susan lifted a final poster for all to see. "The importance of Vitamin A!," it proclaimed above a series of drawings charting the growth of a child from baby to toddler to robust boy playing soccer. "If you eat foods rich in vitamin A, you will have active children like this one," Susan said. "If you eat foods rich in iron, your children will be bright in class. All your children are important. Every one of them. You take good care in these days, and your child won't be malnourished. Your child can achieve great things."

She let that thought hang in the hot, heavy air.

"Maybe you will give birth to a president," she said with a big smile. She was only half-joking. By raising lofty aspirations, Susan wanted to give the moms even more incentive to follow her advice. "Yes, the president of our country may come from this group."

Another wave of murmurs—louder this time, more excited—rolled across the veranda. Some of the women clapped, others whooped with glee. Imaginations were on fire. Esther, smiling broadly, envisioned her child being a success in business, perhaps a manager or president of a company, if not president of the entire country. That would really be something, she thought. That would be her dream come true.

IN CHICAGO, JESSICA, too, dreamed of the possibilities for her child. "I see her being an honor student. I see her playing sports, like me. And there will be music in her life, maybe playing the violin," she told Patricia Ceja Muhsen, a *doula*, a guide through her pregnancy who visited every week.

Patricia smiled as Jessica's words tumbled out. "You want your child to have the best chance in life to do great things, right?" she asked. Jessica nodded. "Well, it all begins now." Patricia, too, zeroed in on the 1,000 days, when mothers' dreams begin to be fulfilled—or dashed.

They were in a community center just off Michigan Avenue, less than six miles south of Chicago's famed Magnificent Mile of chic commerce and fine dining. There was no window shopping here, though; many of the windows in the buildings on this stretch were boarded up. Across the street from the community center was an open field where once stood a section of the Robert Taylor Homes, one of Chicago's most notorious housing projects before its demolition. News reports were emerging that President Barack Obama's presidential library would be located just a couple of miles from here at the University of Chicago, near his old home. That would certainly be a monument to great possibilities. But a couple of miles in another direction were some of the most violent neighborhoods in the United States—Chi-raq, some were calling them. On those forbidding streets, the potential for achievement didn't mean a thing. Life itself was cheap, too often ended by a bullet, intended or stray.

Patricia's message on the importance of nutrition, cleanliness, and exercise in the 1,000 days was the same as Susan's in Uganda. And, similarly, it was new information for sixteen-year-old Jessica, for it certainly wasn't covered in any of her high school classes. "You know you have to eat better for you and your baby," Patricia reminded Jessica. "We've talked a lot about eating fruits and vegetables. What about apples, bananas? Are you eating them?"

"I had mashed potatoes for lunch," Jessica said.

Actually, her boyfriend, Marco Ortega, corrected, *he* had the potatoes. Marco was sitting beside Jessica, holding her hand. "You had a chocolate-chip cookie that you dipped into the potatoes," he said.

"Weird cravings," Jessica conceded.

She smiled and shrugged and confessed her nutritional sins. "I'm addicted to Flamin' Hots," she said, referring to the spicy Cheetos product wildly popular among teenagers. Most days, she didn't bother eating at school—"no time, and the food's nasty," she insisted—even though a government program provided free breakfast and lunch to students from low-income families. After the last bell, she and Marco would often grab a cheeseburger at McDonald's or Burger King, two of the many fast-food joints tempting students within blocks of the school. The burgers were cheaper than the salads, she told Patricia. And then there's the chocolate. "I love Snickers," Jessica said.

Patricia, who knew Jessica was fighting against a strong cultural and commercial pull that favored Cheetos over carrots, had heard it all before in her work with new mothers: one mom saying the only way she knew how to cook chicken was deep-fried; moms filling baby bottles with Coca-Cola or Kool-Aid because it was cheaper than milk; infants chewing on fatty pork ribs once they started eating solid foods. She was determined that Jessica would do better, warning that obesity was also a form of malnutrition with dangerous consequences for mother and child. Every meeting, they practiced exercises and prepared for birth, but mainly they talked about good nutrition. They read labels, with Patricia going over the same nutrients and vitamins that Susan had listed in Uganda. Patricia brought samples of healthy snacks to her meetings with moms. A kiwi, a granola bar, grapes. This time she came with sandwiches: turkey, beef, vegetarian.

Jessica and Marco looked suspiciously at the peppers, eggplant, and lettuce in the vegetarian offering. "What's *that*?" Jessica asked with a scrunched-up face.

They chose the turkey. "Very good," said Patricia.

Jessica took a few bites and wrapped up the remainder of the sandwich. "I'll eat it later at home," she said. "I promise."

At home, in her mother's brick bungalow three blocks from her high school, Jessica compiled a catalog of promises in her diary. In letters to her unborn baby, she confided her hopes and fears. An ultrasound had indicated she was carrying a daughter, and Jessica believed she had selected the perfect name: Alitzel. "It sounds important, unique and one of a kind," Jessica wrote to her daughter. In another entry, she assigned a dream characteristic—her imagined ingredients of a successful personality and life—to each letter of the name:

> A is for amenable, for your easy going nature.
> L is for luster, your shine.
> I is for inspire, others to seek your guidance.
> T is for traditional, somewhat old fashioned.
> Z is for zany, the funny side of you.
> E is for enrich, a quality you have.
> L is for love, everlasting.

Jessica knew she had a lot of work to do in the 1,000 days to lay the foundation for her daughter to reach all that was possible. She penned a promise to her daughter and surrounded it with hearts:

> *I'll give up everything for you, to make you happy, to love you, to give you everything you deserve.*
> *I love you forever, Mommy.*

EVERY CHILD DESERVES a chance to reach his or her full potential. This is the most widely shared human aspiration: the hope for every child who comes into this world to develop the good health, strength of body, and intellectual capacity to achieve all that is possible. It is at the top of the wish list for mothers, fathers, and grandparents everywhere, and matters even to those without any children of their own. We want this not only for the sake of the individual child, but for the sake of us all. For who knows what any child might one day contribute to our common good?

Achieving great things, of course, plays out over a lifetime, and in its own special way for each individual. It could be learning to read in a mainly illiterate community. Being first in the family to finish primary school, or graduate from high school, or attend college. Managing a shop. Supporting the family. Making people happy. Serving the community. Even growing up to be president.

As Esther and Jessica came to learn, it is in the first 1,000 days of life that the stage is set for fulfilling individual potential. This is the time, science tells us, when the brain develops most rapidly and robustly, when the immune system is bolstered, when the foundation of physical growth is laid. But this is also the time, reality shows us, when potential can be undermined by the perils of a mosquito bite or a sip of dirty water (malaria and diarrhea, along with malnutrition, being the greatest threats to child development); by the lack of something taken for granted in the wealthy world, like a toilet or electricity; by discrimination and ignorance.

If we want to shape the future, to truly improve the world, we have 1,000 days to do it, mother by mother, child by child. For what happens in those 1,000 days through pregnancy to the second birthday determines to a large extent the course of a child's life—his or her ability to grow, learn, work, succeed—and, by extension, the long-term health, stability, and prosperity of the society in which that child lives.

Then why don't we? Why do we continue to squander so much potential greatness? The simple, practical advice Susan and Patricia provided to moms and moms-to-be about how to avoid stunting should be a global no-brainer. Good nutrition is the indispensable fuel of growth and development, particularly in the 1,000 days; it is the accelerant of a good start in life. Babies growing in the womb receive all nutrients from their mother. If she lacks key vitamins and minerals in her diet for her own health, so will her baby. For infants, mom's breastmilk provides an array of vital micronutrients and an early immunization against illness and disease that helps fortify the body. Once complementary feeding begins, usually around six months of age, healthy foods ensure continued growth and brain development. Foods introduced at this time also shape a child's life-long relationship to food and the body's reaction to it. Any prolonged shortage of food or persistent lack of vital micronutrients such as iron, zinc, iodine, and vitamin A in the 1,000 days can set back growth and development, sometimes irreversibly. So, too, can repeated bouts of diarrhea that take nutrients out of the body, or an intestinal infection of worms or parasites that prevent the body from absorbing the minerals and vitamins it needs—making clean water, proper hygiene, adequate sanitation, and access to basic health care vital accompaniments to good nutrition.

As obvious and time-worn as all this may seem to educated people in wealthier societies, both the knowledge and its practice remain revolutionary in many places in our world today, whether in Africa, Asia, or the Americas. The commonsense messages of Susan and Patricia are rarely heard, and even more rarely put into play. While the world made dramatic progress on one front, reducing the mortality rate among children under five by 50 percent between 1990 and 2012—thanks largely to the widespread deployment of vaccines, malaria bed nets, and other health innovations—the neonatal mortality rate (deaths in the first month after birth) decreased less dramatically, by only about one-third over the same period. As a result of a lack of attention to the 1,000 days, newborn deaths accounted for a stunning 44 percent of total mortality among children under five in 2012 (that's nearly 3 million babies each year) and represented a larger proportion of under-five deaths now than they did in 1990, according to the United Nations Children Fund, UNICEF. And nearly 300,000 mothers die every year while giving life. Almost all of these deaths, child and mother, are from preventable causes—meaning, preventable in the richer precincts of the world.

The 1,000-day period has always existed, of course, but it has never been the center of attention in public policy. World health and development organizations have in the past usually fixated on age five and primary school as milestone targets for intervention. Getting children into school—universal primary education—has long been a holy grail of successful development, while ensuring proper brain growth and cognitive development in the first 1,000 days—so children are actually capable of learning once they get there—has largely been neglected. In the United States, national Dietary Guidelines have been directed to children age two and up, with a particular focus on school-age children. Interventions to prevent undernutrition, such as school feeding programs, and initiatives to lower obesity rates have also centered on primary school rather than on the 1,000 days when the consequences of malnutrition are most severe and the preconditions for obesity are forming.

Nutrition, which works silently and internally, has long been the neglected stepchild of international development—part agriculture, part health, but disdainfully disowned by both fields. Agriculture's practitioners have often believed their main task to be the production of ever-increasing yields; concerns about the nutritious quality of the food have been dismissed as a nuisance that could only interfere with quantity. And the health ministries of the world have been in a constant chase of dollars to combat the disease *du jour*, desperately scrounging for the resources to vaccinate mothers and children; providing proper nourishment was not their bailiwick. Nutrition? Not our responsibility—it was the one thing agriculture and health ministers could agree on. The leading development organizations also did little to elevate nutrition's profile. For years, nutrition experts were an endangered species in the Washington, DC, hallways of the World Bank, the largest poverty reduction agency. In past decades, less than 1 percent of total international development aid has been spent on nutrition. It was an illogical imbalance: nutrition was everywhere in human development, but virtually nowhere in development strategies.

And so it is that the ancient scourge of malnutrition persists as our planet's most pressing threat to health and prosperity. As I write this in the autumn of 2015, more than half of the world's 7 billion people are malnourished in some way, according to the World Health Organization and the United Nations Food and Agriculture Organization. About 800 million are chronically hungry, enduring a daily grind without sufficient food and calories to maintain an active and healthy life. Two billion people are considered to be micronutrient deficient; it is called "hidden hunger," for the absence of vital vitamins and minerals is largely imperceptible, and certainly less graphic than the bloated bellies and stick-figure limbs and hollow eyes of famine victims, but it can be just as deadly and devastating. At the other extreme of malnutrition, another 2 billion people are overweight or obese. For many of them, their bodies are both over- *and* under-nourished (they are over-consuming calories, but under-consuming healthy nutrients). Malnutrition is responsible for nearly half of all deaths of children under five worldwide and is a main culprit behind many adult chronic diseases. And it all begins in the first 1,000 days.

If it once was easy—or convenient, at least—to ignore the fate of a single child, to compartmentalize malnutrition and stunting as sad problems "over there" somewhere, it is no longer. Malnutrition has not only gone big, it has gone global. A stunted child in Africa is a stunted child everywhere, as the impact, particularly the economic cost, rolls through time and across societies and around the world like the ripples that spread from a single pebble cast into a pond.

It begins with the individual. A child with stunted cognitive development has difficulty learning in school and drops out early, which diminishes the child's prospect for success in the labor force. A study in eastern Guatemala that now spans five decades has found that children who were well nourished in the 1,000 days completed a couple more grades of school than malnourished children. As adults, the better-nourished group earned 20 to 40 percent more in wages, and they were less likely to develop a chronic illness.

Next, the impact spreads to the family of the stunted child, who will likely earn less than a full wage and incur higher health-care costs than would otherwise be necessary, making the family's climb out of poverty that much more difficult. For many families, the impact of malnutrition and stunting steamrolls through the generations in an accumulation of historical insults: stunted girls grow up to be stunted women who give birth to underweight babies. The cycle spins on.

The ripples from stunting then widen to engulf the community, for where there is one malnourished child, there are certainly more. Labor pools are depleted, productivity is sapped, economic growth lags. In the same way, entire countries and continents are crippled. Nations with high child stunting rates—in more than seventy countries, at least 20 percent of children are stunted—calculate that they annually lose between 5 percent (Guatemala and Uganda) and 16 percent (Ethiopia) of their gross domestic product to low labor productivity, high health-care expenditures, and other impacts of malnutrition. Sub-Saharan Africa and South Asia—where aggregate malnutrition stands at about 40 percent and stunting is the highest in the world—each lose an estimated 11 percent of gross national product every year, according to the first-ever *Global Nutrition Report*, introduced in 2014 by Lawrence Haddad, senior research fellow at the International Food Policy Research Institute.

Why do some countries and regions of the world remain poor? Because their mothers and children are malnourished and stunted. They have a lousy first 1,000 days.

The impact of malnutrition in the 1,000 days isn't limited to the poorest places on the planet, the *Global Nutrition Report* makes clear. China and India, the world's two most populous countries, both important drivers of the global economy, are experiencing a significant and escalating impact. For all its billionaire businessmen, high-tech progress, and Bollywood glamor, India has some of the world's highest stunting and malnutrition rates; about half of its children younger than five have low height and weight for their ages. Those physical measures are often signifiers of diminished mental development as well. India's geopolitical position and potential economic power reside in its immense population—more babies are born in India every year than anywhere else—and the demographic dividend it should reap as all these children go to school and become well-educated working adults. But because so many of those children are born underweight to malnourished moms and grow up stunted, carrying the penalties of a poor first 1,000 days throughout their lives, that demographic dividend threatens to become a demographic disaster.

Similarly, obesity is beginning to weigh heavily on national economies. Because stunted children have a higher propensity to be obese as adults (their bodies are conditioned to conserve calories and fat), India now also has one of the fastest-growing obesity rates in the world. It is an emerging phenomenon: the crippling double-burden of malnutrition. In China, a country once plagued by famine and vast hunger, the future economic costs of obesity are projected to more than double, rising from 4 percent of gross national product in 2000 to 9 percent in 2025. And in the United States, where obesity rates have more than doubled in adults and children since the 1970s, the burden has become a leading public health problem, with escalating cases of diabetes and other chronic diseases as well as burgeoning health-care costs. The *Global Nutrition Report* highlighted a peculiar American paradox: while two-thirds of adults and nearly one-third of children and adolescents are overweight or obese, about 15 percent of households are food insecure, which means that at some point in the year they are uncertain they can afford the next meal.

One in every five children is in a family dependent on food stamps; for them, meals often consist of the cheapest food available, which usually means the least nutritious. In 2014, hunger and food insecurity increased health expenditures in the United States by at least $160 billion, according to a study by researchers John T. Cook and Ana Paula Poblacion published in Bread for the World Institute's annual hunger report. No country in the world, no matter how rich or mighty, is immune to the insidious impact of malnutrition.

Which brings us to the final ripple: the cumulative toll of these individual, family, community, and national costs imposes a significant drag on global productivity, international trade, and health care, stunting the world economy by as much as 5 percent. That's the equivalent of several trillion dollars in economic activity, squandered every year.

Those are big numbers. But perhaps the greatest costs of malnutrition and stunting are immeasurable: A poem not written. A song not sung. A novel not imagined. A gadget not invented. A building not designed. A mystery not solved. A horizon not explored. An idea not formed. An inspiration not shared. An innovation not nurtured. A cure not discovered. A kindness not done.

What might a child have contributed to the world if he or she hadn't been stunted in the 1,000 days? A lost chance at greatness for one is a lost chance for all.

THAT WE MIGHT be missing something truly valuable in our neglect of nutrition and the first 1,000 days—that, in fact, we might be doing our world great harm—didn't really register until the dawn of the twenty-first century. Threats to the planet were piling up at the threshold of the new millennium: overpopulation, water shortages, armed conflict, climate change, infectious disease, chronic disease, diminishing biodiversity, environmental degradation, an increasing tempo of natural disasters. In the shadow of such impending doom, a Danish political scientist and environmental analyst named Bjorn Lomborg pondered this question: If we had an extra $50 billion to improve the state of the world, which problem would we solve first to the greatest effect? He challenged economists and development thinkers around the world to ponder with him, to examine the great problems of the day (especially those not making the television news), assess the costs to global society, draft solutions, calculate the benefits, and rank them in the order of potential effectiveness. The goal was to help decision-makers and philanthropists set priorities for their work and thereby ensure better living conditions as well as greater security and prosperity across the world. Dozens of teams of researchers, eager to stake a claim of expertise on the world's greatest problem, scrambled into action. Emails circumnavigated the globe. Evidence was compiled. Papers were written. A group of Nobel-laureate economists was assembled to analyze it all. In early 2004, they gathered in a stately house on the Copenhagen harbor and pored through the papers, quizzed the authors, and came to some conclusions, to be known henceforth as the Copenhagen Consensus. The top priority: develop new measures to control and treat HIV/AIDS. Few were surprised by this, for AIDS was devastating countries and economies in southern Africa and advancing across the world. But the second priority—a close second—shocked the development community and Lomborg himself: attack malnutrition, especially micronutrient deficiency, particularly in the early years of life. The Nobel laureates pointed to an "exceptionally high" benefit-to-cost ratio of providing micronutrients to conquer diseases caused by iron, zinc, iodine, and vitamin A deficiencies, diseases that were cumulatively weakening and impoverishing the planet. The group agreed to reconvene every four years to reassess global priorities.

In the meantime, a worry that had long ago subsided suddenly re-emerged: the threat that food consumption would outstrip food production. Under pressure from an expanding population, the changing dietary habits of a growing global middle class, and an increase in the practice of turning foods into biofuels, stockpiles of the world's major grains had dwindled to their lowest levels in generations. Prices soared with the shortages. By 2007, a full-blown food crisis gripped the world. Food riots rocked dozens of nations. In a dramatic reversal of the steady decline of previous decades, the number of chronically hungry people rocketed past 1 billion.

Josette Sheeran, then the executive director of the World Food Program (WFP), the United Nations agency charged with feeding the swelling ranks of the hungry and preventing mass starvation, barnstormed the world with a red plastic cup. It was representative of a measure of school feeding rations for millions of children in the developing world. She waved the cup in front of parliaments and television cameras, in finance ministries and health ministries as well as in the wheat and corn pits at the Board of Trade in Chicago where commodity prices were set. The food crisis was leaving the cup half empty, she argued; the WFP urgently needed more money to fill it. She also waved a black-and-white photo. It was a brain scan of a malnourished, stunted child. There were white spots that should be darker, truncated branches of connected neurons that should be longer. Look at what malnutrition is doing to our future, Sheeran said. It is limiting our children, squandering their potential. Look!

The World Bank had finally opened its eyes. One of the bank's lonely nutritionists, Meera Shekar, a petite woman with towering persistence, had authored a report called *Repositioning Nutrition as Central to Development: A Strategy for Large-Scale Action*. That was in 2006. It would likely have been consigned to the heap of World Bank documents collecting dust but for the escalating food crisis. The report insisted that improved nutrition be considered a public good that benefited everyone, just like malnutrition was a shared burden. "The unequivocal choice now," the report proclaimed, "is between continuing to fail, as the global community did with HIV/AIDS for more than a decade, or to finally make nutrition central to development so that a wide range of economic and social improvements that depend on nutrition can be realized."

Shekar's jeremiad mirrored what was happening on the ground, and, like Sheeran's pleas, they struck a nerve. The World Bank's new president at the time, Robert Zoellick, gave the report traction. A banking and international trade specialist, Zoellick began speaking of cognitive stunting in economic terms, referring to diminished "human capital formation." And he talked about the most important period in developing that human capital, which he called "minus nine to 24 months." It was a clunky label, but Shekar refined it. She stated, eloquently and bluntly, that "undernutrition's most damaging effect occurs during pregnancy and in the first two years of life," and that "the effects of this early damage on health, brain development, intelligence, educability, and productivity are largely irreversible."

It was the clamor of flinty-eyed number-crunchers and their cold-blooded institutions, rather than the humanitarian crusades of warm-and-fuzzy idealists, that extracted the mission of ending hunger and malnutrition from the preserve of moral imperative and presented it as an urgent, undeniable priority for long-term economic growth. They struck a balance between heart and head; it was not just the right thing to do, but the smart thing. Meeting again in 2008, this time in the shadow of the food crisis, the Copenhagen Consensus team recalibrated its priorities and elevated the task of getting nutrients to mothers and young children to the top of its list of priorities, calling it the world's most compelling and impactful investment. And it kept it there again in 2012. Without these investments, the financial wise men insisted, the planet would surely grow sicker, weaker, poorer, and more unstable.

At the same time, the scientific underpinnings of the economic and moral arguments were crystallizing. Beginning in 2008, the eminent medical journal *The Lancet* published a series of seminal articles that brought hidden hunger out into the open and zeroed in on the particular benefits of good nutrition during what it called "the critical window of opportunity": pregnancy through the child's second birthday. Article after article, authored by doctors and child development specialists, laid out the evidence: the impact of zinc deficiency on a child's growth, the importance of vitamin A, the necessity of iron, the rapid development of cognitive functions in the brain. *The Lancet* series also scolded the global nutrition community for the dysfunctional bickering that allowed its cause to be isolated and ignored. And the authors advanced the idea that childhood stunting was the best measure of malnutrition and its long-term costs to society. They concluded that if the world was to launch an effective assault on stunting, it would need to attack the problem along a wide front stretching across multiple sectors of development—agriculture, nutrition, health care, water, sanitation, education, communications, and behavior change. A palpable urgency seized the report's final words: "There is an enormous unfinished agenda."

Finally, the accumulating evidence began to persuade the politicians and development experts who could translate it into on-the-ground progress that it was time to act. They now had an answer to a question that had long vexed their efforts: Why has all the money spent on international development over the years had so much less impact than hoped for? Because so little of it had been spent on the fundamental prerequisite for individual human development: good nutrition, particularly in the first years of life.

In April 2010, several development groups gathered at the World Bank headquarters in Washington, DC, and sketched out an initiative that would be called Scaling Up Nutrition, or SUN. They calculated the financing needs, and in the months that followed someone actually counted and rounded the days of pregnancy (270) to the child's second birthday (730) and found a crisp, bold number: 1,000. It was easy to grasp, a good campaign hook, a simple rallying cry. A network of leading humanitarian agencies took it from there, drafting a roadmap to actually improve nutrition in the 1,000 days. If SUN were truly to rise, it would demand the emergence of a fresh development model anchored in a new ethic of cooperation in the often fractious humanitarian community. Over the past decades, almost every organization active in this realm had focused on its own pet causes—education, health, water, agriculture, infrastructure, environment—often deploying its preferred solutions in scattershot isolation from others. Development fiefdoms, jealously guarded from criticism or change, prevailed; beliefs and practices were cast in stone. The 1,000-day time frame offered a way to bring all these elements of development together—a place where they *needed* to come together. Here, pet causes could find common cause. Farmers and nutritionists would finally become allies; the world needed not just more food, but more nutritious food. And what good would that food and those nutrients be without clean water and better sanitation to keep away diarrhea and worms and parasites that deprived the host body of the essential nutrients? How could those parasites be identified and treated without microscopes and medicine, and how could clinics and delivery rooms safely operate throughout the day without electricity? How could moms and dads be expected to adopt the necessary behavior changes—diets, cleanliness, interaction with their children—without targeted communication strategies? Without all this in the 1,000 days, how could children fully develop cognitively and physically to take advantage of later educational and employment opportunities? And would any of this be possible without political will and government commitment across the world?

This final piece came in September 2010, at an American-Irish meeting on the sidelines of the United Nations General Assembly. Six months earlier, on St. Patrick's Day, when the US-Ireland kinship is traditionally renewed over a pint of Guinness, leaders from both countries decided to do something together beyond issues of bilateral interest like immigration. Reducing global hunger and malnutrition had already emerged as a priority for both Ireland and the United States. Ireland, given its own history of famine, had declared in a much-trumpeted white paper that it had a national calling to prevent famine anywhere in the world; what Norway was to peace, Ireland would be to hunger. And the Obama administration, seeking to revitalize America's historical leadership in agricultural development, had launched its Feed the Future program to assist smallholder farmers in Africa, Asia, and Latin America conquer their hunger seasons. Domestically, First Lady Michelle Obama had initiated the "Let's Move!" program in tandem with the President's Task Force on Childhood Obesity. And Secretary of State Hillary Clinton, embracing the evidence, saw that improving nutrition in the 1,000 days could move the needle in improving the lives of women and children around the world, a long-standing goal of American diplomacy.

On September 21, 2010, in New York City, Secretary Clinton joined with her counterpart in the Irish government, Micheál Martin, and with other foreign ministers to commit their countries to Scaling Up Nutrition. "There is a unique convergence of the science and research about what works and what needs to be invested in," Clinton said. "It is now time for us to get into action." They stood together as an example for national leaders everywhere to embrace the 1,000 days. And, in relatively short order, many others followed. The 2012 Group of Eight meeting of the world's largest industrial countries forged a New Alliance for Food Security and Nutrition. The governments of Britain and Brazil convened a hunger summit before the closing ceremony of the London Olympics in 2012; the gathering set a goal of 25 million fewer stunted children by the time the Rio de Janeiro Summer Olympics opened in 2016. Governments in the developing world signed on to Scaling up Nutrition by the dozens, and by the middle of 2015, there were fifty-five countries under the SUN.

Yes, it seemed that everything—the science, the research, the awareness, the politics—was in place. A new movement to save mothers and children was born. But, as we shall see, the way to success is strewn with real-world obstacles, big and small: poverty, violence, corruption, misogyny, wretched infrastructure, stubborn local traditions, contrarian mothers-in-law, rain, drought, parasites, mosquitoes.

THIS BOOK IS an exploration of the promise and the challenges of this revolutionary movement. It is a journey through the 1,000 days chronicling the experiences of mothers and their children in four corners of the world where the peril and the potential are particularly acute:

Uganda, hailed as the Pearl of Africa by European explorers, a place where you could put a stick in the ground and it would grow, and yet where more than half of all women of childbearing age are anemic and about 35 percent of the children are stunted.

India, the prime beneficiary of the Green Revolution, the world's largest producer of milk and the second-largest grower of fruits, but home to one-third of all the world's malnourished children.

Guatemala, a verdant land whose nutrient-rich vegetables fill the shelves of American grocery stores, yet where child stunting rates in the western highlands approach 70 percent, the worst in the Western Hemisphere.

Chicago, the capital of the bountiful Midwest of the United States of America, breadbasket of the world, and yet a city where hundreds of thousands of residents have lived in "food deserts"—neighborhoods lacking access to fresh fruits and vegetables—and where one in three children are overweight or obese.

The narrative focuses on women who live in these places, following them from the first months of their pregnancies in 2013. Their personal journeys open into explorations of the science, economics, politics, and innovations of the 1,000 days. This is not an exercise in academic or scientific rigor; rather, it is a journalistic narrative built of anecdotes and observations and research, as well as storytelling by the women and their families. It is a narrative of discovery and dreams, of crushing disappointment and soaring hope, of terrible sorrow and tremendous joy.

Any journey through the first 1,000 days of life is a journey through the obvious and the mystifying, the simple and the complicated. It turns out that your mother was right when she told you to "wash your hands and eat your vegetables."

It is such simple advice. But nothing about the 1,000 days and the first stirrings of possibility is simple. Not at all.

| # PREGNANCY

chapter one

UGANDA

TO THE NEW MOMS AND MOMS-TO-BE GATHERED ON THE veranda of the Ongica health post in northern Uganda, midwife Susan Ejang seemed like a modern-day incarnation of the Angel Gabriel, who two millennia earlier had appeared to one particular young woman with the message that she would give birth to the Son of God. Susan's message that their offspring could achieve great things wasn't quite that momentous, but it was certainly a bolt from the blue. And it also required a leap of faith. For generations, mothers here had not dared to dream of such things for their children, so tormented was life in northern Uganda. In fact, many of these young moms now on the veranda considered themselves fortunate to have merely survived their own childhood. Up until a few years earlier, they and many other villagers routinely scurried through the bush like field mice to escape the terror of the warlord Joseph Kony and his thieving, kidnapping, murdering gang called the Lord's Resistance Army. The LRA aimed to topple the government and establish a theocratic state based on the Ten Commandments while breaking every one of them along the way: raping, murdering, stealing, pillaging, abducting thousands of children to serve as soldiers and sex slaves. At night, mothers and fathers fled with their children to the rocky hills to sleep under the tenuous protection of Ugandan army troops. During the day, girls and boys sat nervously at their school desks, jumping at any loud noise that might signal the beginning of an LRA raid. Rural villages disappeared as residents fled to refugee camps near bigger, slightly more secure cities, such as Lira. One night, in the town of Aboke, down the road from the Ongica health post, 139 girls were abducted from a Catholic school and taken to LRA camps deep in the bush.

It was into this brutal world that mothers delivered their children. The goal was simply survival. Who could dream of anything, especially greatness, beyond their daily nightmare?

Esther's parents prayed that their daughter would stay beyond the reach of the LRA and out of harm's way in the Nile River marshlands where they lived, just south of Lira. The parents of her husband, Tonny, had spent four years on the move to secure the safety of their children, first doing the nighttime shuttle up the craggy hill called Apila and then moving into a camp. Esther and Tonny knew one thing as they expected their first baby: living in fear, terrified of what might happen each day, was no way to raise a child.

Although Kony had fled the area several years earlier, perhaps for the jungles of Congo or the Central African Republic—no one knew precisely where—the years of LRA terror, and the brutality that had preceded them throughout the country, still haunted northern Uganda. Since independence from British rule in 1962, Uganda had endured a series of coups and conflicts and governments of kleptocrats, thugs, and murderers (exhibit A: Idi Amin, who murdered thousands and stole millions) that had scarred the country's beauty and largely squandered its natural abundance. As the twentieth century came a close, the Pearl of Africa had become the Peril of Africa.

One of the legacies of a half century of upheaval was widespread malnutrition and a woeful health-care system that particularly jeopardized the early years of life. Even now, in the second decade of the twenty-first century, Uganda's neonatal mortality rate of 27 per 1,000 live births, infant mortality rate (deaths within the first year) of 54 per 1,000 live births—and worse, 66, in the northern district—and the under-five death rate of 90 per 1,000 live births (about 170,000 children in total), along with a maternal mortality rate of 438 per 100,000 live births, were among the worst in the world. These numbers represented big improvements since the 1990s, but they still put the country "in the top ten"—in other words, at the bottom—of a combination of these woeful categories, as described in a candid assessment released by Uganda's minister of gender, labor, and social development, Wilson Muruuli Mukasa, and UNICEF.

The report, *Situation Analysis of Children in Uganda*, painted a bleak picture of maternal and infant health. The immediate causes of infant mortality were hypothermia (37 percent), premature birth, and pneumonia and infections, with malnutrition being an underlying cause of 40 percent of all under-five deaths. The main direct causes of maternal mortality were hemorrhage (42 percent), obstructed or prolonged labor, and complications from unsafe abortion; indirect causes included malaria, anemia, and HIV/AIDS. Vitamin A deficiency was found to afflict about 40 percent of all children under five and about one-third of all women of childbearing age, while anemia plagued about half of all children between six months and four years of age and 60 percent of pregnant women. The report estimated that Uganda lost nearly $1 billion worth of productivity every year due to high levels of stunting, iodine deficiency disorders, iron deficiency, and the lifetime impact of low birth weight.

"Staggeringly low" was how the report described the availability of basic health services, especially in rural areas. Only about half the country's pregnant women had access to good-quality prenatal-care services, and only 57 percent of babies were delivered in a health facility. In 2011, barely half the children one or two years old were fully vaccinated in the country—despite the government's goal of full immunization. One-quarter of children under four years of age were said to be living in extreme poverty and experiencing profound deprivation.

These were unlikely conditions for producing much greatness. But Esther had reason to believe she was one of the lucky ones, a woman soon to deliver her first child at the time her country had made improving nutrition and reducing stunting a top national priority. "Our children's cognitive development represents Uganda's greatest natural resource," Minister Mukasa had written in the foreword to the *Situation Analysis*. He noted that Uganda's ambition to become a middle-income country by 2040 remained "highly contingent" on the country's children having the best possible start in life.

The women gathered on the veranda of the Ongica clinic were new moms bringing forth a new generation of children—and expectations. Focusing on the 1,000 days was an essential part of the government's Nutrition Action Plan, a document that conveyed a palpable urgency that the nation's future was in the balance. Uganda's stunted children, it reported, had 1.2 fewer years of education than did healthy children. More than half of the country's current adult population had suffered from stunting as children, and as a result these adults were less productive in their jobs and earned lower wages than those who had not suffered from stunting. The combined cost associated with child undernutrition—health-care expenses, lower education, lost productivity—was one of the main factors keeping so many Ugandan families, and their entire country, poor. "Eliminating stunting is a necessary step for sustained development in the country," the report concluded. It was one of the first African documents to embrace the importance of the first 1,000 days.

Esther eagerly stepped up to the front lines to put the plan into action for herself and her baby. She had toiled in the fields all morning, tending to her crops, bending deeply to turn the soil and remove the weeds with a hoe. She was especially proud of two particular plots: her orange sweet potatoes, rich in vitamin A, and a new variety of beans that had a higher-than-normal iron content. Before heading off to the health clinic for the lesson with Susan, Esther had washed the dirt from her feet, legs, and arms and put on clean clothes. She chose her favorite new shirt, which hung loosely on her tall, thin frame. The polo-style shirt was bright orange and proclaimed this message on the back: "Prevent Vitamin A and Iron Deficiencies. Plant and Eat Orange Sweet Potatoes and High Iron Beans."

The shirt was a gift from HarvestPlus, an international research program that was pioneering the fortification of staple crops, a new wave in agriculture that, through conventional breeding, raises the nutrient content of the food people eat every day. It was one of the imperatives of the 1,000 Days movement, bringing agriculture and nutrition together in a marriage called "nutrition-smart agriculture." The program, which was endorsed in the Nutrition Action Plan, had been introduced to the

rural areas around Lira by HarvestPlus and the international humanitarian organization World Vision just two seasons before. Esther readily
embraced the new crops. The timing for her, she believed, was wonderful, the planting in sync with her pregnancy. The harvest would coincide
with the birth of her child. The vitamin A and iron would help keep her
strong and give her baby a good start in life; the nutrients would enrich
her breastmilk and then also the baby's first solid food of mashed-up
sweet potatoes and beans. She was practicing what Susan was preaching.

"Who is planting these crops?" Susan asked the women on the veranda.

Esther enthusiastically and proudly raised her hand. "I am," she said.
Dozens of arms shot up and waved across the veranda. Most everyone
was in on the program.

"Don't grow them just to sell," Susan instructed. "You and your families must eat them. Vitamin A and iron are important for your child's
growth."

I HAD FIRST met Esther the day before in the village of Barjwinya, under a giant mango tree. It was the local gathering spot to discuss matters
of importance. The tree was at the center of a cluster of square one-
room mud-brick houses with thatched roofs. On this day, families had
migrated to this shady spot from miles around, walking along the dirt
pathways from their small settlements.

They had come to celebrate the HarvestPlus program and to learn
more from World Vision instructors based in Lira. As the World Vision
staff arrived, they were greeted with dancing and clapping and joyous
shouts as well as the high-pitched trilling ululation central to an African
celebration. A chorus of women decked out in orange T-shirts and skirts
welcomed their visitors with a swaying song of greeting, a verse for each.
The most animated praise was lavished on the orange-flesh sweet potato
and the high-iron beans. They were the newcomers that had changed the
village. *Ekyokulya Ekyobulamu*, proclaimed the slogan on the women's
orange shirts. *Good Food Good Life.*

Pregnant women and mothers with little children sat on reed mats at
the base of the tree, in the center of the shade. They warily eyed the large,
round mangoes hanging above them, which were nearing peak ripeness

and would be falling soon. Eating the fruit would be good for their health, but the mango season could be hazardous as well. You didn't want one clanking you or your child on the head as it fell. A dozen chickens and one rooster scratched the dirt around the tree. The men stood on the fringe of the gathering, just within the shade cover. Together, women and men, they called themselves *Ocan Onote*: The Poor are United. The village's very name indicated a history of misfortune: in the local Langi language, Barjwinya means "place of jiggers," referring to a past infestation of the parasitic fleas that burrow into the skin, causing infection and great pain.

But this was a day to celebrate a hopefully brighter future. A line of blue plastic chairs was arranged for the elders and the visitors. We sat behind wobbly little wooden tables neatly covered with blue and white doilies. It was a big day for the villagers. From their humble little houses, they brought out the best furniture they had.

First to speak were the elders of Barjwinya, who regaled the gathering with tales of how their eyesight and general health had improved since the introduction of the vitamin A–enriched sweet potatoes. One man insisted he could now see visitors entering the village from a far distance; before they were just blurry ghosts. Another man proclaimed his eyes had stopped watering and he didn't need his glasses anymore. A woman who had lost her front teeth, top and bottom, and almost all her sight, said that before the orange sweet potatoes, she had given up sewing because she couldn't see well enough to thread the needle. Now, she joyfully told the gathering, she was threading again! And she was back sewing. The oldest member of the group, a woman who proudly proclaimed her age of eighty-seven years, to great applause, said, "I didn't see well, especially at night. But now I can see much better. I can see that Roger is sitting there, and he is white!" The laughter nearly shook the mangoes off the tree.

The elders then encouraged the young women, those expecting and those with babies, to speak. At first they described conditions before the arrival of the new crops: pregnancies marked by tiredness, dizziness, miscarriages; babies often sick, listless, cranky. "Tired blood" was their common diagnosis for both moms and babies, confirming the country's statistics showing that anemia was a national malady. One woman said her first two children had each needed a blood transfusion at about six months of age because they were so anemic. But, she added triumphantly, her youngest child—born after the arrival of the sweet potatoes and the beans—had reached the age of one without any illness.

Eveline Okello sat on a reed mat, breastfeeding her one-year-old son Joshua. "There's a very big difference between this child and my others," she said. "I notice I have more breastmilk for this one." Joshua had four siblings. He was barely one month old when he was riding on his mother's back as she planted her first orange sweet potatoes and then her maiden crop of high-iron beans. When he was six months old, the harvest was in, and the sweet potatoes and beans were the first solid foods that he ate. "This child isn't sick so often," Eveline said. In fact, he was so robust neighbors had taken to calling him "little President." Her other children, Eveline noted, had "coughs, malaria, the flu, headaches. But I haven't suffered with Joshua at all." One of the elderly women piped up again to say the area children were quite rambunctious. "Ooooh, they develop very fast now," she said. "They aren't dull."

Grace Akullu, the World Vision nutritionist in Lira who worked with the women as they harvested and consumed the new crops, asked the pregnant moms if they were taking their iron and folic acid supplements. The women reported that the supply of the tablets at the local health post was inconsistent. Sometimes they were available, sometimes not. Instead of receiving a batch of thirty for one month, one woman said she only got fourteen. "Four," said another mom, that's all she had. A third woman said she was only given malaria tablets; she hoped they would be a general cure-all. Even if women received the required number of tablets, there wasn't much follow-up to make sure they took them. The government standard of prenatal treatment was four checkups, but many women just went two or three times, depending on their distance from the health post. Grace, who was pregnant herself, noted that women sometimes stopped taking the iron tablets because they didn't like the taste, or because it made them feel ill or become constipated. A common attitude was, I'm feeling fine, why bother taking something that doesn't sit right with me? They didn't understand the health benefits.

The new crops, which the women would eat almost every day after the harvest, provided a more consistent dose of micronutrients. The amount of iron and vitamin A the food provided may not have met international recommended amounts, but it was certainly more than they had been getting before. And the moms believed in the health benefits of the new varieties of crops.

Brenda Okullu, stylish in a gold dress and a maroon scarf wrapped around her head, said she was feeling much better with this pregnancy, her second. She was six months along, and suffering fewer headaches than she had the first time. She had more energy and expected to be working in her sweet-potato and bean fields right up to the time she would deliver. She thanked World Vision, and the new crops, for her added pep. It must be them, Brenda told Grace; nothing else had changed. "Right now I'm feeling good," she said. "The baby kicks a lot. My life is good."

A shy smile brightened Brenda's cherubic face. Grace was happy to see that, for she knew that Brenda had experienced deep sadness. Despite the smile, Brenda spoke and moved as if carrying an invisible burden; her voice was soft, her head bowed. She began to recount the story of her first pregnancy, two years earlier when she was eighteen. The pregnancy had been difficult. She was always tired, dizzy, suffering headache after headache. But she carried her baby to full term and delivered at the Lira hospital. The baby was healthy and began breastfeeding immediately after birth. The new arrival brought great excitement and joy in her family compound of little thatch-roofed huts. A week after the birth, though, Brenda was still in considerable pain: her ribs and back were sore, and those headaches continued to pound. She had an appointment scheduled to bring the baby to Susan Ejang's clinic in three days, but her pain became so acute that she returned to the Lira hospital, this time to the emergency ward. She was breastfeeding, so she brought the baby with her. The nurses checked Brenda into the hospital for treatment of anemia. They told her she needed rest.

While Brenda recuperated, her baby began fussing and crying; breastfeeding was difficult. The doctors suspected an infection of some sort, but they had little time to investigate the cause or medication to combat it. Brenda was feverish with fear: Was she losing her firstborn? One night, the baby stopped crying. Then the baby stopped everything.

Within two weeks of birth, her child was dead.

"I don't know why," Brenda said. Then she fell silent. That would be all she would say about her first child. It was all she *could* say. She knew nothing more; no one had given her an explanation. Tears welled in her eyes as she looked away, first staring into the soil and then looking into the distance.

No one spoke for a minute or two as the community shared in her sorrow for her lost child. Then another mom, Harriet Ogwal, filled the silence with a hopeful note. "I see things getting better," she said. Harriet was newly pregnant with her fourth child. She was older than Esther and Brenda, about twenty-seven (she didn't know for sure), and a voice of experience for the younger women; her children were ten, eight, and five years old. Harriet knew the importance of good nutrition. During her three earlier pregnancies she and her husband, Moses, could rarely afford any food beyond what they grew themselves. She was often sick with malaria, nausea, or general weariness. And the children were frequently ill as well. Now, bolstered with a better home-grown diet, thanks to the orange sweet potatoes and the beans, she said this pregnancy was her best yet. She anticipated being able to work in the fields, tending to her fortified crops, until the day of delivery. "During previous pregnancies, I'd fall sick over and over. So much malaria," she said. "Now I have more energy to do the planting and a better appetite for food."

Suddenly, from out of the bush, a man stumbled into the gathering, demanding his dinner. "Where is it?" he bellowed. "Why is it late?"

The crowd under the mango tree erupted in laughter. Clearly the man was drunk—or was pretending to be. In fact, his appearance was the beginning of a play. Community theater had proven to be particularly effective in conveying messages to areas where many of the residents were illiterate. World Vision and HarvestPlus also used the nation's network of local radio stations, developing scripts for short spots and a call-in show. But bush drama was more intimate; the actors were neighbors, the language their own. It was also great entertainment.

The drunk's wife, hurrying to offer up an explanation why dinner wasn't ready, said she was feeling sick, tired, and dizzy; she was not seeing well, and her head was pounding. "Well, then," her husband insisted, "you must go to the hospital."

The scene shifted. The wife was now facing a doctor. She repeated her symptoms as the doctor looked under her eyelids. Anemia, he declared. "You should go back to your community and join a group growing high-iron beans that are good for the blood and also the orange sweet potato for vitamin A." Don't fear the orange, he advised; it is an indication that the potato is full of beta-carotene, which the body turns into vitamin A. And vitamin A is good.

Back home, the wife told her drunk of a husband that World Vision was distributing orange-flesh sweet-potato vines and high-iron bean seeds in their village. They should get in on the program, she suggested. The husband angrily waved off the idea.

"We have been planting beans and sweet potatoes all these years and there has been no improvement in health," he complained.

"But these sweet potatoes are orange, not white like our usual ones," explained the wife. "The orange helps to improve eyesight, boost the immune system, soften the skin. And the beans, they may look the same, but they have more iron, which will help our blood." The husband perked up at the mention of softer skin for his wife. "If it will make us better," he conceded, "we should plant them."

Next, the man began strategizing about where to plant the new crops. He paced impatiently, grumbling, "We are ready. Where are the vines and the seeds?"

A World Vision worker appeared and demonstrated how to plant the new crops. Place each sweet-potato vine in a mound of dirt, not just flat soil, he said. The beans need proper spacing, fifteen to twenty centimeters between holes. If you plant them too close together, the beans will have to compete for soil nutrients, sun, and water. "Just like if you have ten children in your house and your neighbor has two. The two will grow up to be healthier than the ten, because ten are too many to care for." It was a family planning message thrown in for good measure.

The scene shifted to the post-harvest period. The wife emerged from a hut carrying a bowl of orange sweet potatoes, and a group of children pounced on it, pushing and tugging at each other to reach the treat. One girl victoriously held a potato aloft and shouted, "Look what I got!"

In a market scene, a seller hawked the sweet potatoes. She also hoisted one above her head for all to see. "This is full of vitamin A. It's very healthy."

Another vendor shouted, "I have beans high in iron, they help your blood and brain development."

A woman selling regular black beans complained to customers: "Why aren't you buying these?"

A customer scoffed, "We don't want those beans anymore. The other ones are healthier."

The drunk reappeared, but now he was sober, cleaned up, robust, strutting. He announced to his family, "Do you see the change in me? I'm a better man now."

His mother congratulated him for using the money he once spent on booze to purchase bean seeds and sweet-potato vines and to provide more nutritious food for his family.

In a final scene, the wife and husband, now wearing orange T-shirts, were back at the hospital, thanking the doctor for his advice about the new crops. They and the other cast members launched into a closing song:

> The new crops are feeding us well.
> Very nutritious, very wonderful.
> The high iron beans have saved our lives.
> The orange-flesh sweet potatoes have saved our lives.

Esther joined in the applause and laughter. She, too, was grateful for the new crops and their promise of better health for herself and her child. She slowly rose to her feet, lifted by the optimism of the gathering, and began the long walk back to her fields, to tend to her beans and sweet potatoes. As did Brenda and Harriet and the rest of the crowd. But a nagging thought remained hanging under the mango tree in the village named for a plague: Could this agricultural innovation truly conquer their poverty and lack of development? Or would it, eventually, be the other way around?

chapter two

INDIA

I N A RURAL VILLAGE IN INDIA, THE POSSIBILITIES OF THE 1,000 days were also praised in song. "Light the lamp of knowledge in every home, transforming our weakness into strength," sang a chorus of pregnant women and new moms in their Hindi dialect.

> If you take care
> you'll need no medicine
> and won't need to spend a penny.
> Before delivery, tend to the mother,
> and afterwards, the baby.
> Share this wisdom
> for the good of everyone,
> transform weakness into strength.

The singing triggered a rare wave of laughter and joy in the downtrodden village of Rampur Khas in the northern state of Uttar Pradesh. Together, the women in their colorful saris formed a glorious rainbow—bright yellows, reds, purples, blues, greens, and oranges. But this wasn't an over-the-top Bollywood exuberance. There was singing, yes, but no one was dancing. The women stayed sitting cross-legged on the ground in the shade of a thatched roof. They were happy for the rest after a morning of backbreaking labor in the fields that began with the rising sun. The peppermint harvest was underway, which meant days of bending and squatting and plucking the delicate leaves of the green bushes. The work unleashed an aroma of menthol throughout the countryside, as if someone had opened an enormous jar of Vicks VapoRub. The soothing scent, though, did little to ease the aching muscles from the work and the discomfort of the season. The annual monsoon rain was still a few weeks away, but the humidity was already thick in anticipation. The temperature swelled past 100 degrees. As they sang in the shade during their noontime respite, the women twirled homemade fans in a desperate effort to budge the reluctant air. Later in the afternoon, they would be back in the mint fields.

Rampur Khas was a village of 120 households, mainly of the lower castes. The men and women were day laborers and farmers, doing the country's hard and dirty work. Sixteen women in the village were pregnant, and an almost equal number were nursing babies. Here is where I met Mohana and Sushma, neighbors whose houses shared a common wall, and friends Meera and Kiran, all beginning their 1,000-day journey. Each one of them was ruggedly dainty—a contradiction of words, but truly appropriate when you matched their calloused hands and feet with their small, thin, frail frames. Mohana was the tallest, just over five feet. The tiniest was Kiran, who was at least a head shorter than Mohana. When I first spotted her, Kiran was draped in a billowy yellow sari, and I thought she was a daughter of one of the other women, maybe twelve years old, and hardly one of the pregnant moms herself. She told me she was twenty. She had just been to the local health post for her first checkup. She winced when she got a tetanus shot, and warily accepted a batch of iron and folic-acid tablets and some pills to ward off malaria. She also stepped on a scale for the first time. At the gathering, she showed me her mother and baby identification card, where all the data from the 1,000 days would be recorded. Her weight was penciled in: thirty kilograms—sixty-six pounds. She was almost five months pregnant.

The nurse at the checkup had warned Kiran that she was very thin and needed to gain weight. She pointed to two illustrations on the card and suggested Kiran follow the advice. One drawing depicted a woman lying on her side. "Get your rest during the day and at night," said the caption. In the other drawing, a woman was sitting up, eating. "A diverse diet is important," it said. "Make sure all food groups are included." It instructed further: "Eat one-quarter more food than you normally would. Eat iodized salt."

Clearly, these moms-to-be gathered on the veranda had been stunted as children and were now stunted women about to have babies of their own. It was a generational cycle that spun viciously throughout rural India, but particularly in Uttar Pradesh. The state's own statistics showed that nearly 55 percent of its children younger than three were stunted (a total of 12 million children), 42 percent were underweight, and 85 percent suffered from some level of anemia. More than 50 percent of the state's pregnant women were also anemic. Undernutrition mixed with poverty, poor sanitation, and paltry education. Uttar Pradesh was home to 20 percent of India's poor; the state's literacy rate was only about 70 percent, about 50 percent for women; and more than 65 percent of households had no toilet facilities.

It was these statistics, and the suffering behind them, that had lured Vishwajeet Kumar back to India. A gregarious young man with a huge smile, Vishwajeet had been researching and teaching public health at Johns Hopkins University in the United States, with a particular focus on reducing infant mortality. He had come a long way from the Indian state of Bihar, where he had grown up in a privileged family. Despite their social standing, his mother, who managed the family's landholdings, had insisted that her youngest son have breakfast with the laborers working on the family's farms. It was there, at those communal tables, that Vishwajeet was first confronted with India's profound caste-based inequalities. Questions about the disparities in living conditions and health care in his country pummeled his conscience. He determined to study medicine and took up clinical work at a large hospital in Delhi, setting out on the well-worn path to becoming a surgeon. But as he honed his bedside manner, diligently taking patients' histories, he found himself longing to work upstream, where the problems began, in order to focus on preventing rather than treating disease. As fate would have it, in the hostel where he was living, he spied a journal describing Johns Hopkins

University's public health program. The anecdotes of work being done in homes and communities far beyond a clinical setting stirred memories of the communal meals of his childhood. Soon he was in Baltimore, studying with some of the top child-health experts in the United States. He flourished there, but his thoughts kept drifting back to the disparities in India. When an opportunity arose to join a new project, studying infant deaths and hypothermia in the state of Uttar Pradesh, Vishwajeet eagerly packed his bags. In his early thirties, he pulled a career U-turn; he was on his way back home, to finally work where the problems were.

And what overwhelming problems he found. Uttar Pradesh, known as UP, was India's most populous state—its population of 200 million would make it the sixth-largest country in the world—and carried 30 percent of the nation's total malnutrition and disease burden and, thereby, a significant chunk of the world's malnutrition. UP was a particularly perilous place to have, or be, a baby. The average infant mortality rate was 63 deaths per 1,000 live births, compared to about 44 in all of India, and there were some pockets in the state where the rate climbed to the astronomical level of 90. The maternal mortality rate was 345 per 100,000 live births, compared to an Indian average of 212, and the global rate of 210. With about 20 percent of India's annual births, UP also had a disproportionate amount of the country's neonatal and maternal deaths (28 percent and 35 percent, respectively).

Vishwajeet believed that if the international development community really wanted to move the needle on global levels of malnutrition, stunting, and infant and maternal mortality, it would have to come through Uttar Pradesh. Back at home, he argued that India's maternal and child health statistics—30 percent of the world's stunted children, 27 percent of the world's newborn deaths—were utterly unacceptable for a country that had made great agricultural and technological progress in recent decades. In the years after the Green Revolution of the 1960s, which rescued the country from a ruinous cycle of famines, India's farmers produced surpluses of wheat, rice, maize, and pulses (such as beans and lentils) that were so great they overwhelmed the country's storage facilities. India also had a White Revolution, which turned it into the world's top milk producer. And a Sweet Revolution that made it a leading grower of fruits. The country's stack of antipoverty and food distribution legislation could fill a library. So India's problems of malnutrition, stunting, and infant mortality were rooted in issues beyond food production and access. Vishwajeet insisted that what needed to change were cultural attitudes and behaviors toward maternal and child health, particularly in the 1,000 days. Too many children in India were getting off to a horrible start in life.

Vishwajeet plunged into the rural villages around the town of Shivgarh, in the central region of UP. They were some of the poorest in the state. Open defecation was commonplace, as it was throughout much of India, leading to rolling communal health crises of diarrhea, parasitic infections, and intestinal illness. In the Shivgarh villages, nearly all the children appeared to be stunted and looked young for their age. You might think a child was four years old by appearance, but upon asking learn that she was eight, or ten. The adults were uniformly tiny, too, for most of them had been stunted as children. A person taller than five and a half feet was a giant. In this setting, villagers didn't see stunting as a problem; it was the norm.

As he began his work, Vishwajeet likened himself to an amateur diver, exploring a new world of strange phenomena. What he discovered in the villages were traditional practices and superstitions, deeply rooted in the region's caste system, culture, and spirituality, that were having a profound impact in the 1,000 days. Folk wisdom and common custom encouraged families to make choices discordant with all he had learned in medical school. Women were still insisting on delivering their babies at home (upward of 80 percent of them) even with the proliferation of clinics and hospitals in the countryside. The newborns would be taken from their mothers and thoroughly washed—sometimes heavily scrubbed, even cleansed with mud from a pond—and then left on their own, unclothed, lying on the ground for up to an hour, while the home birth attendants turned to caring for the mother, as the risk to her life after giving birth was perceived to be higher. This washing and scrubbing was a ritual meant to cleanse away evil spirits, but it dangerously exposed the babies to the deadly evil of hypothermia. Cutting the umbilical cord after home deliveries was a job for the traditional cord-cutter, a woman from the lowest caste. If she was delayed in arrival, the baby remained attached and often unheld by the mother; when the cord-cutter performed her task, the knife was likely one that had been used elsewhere, escalating the chance of infection. Breastfeeding didn't begin for several hours, at the earliest, or in some instances several days; less than 20 percent of newborns in Shivgarh were immediately breastfed. Instead, the first breastmilk, containing the antibody-rich colostrum, was discarded; yellowish in color, it was considered unclean, like a pus, part of the afterbirth. The first liquids given to a baby would be cow's milk or water (unpurified, straight from the well) or a drop of honey. Massaging the newborn with mustard oil was also common, though it meant more time that the baby was unwrapped and exposed to the environment, and had a deleterious effect on the skin barrier function, which would lead to increased loss of water and heat. Then mother and child retreated alone into a room for a ritual period of confinement, called *saur*, that would last for a week or two, at least. Cow dung laced with incense would be burned at the entrance to the room to ward off spirits, but the stinging smoke was toxic to an infant's lungs.

Given all that he discovered, Vishwajeet was hardly surprised as an explorer—though appalled as a doctor—to learn that the newborn mortality rate in the villages around Shivgarh was an exceedingly high 80-plus per 1,000 live births. When he spoke to the communities, he initially found few who believed that change was necessary. He told them 80 deaths for 1,000 births should be unacceptable; the elders in the community, especially the older women who had abided by the old customs, told him that 920 surviving babies sounded pretty good. And Vishwajeet had to admit that 92 percent was an A on any test at any school he had attended. He was frustrated that the communities were looking at survivability; he wanted them to focus on the mortality. The women said the infant deaths were fated; he insisted they were preventable. Your babies didn't have to die, he told the women. You have the power to ensure they will live. Vishwajeet defined his challenge: move the women and the communities from a state of fatalism to a state of control.

To do this, Vishwajeet forged a merger between modern medicine and community beliefs. His team of medical scientists worked with local community leaders to agree on a common objective: increasing infant survival. And then they aligned the traditional belief that evil spirits, called *jamoga*, harm newborns with the medical science of how infections harm newborns. Infections were *jamoga*, too, Vishwajeet told them. He began calling infections *germoga*. A tetanus shot during pregnancy, a new intervention in the women's lives, could defeat *germoga*. And his team capitalized on the local fear of fevers by giving hypothermia, a leading cause of infant death in rural India, a new name: they called it *thandabukar*, which in Hindi means "cold fever." Together, Vishwajeet's team and the community leaders came up with a package of behavior changes—hygienic delivery, light cleansing of the newborn rather than a thorough scrubbing, skin-to-skin contact between mother and child, immediate breastfeeding with the colostrum—that could conquer the evils killing infants. Vishwajeet called his budding organization the Community Empowerment Lab. In the homes and up and down the dusty streets of the villages, the women called it simply *Saksham*. Empowerment.

Vishwajeet's favorite visual aid was a mother's hand with the fingers spread wide. "There are five secrets to success," he would tell the women, assigning one secret to each finger. "One, love. Two, warmth. Three, food—breastmilk. Four, hygiene. Five, care—know the signs when your baby is sick and go to the doctor. These behaviors are all in your control. They are in your hands." It was a revolutionary concept—empowering mothers—in a country where women often have little say in their own homes, even over reproductive and family planning decisions. And especially in a highly patriarchal place like Uttar Pradesh.

The Community Empowerment Lab hired a team of frontline workers—young women from the villages, most of whom had attended high school—and dispatched them into the communities to listen to the women, understand their practices, and spread the word about how some simple behavior changes could save their lives and the lives of their children. The frontline workers were well known and trusted by their neighbors, and admired for having a better education than most. On basic bicycles, they peddled furiously over rutted dirt roads and cobblestone lanes from village to village, toting Samsung Galaxy tablets to record data on all the pregnant women in the vast study area. On the verandas of the humble houses in dozens of villages, they met with moms and moms-to-be and other important caregivers, including mothers-in-law, fathers, midwives, and spiritual leaders. The frontline workers discussed the importance of good nutrition and rest during pregnancy, and they advised mothers to go to the clinics and hospitals for delivery and to bring a clean blade of their own to cut the umbilical cord. They taught the women how to lightly clean and swaddle a newborn. They introduced the practice known as "kangaroo mother care," where the baby is immediately placed on the mother's chest for skin-to-skin warmth and bonding. They didn't just tell them what to do; they told them why it was important. They explained that initial breastfeeding provided essential nutrients and antibodies to the baby; that first milk, they said, was far too valuable to throw away. They explained that anything else, such as water, cow's milk, or honey, was dangerously unclean and too difficult for a baby to digest. There were questions raised, particularly by mothers-in-law, who argued that the old practices had been good enough for them. But as they witnessed a group of younger moms—the early adopters—eagerly welcoming the changes, and saw infant deaths and illnesses become less common, their resistance waned. Particularly powerful were the examples of mothers who had lost a child and embraced the new information and practices in the hope that it wouldn't happen again.

Saving newborns unified communities divided by caste and income. There was now a common goal and all hands shared control. In this endeavor, all were equal. The impact was astonishing, even to Vishwajeet. Within 16 months, neonatal mortality in the Saksham villages was cut in half; it had fallen to 41 deaths per 1,000 live births, compared to 84 in neighboring villages where the changes hadn't been introduced. Mothers dying while giving life became ever rarer. Here, Vishwajeet proclaimed, was evidence of what can happen when mothers are empowered. In short order, the UP government followed the Saksham lead and incorporated the basic tenets of care for pregnant women and their newborn children into the state's public programs and the duties of its legion of local health workers, the accredited social health assistants, or ASHAs. Vishwajeet was proud of what had been accomplished, but the work had just begun: More infants would now survive, but what could be done to help them thrive?

IN RAMPUR KHAS, the women put all they learned into verse.

Mothers listen to this advice.
Press your child to your bare chest
It won't cry or be afraid.
Increase your motherly love
Press your child to your bare chest.
You must increase the weight of the child.

Wrap yourself and your baby in a blanket.
That's how you press your child to your bosom.
Mothers listen to this advice
Press your child to your bare chest.

The songs helped bring more women to the gatherings, particularly the illiterate ones who couldn't read the written materials and often felt intimidated at other community meetings. The simple lyrics were a combination of Hindi and a rural dialect incorporating old Sanskrit phrases. When a Saksham frontline worker put the words to paper, even Vishwajeet and his learned colleagues had difficulty translating some of the passages. But there was universal understanding in the villages.

From village to village the messages spread, carried by a Saksham frontline worker—such as Gayatri. She was a young woman, slender with long black hair, friendly with all the mothers in the communities. She knew where every pregnant woman lived. After leading the meeting in Rampur Khas, she guided me through a maze of narrow lanes to the homes of Mohana and Sushma, who lived side-by-side at the edge of the village. (Most of the women of Shivgarh go by only one name; Mohana would be identified as "Mohana, the wife of Krishan.")

Their one-room houses shared a common mud-brick wall. Thick thatch roofing angled out in both directions from this wall and extended past the front doors to give each family a broad veranda. This is where water and grain was stored in clay vessels and food was cooked over a fire in an earthen stove. A couple of *charpoys*, the ubiquitous homemade woven cots, served as seats and beds; the open veranda was both living room and bedroom. On the wooden door of each house, pictures of Hindu icons mingled with stickers of Bollywood actors.

Mohana, thirty years old, was painfully aware of what was at stake in the 1,000 days. Her first three children were born before Saksham came to the village. She gave birth at home and followed the traditional practices of scrubbing and oiling the babies. She remembered discarding the colostrum and the first breastmilk; the home birth attendant had insisted on it. Instead of her own milk, she fed her newborns goat milk or milk produced by the water buffalo tethered to a pole outside their house. She started breastfeeding her babies on the third or fourth day after their births. Neither she nor her children got any vaccinations.

Wearing an orange sari and fiddling with red plastic bangles on her wrists, Mohana wondered about her first children. They were frequently ill, and diarrhea was common. Her oldest, a son, had stayed in school for only a couple of years; he had not done well and had no interest in continuing. Now, at fourteen, he lethargically idled around the village. Mohana worried that he had missed something in his early development, and she feared that the second and third children, now eleven and ten years old, were also behind. By the time she was pregnant with her fourth child, Saksham's team of frontline workers had arrived, and Mohana was ready to try the new behaviors she was learning. She delivered a girl in the local hospital a few miles away, swaddled the baby on her chest, and immediately started breastfeeding. She named the baby Lakshmi, for the Hindu goddess of wealth and prosperity.

Mohana believed Lakshmi would have a better start to life. In the months after the birth, Mohana often testified at village gatherings about her youngest daughter's good health. "This one is rarely ill," she would say. "Feeding the first milk to a child is a major difference. I can see the child gets stronger to fight diseases, more intelligent."

But as Lakshmi approached her first birthday, her health faltered. In weaning her child from exclusive breastfeeding, Mohana had begun feeding her milk from the family buffalo, as she had done with her other children. Buffalo milk is creamier and heavier than cow's milk, and Lakshmi's body seemed to reject it. She became very ill. What kind of *jamoga* was this that gripped their daughter? wondered Mohana and her husband, Krishan.

Mohana held Lakshmi on the back of her husband's bicycle as he pedaled to the regional hospital about ten miles away. There, a doctor diagnosed Lakshmi's problem as an intestinal blockage. He said he could cure her, but his time and the medicine would cost 25,000 rupees, or about $400. It was a huge sum for Mohana and Krishan. They hurriedly negotiated with a neighborhood lender to borrow a considerable sum, but it wasn't enough. So they sold some of the wheat and rice they had been storing to eat later in the year. They made the payment to the doctor. The treatment and medicine worked; the blockage was relieved. Lakshmi survived.

But Mohana worried about the toll on her daughter. Now almost three years old, Lakshmi was small, and she was often sick with diarrhea and bronchitis. Throughout her current pregnancy, Mohana prayed that the baby she now carried would be healthy. Maybe this would be the one who remained strong, grew well, and advanced in school. When the Saksham workers visited, she listened very carefully, for she obviously still had much to learn.

Sushma, on the other side of the wall, was further along in her pregnancy and was ready to give birth. She had bought a new blade to cut the umbilical cord and new thread to tie it off, and was preparing new light cotton cloths in which to swaddle the baby. It would be her third child; the first two—a seven-year-old son and a two-year-old daughter—had also been born after Saksham began its work in Rampur Khas, and they appeared to be thriving. Sushma, a few years younger than Mohana, had been a believer from her first meeting with Saksham and the ASHA worker. "I felt that they were educated people, so I trusted them," Sushma told me. She herself had only a few years of classroom education. "I know now I am doing all I can for my babies," she said. "I know what I do can make a difference."

But her mother-in-law, who kept a close eye on her and also attended the meetings, had serious doubts. Relations were frayed, as the mother-in-law insisted on adherence to traditional behaviors. Two, three, four times she listened to the Saksham principles, and still she resisted. Home delivery, a good scrubbing after birth, and a bit of honey for the newborn—it had been good enough for her generation. "You just don't like new things," Sushma told her. But as she saw over time that the newborns in the village were healthy, and that the mothers were healthy, too, Sushma's mother-in-law relented. When I met her, she shrugged, treating the new practices as the latest fad. "It goes with the wind," she said. "This is what people are doing now."

Kiran's mother-in-law, Tulsa, who also lived in Rampur Khas, needed no convincing, for she had herself experienced the wonders of the new practices. She had already given birth five times—and lost two of her children—and was pregnant for a sixth time when Saksham arrived in the village. She attended the meetings with great curiosity, an openness to change, and a morbid anxiety that she would lose another child. Her fear skyrocketed when she went into labor at seven months. When her baby, a tiny girl, was born, the odds of survival were slim. Tulsa insisted on kangaroo mother care, immediately wrapping her daughter on her chest and initiating breastfeeding. She followed Vishwajeet's first three secrets: love, warmth, food. The baby, a girl she named Meenu, survived and was proclaimed a miracle. Tulsa told everyone: "Saksham saved my baby's life."

Word of these remarkable happenings traveled throughout the neighboring villages, giving more credibility to Saksham's frontline workers. It even reached places where Saksham wasn't visiting, the original "control villages" for Vishwajeet's study. In one of them, a small cluster of houses called Pure Baishan, a woman named Shyamkali had heard about the Saksham practices from women she worked beside in the fields. She was already a mother of four children, all girls. Now, pregnant for a fifth time, she was ready for some behavior change.

Shyamkali, who had no formal education, didn't know her exact age, but believed it to be thirty or thirty-two. She was in the clutches of a powerful desire that gripped much of India: the cultural preference for having male children. Boys would carry on the family line; they were seen as having a greater economic value through their earning potential; they would bring honor to the house. Thus they often received a greater share of food and education within the family. Girls, on the other hand, were seen as bringing certain economic loss. A girl left her home after marriage, and a "giving away" dowry was paid to the husband's family, which then also received the benefits of her labor and her children. So why invest in a daughter's nutrition, health, and education? Common social and cultural practices had girls and women eating last and least in households, passing malnutrition from one generation to the next—stunted girls became stunted women who in turn gave birth to low-weight babies. Indeed, why even welcome the birth of a daughter to begin with?

This attitude has left India with tens of millions of girls "missing" as a result of female infanticide and feticide and the neglect of the well-being of daughters. India's skewed sex ratios reflect these practices; it is one of the rare countries with far fewer girls and women than boys and men. In his book on India's history of hunger and malnutrition, *Ash in the Belly*, Indian social worker and human rights activist Harsh Mander plunged into the 2011 census that revealed there were 940 females to every 1,000 males in India. (In Uttar Pradesh, it was only 904.) He also charted a continuing decline in the ratio of girls to boys in the age group of zero to six years, from 927 in 2001 to 914 in 2011. He noted that this gender gap was particularly pronounced in some of the wealthier, more prosperous areas of the country, perhaps because there was greater access to ultrasounds and people who performed abortions. It seemed to matter little that the government had made it illegal in India for parents to even ask a doctor about the sex of a child after an ultrasound, or that doctors who disclosed the gender could be stripped of their medical license and thrown into prison. Mander concluded: "What these figures establish beyond doubt is that social and cultural—and increasingly technological—processes of discrimination, neglect and hostility extinguish the life chances of these many million 'missing' girls and women. . . . And the declining ratio of females illustrates the greatest paradox, that modernity—and with it wealth, education and reproductive health care—has not reduced but further aggravated this country's aversion to its daughters."

Having a boy was certainly the top priority of Shyamkali's husband, Rajender, a day laborer who traveled far and wide to find work of any kind. Shyamkali told me that each of their first four children was conceived to be a boy. And so it was, too, with this fifth child. Each of her pregnancies had been weighed down with this pressure to have a son. She worried that her husband would persist in having more babies until she delivered a boy, even though they were already struggling to feed and clothe and educate their four girls, who were twelve, ten, seven, and five years old. The girls all had dark, soulful eyes and delicate features that radiated beauty beyond the tattered dresses and smudges of dirt. They were thin, very thin. The two oldest daughters took turns staying home from school to look after their younger sisters while their mother worked in the fields, trying to earn a few rupees.

Greatness? That was a luxury not worth thinking about. How many more children can we support? Shyamkali wondered instead.

Shyamkali, herself a wisp of a woman, barely four-and-a-half feet tall and rail thin, often hid her face behind the hem of her sari. She had little power in the matter of family size. That was one dynamic that Saksham—empowerment—had yet to impact, and one that would continue to undermine the possibilities of the first 1,000 days of India's children.

chapter three

GUATEMALA

I N GUATEMALA, THE POTENTIAL OF THE 1,000 DAYS CAME TO A boil in a cauldron of cream of potato soup.

"You want your children to grow up healthy and strong, right?" asked Susana "Susy" Menchu, a nutritionist for a local nonprofit clinic called Primeros Pasos, or First Steps.

"*Si,*" came the unanimous reply from a dozen moms and moms-to-be gathered for a cooking class in the hillside village of Chuicavioc. "Healthy and strong."

"Then what we learn today can't go in one ear and out the other. It must stay inside," Susy said, tapping her head.

The women huddled around a stove in a chilly, dank, gloomy community health center, tucked away inside a warren of brick homes and shops. This is where prenatal checkups were administered, vaccinations given, babies weighed and measured, and medicines dispensed—that is, when nurses, vaccinations, scales, and medicine were actually available, which was rare in Guatemala's impoverished western highlands. It was also where Susy freely dispensed her nutrition and hygiene advice. She came once a week, riding in a converted American school bus that now

49

plied the bumpy, perilous roads between the city of Quetzaltenango and the Palajunoj Valley, a largely neglected stretch of indigenous Maya villages languishing in the shadow of the dormant Santa Maria volcano. The colorful bus, festooned with decals of both Jesus Christ and Speedy Gonzalez, careened over the potholes as if dancing to the jaunty rhythm of the marimba music blaring from the radio. Susy held on tight in the front of the bus, clutching a sack filled with the day's ingredients, as well as a scale and measuring board.

The moms had walked to the community center from their homes, some for thirty minutes, gingerly making their way down the hillsides. They wore the traditional dresses of the Maya women of this area, brightly colored and intricately embroidered; many also wore a red apron with pockets for their cellphones and snacks. Those with babies carried them on their backs; the little ones were bundled up in sweaters and knitted caps to ward off the highland chill. The moms here were also uniformly short, almost all of them less than five feet; as in India, it was difficult for local people to perceive a stunting problem when stunting was the norm, and to see that malnutrition, not just ancestry, was a factor in children's stature.

"What do we do before anything else?" Susy asked the gathering.

"Wash hands!" the moms shouted.

"Yes, you must have clean hands before you prepare food. Because you use your hands to touch everything." And most everything around here, Susy reminded them, was dirty. In the valley, most children and adults were riddled with parasites and worms that consumed the nutrients meant for their bodies. Poor eating habits, poor water, and poor sanitation made the valley one of the unhealthiest places in the country. "And don't forget," Susy added, "you must wash the vegetables and fruit as well." For the parasites were also in the soil.

Susy scrubbed and peeled the day's ingredients—potatoes, onions, garlic. She dropped the potatoes into a boiling pot of water and sautéed the onions and garlic with vegetable oil in a frying pan, sending a glorious aroma into the dusty alleyways of Chuicavioc. "Just fry lightly, until they are clear," Susy said. "Don't burn them, for you will lose the nutrients." She mashed the potatoes, stirred in onions and garlic, filled the cauldron with milk, and added a block of processed vegetable protein with the texture of ground beef, called *Protemás*. While the soup simmered, Susy reviewed the benefits of a balanced diet.

"Remember, the potato provides energy, carbohydrates. Milk provides protein and calcium. The oil provides fat, use only a little. The onion and garlic and Protemás provide vitamins and minerals. It is important to understand the mix of the ingredients and how it helps us. You can get a lot of benefits from this recipe."

It was a simple recipe, but the women were astonished at the mixture. Dianet (pronounced Yanet) Coyoy, who was seven months pregnant with her first child, took precise notes. She had always eaten her potatoes boiled and plain. Seeing vegetables combined in a soup like this was a revelation for her. The other moms were likewise wide-eyed as they followed Susy's cooking.

"You will see that this is a meal in itself and it is very healthy," Susy said. "You can make it for lunch or dinner. You can eat it with a tortilla or tamale." This last point was most important, for corn tortillas were central to almost every meal, and they were filling, but thin on nutrients. "When you are pregnant, you must eat more than tortillas," Susy insisted.

The women noted how good the concoction smelled. Others walking past the open door leaned in for a sniff. A black dog wandered in and was promptly chased away by the moms. "Whatever you have in your garden you can make into a thick soup," Susy said. "Cream of carrot, broccoli, spinach. These things are growing all around us."

In fact, these vegetables grew all around Guatemala. It was a jarring paradox to observe this simple cooking class and see the astonished response of the women after my journey to Quetzaltenango from the capital of Guatemala City, a four-hour drive along one of the most verdant stretches of the Pan-American Highway. In midsummer, corn grew up and down the many hills and blanketed the valley floors. It grew to the edges of the roads, to the doors of the houses, to the gates of the cemeteries, to the banks of the rivers. It grew between the legs of billboards, in the bends of hairpin turns, in the clearings of forests. Looking down from the hilltops you saw breaks in this vast corn quilt where farmers had sown patches of beans, broccoli, Brussels sprouts, cabbage, cauliflower, carrots, onions, peppers, and a vast array of other vegetables. These weren't ordinary, pedestrian vegetables. These were vegetables on steroids. Roadside stands and city markets displayed radishes bigger than tennis balls, cucumbers the size of toy blimps, and carrots so cartoonishly large they would have Bugs Bunny drooling. Surely, you would think, the people living in this super-sized cornucopia must be among the healthiest in the world.

You would be wrong. Actually, they were among the most malnourished people in the world. For all of its vegetable-growing prowess, Guatemala had the fourth-highest malnutrition rate in the world and the worst in all of the Americas, with half of its children under five chronically malnourished. In some of the indigenous areas, such as the western highlands, where the Maya communities were concentrated, almost 70 percent of the population was malnourished, with nearly half of the children stunted. The vegetables were Leviathan, the people Lilliputian. The reasons were varied, and vexing. Much of the vegetable harvest was for export rather than local consumption. Guatemala was a prime example of the paradox of globalization: it was one of the top suppliers of broccoli and Brussels sprouts to the US market, but the local population—the farmers who grew the vegetables—could rarely afford them, and even if they could, had little taste for them.

On the drive to Quetzaltenango, I stopped to talk with farmers working in the lush vegetable patches. One women, Maria Pillar, toiled in a field of green peas; she hacked away at weeds while her five-month-old son Hector slept on her back, securely bundled in a blanket.

Hector was in his first 1,000 days, and Maria spent that time surrounded by nutrition. Plots of carrots, broccoli, and green beans flanked the peas. Will you be eating these? I asked Maria.

"No," she said. "But I am told other people do." At harvest time, she explained, trucks would come by and haul away her peas—somewhere, to those other people, she presumed.

What does she eat?

"Corn." She answered with an air of astonishment that anyone would even ask.

Corn, of course. The ancient Maya had cultivated and revered it; they believed they were descended from cornstalks. And corn remained the dietary deity today. No meal, day or night, was complete without corn in some form, most often tortillas or tamales. Corn made up about three-quarters of the local diet. Almost everyone grew some corn, even if only on a small, steep patch on the side of a volcano. Farmers spent much of the money they earned from the export of other vegetables buying more corn. Corn chips were the most popular snack food, especially the multi-flavored ones called Tortrix. They were cheap and devoid of significant nutrients. Guatemala had become a graveyard of well-intentioned programs designed to improve nutrition by boosting income through growing crops for export; alas, absent any corresponding push to change buying behavior, the program evaluations found no correlation between increased income and lower malnutrition. Instead, sales of Tortrix and other snacks soared into the millions every month—all washed down by Coke or Pepsi. The plastic snack-food wrappers littered the countryside. They were there at Maria Pillar's feet, modern-day junk-food tumbleweeds rolling through the rows of peas, broccoli, and carrots.

The country's huge wealth gap, one of the widest in the world, heightened this Guatemalan paradox. Rural poverty and neglect helped spark a civil war that raged for more than thirty years, just ending in the mid-1990s, and they remain an enduring legacy. The war was particularly brutal in the highlands, where the government fought to suppress rebel groups who had support among the indigenous communities. The infrastructure collapsed, health services vanished, the agriculture-based economy was ravaged. Widespread atrocities and human rights violations by government forces triggered claims of genocide. It is estimated that up to 200,000 people were killed or "disappeared" during the war.

Nearly two decades later, poverty and neglect still reigned in the highlands. More than half of Guatemala's population struggled below the poverty line, and more than one-quarter of the rural population lacked access to clean sanitation facilities. The residents of the western highlands, themselves divided among a multitude of indigenous languages, were largely marginalized in national economics, communications, and education, as government services were provided mainly in Spanish. Meanwhile, members of the wealthy social elite in and around Guatemala City often enjoyed weekend shopping excursions to Miami and Houston, both reachable in a couple of hours by plane. It took less time to fly to the malls of America than to drive to the villages of the Palajunoj

Valley. But why would the jet-setters bother to drive to a place where nearly three-quarters of the children were malnourished, stunted, and plagued with parasitic infections? To the residents of Guatemala City, the western highlands were in another world—a poorer, sicker, hungrier, dirtier world than the one they inhabited in the capital.

Willful indifference and debilitating ignorance of malnutrition prevailed among the country's government and business classes. Because no one making policy or making money knew how bad it was, and didn't much care, the situation steadily worsened. Only with the rise of Scaling Up Nutrition had politicians and the private sector begun to champion the 1,000 days and the importance of nutrition and sanitation to maternal and infant health and to the health and prosperity of the country. A month after taking office in 2012, Guatemalan president Otto Pérez Molina, a high-ranking military officer during the war, launched the *Pacto Hambre Cero*, or Zero Hunger Pact, with the ambitious goal of reducing malnutrition by 10 percent by the end of his four-year term. An internal government report estimating that malnutrition annually costs the country—and the pockets of the capital city elites—at least $300 million in economic activity had provoked his concern.

The new president dispatched members of his government to spend a night with a poor family—many leaders of the business community did the same—and his administration ordered up an anthropologic study of malnutrition in the western highlands. Between the home visits and the study, the ruling class discovered the realities of their own country: the heavily corn-based diets; the fact that women often ate last (and usually least); the tiny houses; the sleeping on floors; the lack of sanitation.

Juan Carlos Paiz, a leading businessman and member of the country's Competitiveness Commission, tossed and turned all night during his family visit, trying to get comfortable sleeping on a thin mat. "I laid on one side for thirty minutes, the other side for thirty minutes, then fifteen minutes each side, then five minutes, then two minutes," he told me. "It was my most difficult night." His conscience was harder on him than the floor. "They had two children, not in good shape. They had big eyes, you could see they were malnourished. The father would eat first, the boy would eat second, then the wife and daughter. The wife was sick. It was surprising."

For the first time it became clear to Paiz and others that malnutrition was stunting the entire country. As a businessman, he translated the stunting numbers to the impact on his workforce: "I'll lose 20 percent of the brainpower of 50 percent of my employees," he said. The president declared that every investment in better nutrition was also an investment in better education and improved security for the country.

Guatemala's established business sector and emerging entrepreneurs latched onto the Zero Hunger Pact. They could see the country's competitiveness flagging: How could it keep up with other countries in the region, and the world, with so many malnourished and stunted children? What future did it have? Business leaders created a group to lobby for improvements on the nutrition front. Civil society, rallying under the banner "Wake Up Guatemala" at large street demonstrations, clamored to end the neglect and ignorance. All this declaring and clamoring and waking up elevated Guatemala to the top of the Hunger and Nutrition Commitment Index compiled by the Institute of Development Studies in the United Kingdom. The Guatemalan president and his colleagues shuttled to ceremonies and galas in Washington, DC, and New York City, collecting the accolades.

"We have the political will to attack malnutrition. That is important, but we also need the funding to make it work, and we need to have the belief of the people," Luis Enrique Monterroso, the head of the government's Secretariat for Food Security and Nutrition, told me in Guatemala City. He handed me a glossy thirty-six-page magazine his office had produced to describe the ambitions of Pacto Hambre Cero. Two full-page photos bookended the pact's promises. One showed President Pérez Molina embracing children over the caption, "They are not just numbers; they are thousands of boys and girls for whom we work every day." In the second, children surrounded Vice President Roxana Baldetti; the caption quoted her saying, "We all have something to give to put an end to malnutrition." The question beneath all the gloss, given the history of corruption and neglect by past administrations, was whether it would be something the politicians gave to the malnourished children of Guatemala, or to themselves.

In Chuicavioc, Dianet and the other moms who had gathered for the cooking class were hoping that something would finally trickle down to them in the valley. Dianet prayed that the growing awareness of their malnutrition problem would make this a more propitious time to be pregnant. "We've heard promises before, but nothing happens," she warily told the gathering.

While the cream of potato soup boiled, Susy tried to hold the attention of her pupils by playing a game called "Tick Tock Clock." She would move around the room, pointing to each mom for a response. The first would say, "Tick," the next "Tock," the next "Clock," and so it would go. If anyone missed, they would have to answer a question.

Tick. Tock. Clock.

Tick. Tock. Tock. A mistake. Everyone laughed.

"What are the ingredients in the soup?" Susy asked.

"Potatoes, onions, garlic, milk, oil, Protemás," the mistaken mom said. Applause.

Tick. Tock. Clock. Tock. More laughter.

"What's the first thing we do?" Susy asked.

"We wash hands," replied Griselda Mendoza, who had made the Tock mistake. She was seventeen and expecting her first child in a couple of months.

"Why?"

"Because we handle animals, we change diapers," Griselda said.

More applause.

Another mom, a woman not in their group, entered the community center to have her baby weighed. Not far from the stove, a scale hung from a ceiling beam. The mom placed her baby in a white cloth sling—it looked like a jumbo diaper—attached to a hook at the bottom of the scale. It was the same type of contraption that a market vendor would use to weigh a bag of fruit, or a butcher a slab of meat. The baby's head and arms stuck out the top of the sling, his legs protruding from holes in the bottom. He looked to be about four months old. The moms in Susy's class shifted their focus from the stove to the scale's black needle as it bounced around the numbers. It settled on five kilograms. Eleven pounds. It seemed like a meager number; at four months, the baby should have been a couple of pounds heavier. Susy's moms shook their heads. They were now well aware of the malnutrition all around them in Chuicavioc.

"We see a lot of malnutrition here, not just the children but the mothers as well," Dianet told Susy. Dianet, twenty-three years old, was small herself, several inches shy of five feet. She was determined to deliver and raise a healthy child, and beat her country's odds. "You have told us that as the baby grows inside the mother, it needs to get enough vitamins and nutrients. I now know that this is important. I need to eat better, for myself and the baby."

Susy's class, which she repeated in several villages during the week, was the only nutrition instruction in the Palajunoj Valley, and Primeros Pasos was the only organization offering reliable health care for women and children. Despite the central government's commitment and rhetoric about nutrition, little was happening in the countryside. The government deployed only several dozen nutritionists around the country, and many of them were in the big cities and public hospitals. Instead, the government was putting the emphasis on improving agricultural yields, training about 1,000 new government agricultural extension officers to advise farmers. There was education on how to best grow food, but none on how to best eat it.

Public health services had been rare in the valley until a young and restless American, Brent Savoie, working with equally restless Guatemalan university students, established Primeros Pasos. Brent was between college and medical school, on a fellowship from Vanderbilt University to explore global health issues. He had been in Africa, about to begin researching a tick-borne relapsing fever in Tanzania, when al-Qaeda terrorists attacked the United States on September 11, 2001. Since the US embassy in Dar es Salaam had been bombed a few years earlier, Tanzania was again seen as a heightened security risk for American citizens, and the State Department urged them to leave. Brent still had time on his fellowship, and he thought about continuing his work in Central America, from where he could more easily shuttle back and forth to the United States. But first he would have to learn a new language. Web surfing at an Internet café in rural Tanzania, he spotted a Spanish class in Quetzaltenango. In early 2002, Brent, at the age of twenty-two, set off for Guatemala.

Brent wasn't long in the western highlands before he realized he had arrived at a deadly crossroads of malnutrition and parasitic disease. He met a group of Guatemalan medical students and learned about an abandoned mission clinic in the valley. It had been empty for more than a decade, having been shuttered during the war. A local doctor wandered into the clinic from time to time, but there were no patients. Everyone in the valley assumed it was closed; after all, residents had taken to calling the Palajunoj "the forgotten valley." Poking around the clinic, Brent noticed that a microscope and some rudimentary equipment had been left behind. Here was the possibility for a new research project: the impact of parasites on child development. Brent began going to primary schools in the valley and encouraging parents and teachers to bring children to the clinic for testing.

As they came, Brent implemented an educational component as well, teaching the children about good sanitation and eating habits. His research findings—"It was very glamorous, examining clumps of poop," he would later tell me—were disturbing: a vast majority of the children were heavily infested with parasites, and the parasites were keeping them sick and underdeveloped. And there was no access to medicine to make things right.

Brent finished his report and prepared to leave the valley—and then stopped himself. He anguished over his departure. Was he doing the expedient thing, something he had railed against himself: writing a paper to validate a grant, describing how bad things were, and then leaving with a wave and a "Good luck with all that" farewell? He had revived the clinic, restored services, built up the expectations of the community . . . and that was it? He felt ashamed. The people of the valley deserved better, he thought. He wouldn't add to their feelings of abandonment.

So Brent stayed, putting off med school for as long as possible, at least until he had found a way to keep the clinic operating in his absence. He scoured the local pharmacies for the cheapest deworming medicine. With the help of Guatemalan med students who were dispatched to the valley to get practical experience, Brent set up a schedule for the local school kids to come by the clinic for a broader range of care. They painted the building blue and white and designed a logo of little footprints; then they commenced raising funds to restock the clinic with equipment, medicine, and staff. Primeros Pasos was born.

Before he left to resume his studies in the United States, Brent set up a volunteer program, searching Idealist.org for a coordinator who could keep the projects running during his absence. The clinic expanded to include a dedicated doctor, a parasitologist, and a dentist—many kids were coming in with so much tooth decay they could barely chew the foods they were being encouraged to eat, particularly the fruits and vegetables. Primeros Pasos started a Healthy Schools program, expanded care to adults, and began working specifically with pregnant moms. The local staff treated thousands of patients on a shoestring budget as donations trickled in, particularly from former volunteers. In a dozen years, about 1,000 volunteers, mainly students from around the world, had come through the clinic and worked with the staff. It became a core part of the clinic's mission. "If you don't see it and smell it, you can't really get it," Brent would say over and over to volunteers. He wanted them to look beyond the woeful statistics of Guatemala and see the people. The statistics, he would say, were overwhelming, and you can't help a statistic. But people you could help, one by one. One person isn't overwhelming. "At the clinic that people forgot about, in the valley that people forgot about, filled with children that people forgot about," he would say, "we can make a difference."

Throughout med school and law school in the United States, Brent kept coming back to the valley. In 2012, Primeros Pasos began a nutrition recuperation project that focused on the treatment and recovery of underweight and underdeveloping children in twenty-five families. By the end of the year, most of the children in the program—each under five years of age—had begun recovering weight. They were approaching sizes considered normal for their ages. Next, the project expanded to focus on women and children in the 1,000 days. "In the 1,000 days, we can do something that impacts a life forever," Brent told the clinic staff. "That's crazy."

That was when Susy began making her weekly rounds.

THE CREAM OF potato soup was ready. Susy poured it into small bowls and passed them around. Everyone—all the moms and the babies old enough to eat solid food—got a taste.

"Do you like it?" Susy asked.

"Yes!"

"Are the children eating it? Are they enjoying it?"

"Yes!"

With each spoonful, the moms' dreams of healthy children brightened. The moms excitedly told Susy about the progress they were seeing. Maria Delfina Camacho, an eighteen-year-old who had given birth to a son, José Alexander, just six weeks earlier, beamed as she boasted of his weight. "He was born healthy," she said, "nearly seven pounds." And at one month, he weighed close to ten pounds, "more than a four-month-old" who had been on the scale before her son.

Dianet, awaiting her first child, cheered the progress. "I've seen a difference with the children in our group. They are chubbier, growing more, they have more energy. It is wonderful to see," she said. "We are learning how to take care of ourselves, how to feed the baby, how to keep clean, keep flies off the pacifier." She and Maria Delfina promised they would try the cream of potato soup recipe at home.

Susy smiled, happy that her teaching seemed to be sinking in. She left them with a reminder: "Put cotton in your ears tonight so the lessons of today don't escape."

Dianet left the community center and trudged up a hill to her home, an arduous trek for a tiny woman two months from delivering a baby. The cinderblock house was surrounded by her family's fields. There was maize, of course, growing tight to the edge of the house. And there were patches of squash, tomatoes, cauliflower, and chard, all destined for the export market. But Dianet now knew they would make good ingredients for soup, or any meal; she was determined to lobby her parents to store some of the future harvests at home for the family to eat, especially for her during her pregnancy.

Her argument was powerful: "Do it for your healthy grandchild."

chapter four

CHICAGO

I N A FAR DIFFERENT COMMUNITY CENTER—THIS ONE BRIGHT, AIRY, and welcoming—Jessica opened the door to the Ounce of Prevention Fund office. She was apprehensive. Was this truly a portal to better opportunities for her and her child, a possible refuge from the poverty and violence that threatened their 1,000 days? A sign beside the door buoyed her hope:

> The Ounce of Prevention Fund gives children in poverty the best chance for success in school and in life by advocating for and providing the highest quality care and education from birth to age five.

Jessica was even getting a jump on that, enlisting in the Ounce's doula program for guidance during her pregnancy. She was also taking advantage of another community program, Metropolitan Family Services, that had been working in Chicago for more than 150 years as, it claimed, "part mentor, part motivator, part advocate that empowers families to reach their greatest potential."

As a teen mom, Jessica needed all of that. Becoming a mom so young certainly hadn't been part of her life plan; she dreamed of going to college, becoming an architect, maybe even moving to New York City. Now that she was pregnant, her goals were more immediate: having a healthy baby and graduating from high school. She was prepared to give up sports and after-school socializing so she could spend as much time with her baby as she could and still get her homework done. Jessica's mother was ready to help her with the pregnancy and in raising the child, but she worked nights at a restaurant and knew she wouldn't always be around, so she encouraged Jessica to embrace the community offers.

Jessica had resisted at first; she wasn't keen on the idea of hanging around older pregnant women. But she loved learning—she had become a good student in high school—and she realized that she had a lot to learn about pregnancy. It would become her new favorite subject. She also appreciated the discipline needed to do well, especially in sports. She had liked the rules set by her softball and volleyball coaches, particularly when it came to staying in shape. In season, she often began the day with milk and a granola bar. A water bottle was always within reach during practices; no Kool-Aid or lemonade. She ate sunflower seeds during games. When her coach told her too much sugar would slow her down over time, she laid off the sugar.

Now she missed that discipline. There were no pregnancy coaches in high school, no nutrition coaches for expecting moms. So Jessica caved in to the cravings: the soda pop, the chocolates, the Flamin' Hots, the chocolate-chip cookie she plunged into a mound of mashed potatoes. Her boyfriend, Marco, who worked at a nearby pizzeria, would sometimes bring home dinner. At one checkup, Jessica was alarmed at how much weight she was gaining; she was afraid of becoming obese. She decided that the freedom to eat as much as she wanted wasn't such a good thing.

Patricia, Jessica's doula from the Ounce, would be her nutrition coach. During the home visits and meetings at Ounce offices in the Charles Hayes Family Investment Center, Patricia insisted that Jessica maintain a healthy diet just as if she were still playing softball and volleyball. Stay with the milk and granola bars, she told Jessica. Drink plenty of water.

Don't go overboard on the sugar. Several times she caught Jessica trying to sneak a bite of chocolate during their meetings.

"We've talked about eating vegetables and fruits instead," Patricia gently scolded her. She offered some purple grapes.

"I love peaches and bananas," Jessica said. Marco insisted she eat oranges, so they became an almost daily snack.

Jessica found that pregnancy was changing her tastes and eating habits over time. She was drinking much more milk, several cups a day, mainly because it soothed her nausea. She eventually lost her tolerance for the spicy Flamin' Hots. And she had given up eating the ramen noodles that were once a frequent meal. "I'm trying to avoid them now," she said to Patricia's head-nodding approval. "Too much salt. They make my stomach hurt. I don't want to go through the pain." Jessica also proudly reported that she was eating more salads. If Marco took her to a fast-food restaurant, she opted for the chicken instead of the burgers.

Patricia had given Jessica a homework assignment: read labels. Jessica took up the challenge. Cereal labels: she agreed with her mother that Cheerios were better than Lucky Charms. Soda labels: she switched to juices from soda pop. And then there were the chips labels.

"Did you know," Jessica reported back to Patricia, "that chips have folic acid? Even the extra, extra hot ones have it." She sensed the skepticism in Patricia's widening eyes. "That's what the labels say!"

"What?" Patricia shot back with alarm. "I have to check out that label."

"That's what my mom said, too." Jessica laughed. "She said, 'Still best not to have them.'"

Jessica and her mother often went grocery shopping together, sometimes driving several miles to a store—either Cermak Produce or Pete's—that stocked a good variety of fresh fruits and vegetables. Jessica had also signed up for Women and Infant Children (WIC) services, a federally funded supplemental nutrition program for low-income pregnant women and postpartum and breastfeeding mothers and their young children. Four decades after it began operations in the early 1970s, WIC was serving half of all the babies born in the United States.

Every month, Jessica received coupons for foods specifically designated for pregnant women: whole grains and reduced-fat, high-nutrient, low-sugar items. The WIC store, which only offered these authorized foods for moms and infants—no junk food allowed—was a fifteen-minute drive across the South Side from her house; it was farther than the local grocery stores, but worth the trip for her allotment of milk, juice, and cereal. WIC also provided an additional $10 worth of vouchers for fresh fruits and vegetables; it wasn't much, but at least it was something, and Jessica appreciated it. She favored sweet potatoes, cucumbers, squash, and whatever fruits were in season. She would grab a bag of oranges whenever they were available.

The WIC store on Western Avenue and Fifty-Third Street was in a tidy brick building in a neighborhood that had seen better days before the poverty deepened and the crime thickened. It looked like an ordinary supermarket, until you stepped inside. A security guard stood watch at the door. To his left was a row of desks and computers where moms could complete an online nutrition course required for WIC recipients and also check out the latest community social services programs. To his right was a Kiddie Corral offering child care while moms shopped. In a back corner, a brightly lit room hosted cooking demonstrations and nutrition education classes. In between were aisles of shelves stocked with goods in boxes, bags, bottles, and cans; a chilled area featured fruits, vegetables, eggs, and dairy. Shoppers pushed carts and waited in line at the cashier—all a typical shopping experience. But closer inspection revealed important differences. The breads and pastas were whole-wheat varieties. The rice was brown, the beans black (they were among the stars of the WIC food roster, packed as they were with protein, fiber, iron, folate, and zinc). The cereal shelves sported boxes advertising oats, brans, multigrains, and other nutritious qualities; there were plenty of Cheerios and Special Ks and nary a Lucky Charm or Chocolate Crunch. Juices were abundant, soda pop absent. There wasn't a potato chip or a Flamin' Hot or cinnamon bun in sight. Instead, tangerines, nectarines, bananas, plantains, grapes, plums, kiwis, apples, oranges, blueberries, strawberries, mangoes, and watermelon beckoned the shoppers, along with sweet potatoes, tomatoes, carrots, onions, sweet corn, kale, broccoli, jalapeños, collard greens, cucumbers, celery, lemons, and limes.

These aisles were a fresh-food oasis in a nutrition desert where many residents did their food shopping at gas stations and liquor stores. Larger chain grocers had come and gone; their sales were inconsistent and meager, so they boarded up and left. What set this store apart from them was evident in the cashier line. There were no candies or magazines, but more significantly, payment was with the coupons that were distributed to the moms at the WIC clinics when they attended regular health checkups and nutrition information sessions. Each coupon specified categories of food, depending on the stage of pregnancy or the age of the child. A mom might save more than $1,000 a year using her WIC coupons.

This store, and fifteen others like it in Chicago, was operated by Catholic Charities in partnership with the Illinois Department of Human Services and the US Department of Agriculture. Located in some of the city's most impoverished and troubled communities, the WIC stores did brisk business. More than 3,000 customers shopped at Western and Fifty-Third each week; annually, Catholic Charities served more than 120,000 people at all of its operations.

QUINTANA WOODRIDGE ALSO shopped at this WIC store. A single mom, thirty-two years old, she was expecting her second child. Patricia was her doula as well. They both worked at the Hayes community center. Quintana was a writer for We The People Media, which published a newspaper for residents of Chicago's public housing. She also coordinated an urban youth journalism program at South Side high schools. She was trying to scale back some of the more hectic work as her pregnancy progressed.

Patricia kept a close eye on Quintana at the office. "I see a pop there," Patricia said as she strolled by Quintana's desk, spying an orange soda.

"It's just one," Quintana protested playfully. "I know, it's one too many."

The one thing Quintana knew above all else was that she, too, needed the nutrition discipline. During her first pregnancy, with her son Alex, now nine, "I was eating everything under the sun," she told Patricia. "Whenever I was hungry, I'd eat. I'd eat snack foods, whatever I could grab. Flamin' Hots, they were my friend. Hot Crunchy Kurls. I drank soda pop. Orange Crush."

It continued with her second pregnancy. The Hot Crunchy Kurl habit was particularly hard to kick. Mustering the willpower, she set a strategy of downsizing her munching, from eating a big bag all at once, to a small bag, to just a few Kurls.

Quintana had plenty of incentive to change her diet for this pregnancy. Her doctor had warned her that she was overweight and at risk for preeclampsia, a potentially dangerous pregnancy complication characterized by high blood pressure. Quintana also wanted to set an example for her son. She worried that he might not be getting the proper nourishment; he ate all the time but stayed so skinny. She also thought better nutrition might improve his concentration at school.

So Quintana pushed herself to kick her junk-food habits. Instead of pop, she gulped water or milk. Rather than chips, she munched carrots and celery. She baked more and fried less. And she got hooked on a new thing: yogurt for late-night snacking.

"Less noodles, more oatmeal!" Patricia told her.

Quintana looked for support from her family, friends, and surroundings. More nutritious food options had slowly been arriving in her neighborhood. The local Walgreens began offering more vegetables and fruits. "Now I can get a fruit cup there," she enthusiastically told Patricia. A large Jewel supermarket offered a full range of groceries about seven blocks away, across the street from a McDonald's, but Quintana favored cheaper stores that were a couple miles distant. Shopping at one of them, Fairplay Foods, she bought lettuce, cherries, apples, and green beans. She also picked up a frozen Italian vegetable mix she had come to like; it was heavy on the zucchini.

During the early months of pregnancy she rode the bus with a friend who helped her carry the grocery bags. Then her boyfriend began driving her to the stores. She would shop twice a week, spending up to $80 a week on food. Her family pooled their resources. Quintana received $200 a month in food stamps, an increase of $50 since she had become pregnant. She also had her WIC coupons.

Quintana implored her son, boyfriend, and siblings to join her in eating more healthily. She trained them to eat vegetables with each meal. And she introduced salads, adding cranberries and apples to give them a fruity taste. She served whole broccoli with ranch dressing—"lite" ranch, she insisted. They tried new recipes and liked them, especially the thin-cut pork chops she fried in raspberry balsamic vinaigrette instead of butter.

She was happy they were supporting her. On one shopping trip, Quintana was strolling through the beverage aisles. An old temptation loomed. She idled in front of shelves laden with soda pop. Quintana longingly eyed the Orange Crush. But her boyfriend led her away, further down the aisle, and reached for cranberry juice.

"Yes!" Quintana exclaimed, pumping her fist.

Still, one major weakness remained, she confessed to Patricia: desserts. "I need cookies and cakes."

Patricia countered: "Oatmeal."

NEITHER JESSICA NOR Quintana were pregnant yet when Chicago mayor Rahm Emanuel hustled north along Lake Michigan early one afternoon in May 2012, shuttling between two international summits on global security issues being held in the city that day. In the morning, at McCormick Place on the South Side of downtown, the mayor welcomed heads of state, diplomats, and all manner of generals and admirals to the annual gathering of the North Atlantic Treaty Organization (NATO). In the vast convention center, the military alliance that had prevailed in the Cold War wrestled with defending against new threats in the age of international terrorism. Increasingly, those threats were coming from within, from enemies infiltrating Western societies. Then, shortly after noon, the mayor rushed across town, to the Chicago History Museum on the North Side, to salute an assembly of nutritionists and development specialists at the Scaling Up Nutrition summit. They, too, were on the front lines, confronting another enemy that attacked from within: malnutrition.

"This is an essential topic for all cities and all countries," the mayor said. "It is a problem that touches every part of every society, regardless of where it is in the world." Poor nutrition, he declared, wasn't just a problem in some distant land. It was also a problem right here in America, the richest country on earth. And right here in his city, the City of Big Shoulders.

The mayor's words were an echo from six decades earlier when President Harry Truman signed the National School Lunch Act in 1946. That legislation, passed by Congress at the urging of the nation's military leaders at the time, was in response to so many young American men being rejected for World War II military service because of diet-related health problems related to undernourishment. President Truman insisted that getting more nutritious food into the schools, and providing lunch to those children who needed it, was "a measure of national security, to safeguard the health and well-being of the nation's children." He also proclaimed, "No nation is any healthier than its children."

Several generations later, malnutrition was again a core concern of American military leaders, but this time the focus had shifted from undernourishment to overweight. Mission: Readiness, an organization of more than four hundred retired generals, admirals, and other military brass, had published a report warning that obesity was a looming threat to national defense. The report's title: "Too Fat to Fight."

Mission: Readiness claimed that more than 70 percent of seventeen- to twenty-four-year-olds in America couldn't serve in the military because they were too overweight, too poorly educated, or had a serious criminal record. The report indicated that poor nutrition in the 1,000 days influenced some of the problems, particularly weight and learning issues. "Investing early in the upcoming generation is critical to securing our nation's future," the military officers said.

Mayor Emanuel was staking Chicago's future on an improved 1,000 days. Before he took over in City Hall, it was clear that poor nutrition was diminishing his city's potential. Chicago had been the first big city to be mapped for food deserts. In her groundbreaking 2006 report, *Examining the Impact of Food Deserts on Public Health in Chicago*, research consultant Mari Gallagher linked the health of a city and its residents to nearby access to fresh fruits, vegetables, meat, and dairy products. "Residents of food deserts—large geographic areas with no or distant grocery stores—face nutritional challenges evident in diet-related community health outcomes. Those outcomes worsen when the food desert has high concentrations of nearby fast food alternatives. We call this the Food Balance Effect."

Gallagher discovered that the more out of balance a neighborhood was—less fresh food, more fast food—the greater the loss of life to diabetes, heart disease, and cancer. She also found that as grocery-store access decreased, obesity generally increased. "It is clear that food deserts, especially those with an abundance of fast food options, pose serious health and wellness challenges to the residents who live within them and the City of Chicago as a whole."

The study estimated that more than 500,000 Chicagoans lived in a food desert, most of them African Americans and Latinos on the south and west sides of the city, and a substantial number of them were single mothers and children. The very nature of food deserts—the paucity of fresh food options, and generally higher prices of fruits, vegetables, and meats even when they are available—led to unhealthy diets centered on cheaper junk food and readily available fast food, diets packed with calories rather than nutrients. Subsequent studies found that obesity was indeed rising at an alarming rate in Chicago. More than a quarter of the adult population was obese, with higher rates in the low-income neighborhoods. And obesity among Chicago's children had soared past the national average. About 15 percent of Chicago's children were already obese at two to five years of age; one-third of children entering kindergarten in Chicago's public schools were also overweight or obese. The City of Big Shoulders was becoming the City of Big Waists, with all the attendant health problems, particularly diabetes and heart disease.

Chicago manifested the same paradox I had noticed in Uganda, India, and Guatemala: malnutrition amid abundance. The food deserts had developed in the shadow of the Chicago Board of Trade, an imposing tower topped by a statue of Ceres, the Roman goddess of grain. The Board of Trade was a shrine of the global agriculture industry, and what happened there touched the lives of almost everyone on the planet. Inside, traders shouted buy and sell orders and concluded deals with intricate hand signals. This manic ritual (the last redoubt of old-fashioned bargaining before the spread of electronic trading) set prices for all manner of commodities around the globe and thereby impacted farmers and food consumers everywhere. The Board of Trade helped spur the development of agriculture in the Midwest and, in turn, the growth of Chicago's food-processing and distribution industries, which were the early foundation of the city's financial and manufacturing might.

"Hog Butcher for the World . . . Stacker of Wheat . . . the Nation's Freight Handler," was how Carl Sandburg described the city (along with the "Big Shoulders") in his 1914 poem "Chicago." Drive west from downtown on any summer day now, and it won't be long before you are cruising past fields thick with corn, wheat, and soybeans sprouting from some of the richest soils in the world tended by some of the most skilled, technologically advanced farmers.

And yet, in the southwest corner of the city—near where both Jessica and Quintana lived—the Greater Chicago Food Depository, a state-of-the-art food bank, was, lamentably, doing a booming business serving the city's poor and hungry, exactly one century after Sandburg had also observed in his ode to Chicago: "And they tell me you are brutal and my reply is: On the faces of women and children I have seen the marks of wanton hunger." In 2014, one in six Cook County residents received food from one of the depository's member agency grocery or meal programs. The depository provided about 70 million pounds of food annually, of which 35 percent was fresh fruits and vegetables. Nearly 40 percent of the households it served included at least one child.

In addition, about 20 percent of Chicago's households (including those of Jessica and Quintana) received food stamps under the Supplemental Nutrition Assistance Program, or SNAP, the largest service in the country's domestic hunger safety net. In Cook County, nearly 1 million people were living below the poverty line of about $23,000 for a family of four. Nationwide, about 45 million people participated in SNAP, nearly half of them children.

In contrast to the WIC program, SNAP didn't have restrictions on the type of food that could be purchased at stores. And there was less nutrition education. To stretch their monthly SNAP allocations as far as possible, most recipients bought the cheapest, most-filling food, which is usually the least nutritious. They generally got more for their government-assisted dollars buying chips, soda, white bread, and sugary cereals than they did from purchases of meats, whole-grain items, and fruits and vegetables. Their purchases tended to favor calories and sugar rather than nutrients.

A SNAP diet emerged that was generally high in sugar, sodium, and calories and low in protein, fiber, calcium, and other micronutrients. Research by the US Department of Agriculture, which administers SNAP and WIC, analyzed data from the National Health and Nutrition Examination Survey and noted that SNAP participants consumed fewer fruits and vegetables than nonparticipants and were more likely to consume regular sugar-sweetened sodas and less likely to consume sugar-free sodas, whether they were cheaper or not. As a result, SNAP participants were more likely to be obese than the general American population, which was already heavier than the populations of nearly every other country in the world. While SNAP alleviated hunger and food insecurity, it could also lead to malnutrition through unhealthy eating habits.

"If we don't deal with this issue of nutritional standards, we'll have a health care crisis on our hands," Mayor Emanuel warned at the Scaling Up Nutrition summit. "It leads to obesity and diabetes that are driving up health care costs."

The mayor could see poor nutrition weakening all pillars of his city. "Food deserts are also opportunity deserts," he said. Where there is a food desert, you would also find education deserts, job deserts, security deserts, health deserts. "We know food deserts for their nutritional component," he said. "But there's an economic aspect to this problem that's more than just food. Food is a manifestation of that problem."

It was in the 1,000 days, he noted, where the city's social problems began: failing health of moms and children and, by extension, failing schools, a weakened labor force, higher crime rates. And it was in the 1,000 days where his vision of a "Healthy Chicago" began. He had come to office a year earlier with an initiative relying on innovations that would benefit mothers and children in the 1,000 days: dedicated "baby-friendly" hospitals that support breastfeeding; a city agricultural program that would train hundreds of new farmers to turn derelict empty lots into urban farms to produce vegetables and fruit for the local residents; commitments from retailers to locate and expand availability of fresh foods in food deserts; school reform that would focus on early education, making sure children were prepared to learn when they started kindergarten; educational outreach, beginning with pregnant moms, that would teach the basics of good nutrition. (Mayor Emanuel would later announce that $1 million left over from the NATO summit would be used to develop "learning gardens" to provide students with hands-on nutrition education at sixty schools in the city.)

The mayor said he had first seen the physical consequences of mal-nutrition when he accompanied his father, a pediatrician, on visits to his patients. What will happen to those children? he would ask his dad.

Now, as mayor, he asked himself and his city: What becomes of kids who grow up seeing liquor stores as places where they buy their food?

"Young mothers and young families need to start early in life dealing with nutrition," Emanuel said. "There is a better option for dinner," he added, "than Twinkies and chips."

The mayor may never have uttered anything more obvious—or more profound. Behavior change on the nutrition front in the 1,000 days would be as important for the future of Chicago as it would be for the futures of Uganda, India, and Guatemala.

chapter five

THE BURDEN OF KNOWLEDGE

"THINGS ARE HAPPENING THAT YOU CAN'T SEE."

This was Patricia's favorite way to grab the attention of her expecting moms in Chicago. It was a powerful sentence, mysterious and challenging. So much development was taking place in the womb; there were so many things the moms were already influencing unbeknownst to them. With that one sentence, Patricia had them hooked. She hardly needed to add the next exhortation, but she did anyway, over and over: "Listen carefully, for this is very important."

That admonition—"Pay attention, things are happening that you can't see"—echoed from Chicago to Ongica to Rampur Khas to Chuicavioc. It was spoken in Langi, Hindi, K'iche', Spanish, English. And everywhere, mothers leaned in to listen.

The women speaking those words—Susan, Gayatri, Susy, Patricia— had all noticed the same phenomenon: the most common craving among pregnant moms worldwide is knowledge. It is a universal yearning; new moms are incredibly eager learners. Even women with older children, who had been through the 1,000 days before, were curious to find out if there was anything new this time, anything they could do better for this new baby.

The teaching was universal as well. The messages, the posters, the food pyramids, the cooking demonstrations, the handwashing—all the same. Susan, Gayatri, Susy, and Patricia talked about the same vitamins, the same nutrients, the same food groups, the same risks and opportunities. Their voices conveyed the same urgency.

Their messages were uniformly mundane—and revolutionary. They were simple, low-tech, intuitive—and brilliant. The way the health educators reached the moms in their respective locales may have varied—by foot in Uganda, bicycle in India, bus in Guatemala, car in Chicago—but they all moved in the same essential pattern: community by community, mother by mother.

THE MOST IMPORTANT "invisible thing" happening during pregnancy is the work of various nutrients in the development of the child's body and brain. Whether rich or poor, urban or rural, educated or illiterate, every pregnant mom needs the same vitamins and minerals for herself and her baby. No one is above these nutritional demands, no one is beneath them. The nutrients are the great equalizer. They are humanity's common denominators.

The physical and cognitive development of a child starts off the same all over the world. The World Health Organization (WHO), through a series of studies, has compiled a universal growth standard on the basis of evidence that children from all precincts of the globe have the same potential for physical and mental growth in utero and during early childhood, and that good nutrition is the essential fuel they need to reach that potential. In the womb, the baby is solely dependent on the mother for nutrition. Whatever causes maternal malnutrition—be it a shortage of food, a deficiency of micronutrients, an illness triggered by poor water or sanitation, a disease like malaria, or aflatoxin poisoning from crops spoiled by a fungus—can also lead to fetal and infant malnutrition, with devastating consequences.

This impact was at the heart of the decision by the Copenhagen Consensus to rank delivery of micronutrients to pregnant mothers and their babies as the world's most valuable investment. In their Copenhagen paper, researchers John Hoddinott, Mark Rosegrant, and Maximo Torero of the International Food Policy Research Institute explained what was at stake with a forceful riff on the dire consequences:

> Chronic nutrient depletion, resulting from inadequate nutrient intake, infection, or both, leads to retardation of skeletal growth in children and to a loss of, or failure to accumulate, muscle mass and fat; this linear growth is never fully regained. Chronic undernutrition (also) has neurological consequences. . . . The greatest concern lies with deficiencies in Vitamin A, iron, iodine and zinc. Vitamin A deficiencies are associated with increased risk of infant and child mortality. . . . Iodine deficiency adversely affects development of the central nervous system leading to mental retardation and stunted growth. . . . Anemia is widespread in the developing world. In women, this leads to increased risk of maternal mortality and ill-health, and low maternal iron availability leads to reduced iron stores in newborns. Iron deficiency in children constrains cognitive development. . . . Zinc deficiency affects children's physical growth and leads to increased susceptibility to a number of infections including diarrhea and pneumonia.

Restricted growth in the womb due to maternal undernutrition is estimated to be responsible for more than a quarter of all newborn deaths. Research has found that women who are overweight or obese before and during pregnancy are also more likely to have birth complications, and their children run a higher risk of birth defects, obesity, and chronic diseases later in life.

The carry-on impact of early malnutrition throughout life is called the fetal origins theory—that chronic conditions such as coronary heart disease, type 2 diabetes, and hypertension can originate in response to undernutrition and malnutrition during fetal life and infancy. The research of Dr. David Barker and his colleagues in the United Kingdom in the 1980s found that a high percentage of middle-aged men with coronary heart disease had been born with low birth weight. At the time, it was generally thought that such chronic diseases were mainly a preserve of a wealthy, high-stress lifestyle, but this new finding put the focus on poor fetal growth. Most of the men in the study were of low socioeconomic status, and Barker found that infants carried to full term with birth weights between 8.5 and 9.5 pounds had a significantly lower risk of developing heart disease later in life than babies born at 5.5 pounds or less. The risk declined steadily between 5.5 pounds and 9.5 pounds, but started to increase again as birth weight rose past 9.5 pounds. Later studies showed that low birth weight is also associated with an increased risk of stroke, insulin resistance, and development of high blood pressure in adults.

Another batch of data emerged from a study of the impact of the Dutch "hunger winter" near the end of World II, when food was so scarce in the Netherlands that people resorted to eating tulip bulbs. The study found that undernutrition during pregnancy increased the risk of many diseases by disrupting the critical development of organs and tissues in utero; babies conceived during the famine had higher rates of heart, respiratory, and renal diseases, diabetes, and certain types of cancer as adults. Similarly, an extensive study in eastern Guatemala that has been tracking moms and their children over the past five decades has found that food supplementation trials during pregnancy and early childhood in otherwise undernourished populations led to lowered risk for cardiovascular disease in adulthood.

The ability of the fetus to respond to the mother's diet is known as *developmental plasticity*—the fetus develops to suit its expected environment. Nutritionists and other scientists note that the baby of a poorly nourished mother prepares for a harsh, resource-scarce environment by adapting a protective mechanism—a *thrifty phenotype*—that reduces body size and alters metabolism. Early nutrient deficits can prompt epigenetic changes that turn certain genes on or off. This type of fetal programming leads to changes in the growth and operation of organs such as the kidney, the liver, and the pancreas. It alters genes to preserve fat and sugar, to conserve calories and energy, and to help the baby survive a shortage of food and nutrients after birth.

This adaptation can backfire if a child conditioned in the womb for a life of nutrition scarcity grows up in an environment of food surplus or of high-sugar, high-fat, high-calorie diets. The babies conceived during the Dutch hunger winter later grew up in a time of postwar prosperity and food abundance. In addition to increased risk of chronic disease, they also experienced higher obesity rates as adults. This phenomenon, tracked by Florencia Vasta at the Global Alliance for Improved Nutrition (GAIN) and other researchers, now plays out in the modern paradox of low-weight babies and stunted children having a higher propensity to become overweight or obese as teenagers and adults. The result is a burgeoning "double burden" of malnutrition: the coexistence of under- and overnutrition that can be present at the individual, family, or national level, impacting rich and poor communities alike.

India and Guatemala, along with other countries like China and Mexico, are leading this trend, which follows a shift in many traditional diets. Rising income levels may facilitate more abundance, but modernization and industrialization are also marked by a turn toward more westernized, industrialized diets featuring greater amounts of processed foods high in fat, sugar, and salt as well as high-energy snack foods—diets that have led to obesity booms in the United States, the United Kingdom, and elsewhere in the rich world. In Guatemala, for instance, about 50 percent of women of reproductive age were overweight or obese, even though most of them were stunted as children. In the years between their infancy and adulthood, Guatemala's fast-food industry boomed and diets changed. It was in Guatemala where the McDonald's Happy Meal originated, as an initiative of a franchisee: the inventor called it "Menu Ronald," and its success caught the attention of the chain's management. A popular purveyor of fried chicken, Pollo Campero, also has its origins in Guatemala.

Everywhere that researchers look while studying the spread of the "double burden," they find an increasing dependency on ready-made foods consumed on the run and a proliferation of convenience stores and fast-food outlets. They estimate that middle-income families in eastern and southern Africa, in both urban and rural areas, devote about two-thirds of their food expenditures to processed, packaged foods. Even mothers in remote regions, who spend so much time working in the fields and fetching water, are starting to prefer the ease and quickness of opening a package of processed flour to the strenuous and time-consuming task of pounding their own maize or wheat with a mortar and pestle. Patrick Webb, professor of nutrition at Tufts University, began collecting discarded snack-food bags—those modern-day tumble-weeds—wherever his research took him, be it in the mountain villages of Nepal or the remote bush of Uganda. It should be little wonder then that since 1990 the number of overweight children under five in low-income countries nearly quadrupled. Researchers at the McKinsey Global Institute estimated that approximately 30 percent of the global population was overweight or obese, with the economic impact soaring to about $2 trillion annually, or nearly 3 percent of global gross domestic product—about the same economic toll as smoking.

Market forces have also been driving this trend. In countries with an expanding middle class, prices for more nutritious foods have generally soared while junk foods have become cheaper. A study by the UK-based Overseas Development Institute found that prices of fruits and vegetables rose by 91 percent from 1990 to 2012, while the costs of processed, ready-to-eat meals dropped by up to 20 percent in many countries, including Brazil, China, and Mexico. At the same time, obesity rates have surged in those countries, all of which have a history of hunger.

In addition to the amounts of nutrients passed on from mother to child, mom's eating habits during pregnancy and while breastfeeding also influence her baby's tastes for them. High-sugar diets can create sugar cravings in offspring. Healthy eating habits, such as preferences for vegetables and fruit, can also develop in the womb.

THE SAME FETAL plasticity that shapes the growth of the body is also crucial in the development of the brain. The brain grows more during the 1,000 days than at any other period of life. The basic architecture of the brain, which provides a foundation for all future learning, behavior, and health, is constructed through an ongoing process that begins before birth and continues into adulthood. The first months and years are a time of rapid proliferation of the brain's circuitry. It is these neural connections, billions of them, that enable lightning-fast communication among neurons that specialize in different kinds of brain functions. This is the beginning of the development of basic skills and capacities such as visual conception, hearing, speech, and taste, and then more complex tasks, including language and the executive-function skills of memory, problem-solving, and self-control. The brain develops in a way that adapts to prenatal experiences. The Center on the Developing Child at Harvard University compares this "invisible" happening to the very public construction of a building: "Just as a weak foundation compromises the quality and strength of a house, adverse experiences early in life can impair brain architecture, with negative effects lasting into adulthood."

Good nutrition, again, is the cornerstone of this cognitive foundation. Nutrients are needed for the creation of new neurons, the growth of axons and dendrites (the branches of wiring that conduct nerve impulses in the brain), the formation of synapses, and the covering of axons with myelin, a dense, fatty substance that increases the speed of nerve impulses traveling from one cell to another. Inadequate availability of protein, omega-3 fatty acids, and micronutrients such as iron, zinc, iodine, thiamine, selenium, folate, and vitamins A and D impairs these neurodevelopmental processes. Folic acid is vital in reducing the risk of neural tube defects such as spina bifida; fat in the diet is important for the myelination process. Scientists have found that moderate undernutrition during this period of development, even in the absence of overt signs of malnutrition in the mother, can impact the brain. For instance, iodine deficiency has been connected to a lower IQ. To counteract these "hidden hunger" impacts, programs supplying pregnant women with iron and folic-acid supplements and projects fortifying basic foods with iron and iodine have spread across the world.

Evidence of the long-term benefits of nutrition on cognition has also been mounting. The same large-scale trial in eastern Guatemala that studied the link between early malnutrition and chronic disease has also charted the impact on cognitive development—the ability to learn and earn—over five decades. Children who received a high protein and calorie drink with added micronutrients as infants stayed in school longer than those children in the control villages; had higher cognitive test scores, particularly for reading, vocabulary, and math; and earned up to 40 percent more in average wages as adults.

And yet, on the other side of Guatemala, in the western highlands, just five hours' drive from these eastern villages that have yielded so much valuable information on the importance of good nutrition in the

1,000 days, some of the world's worst malnutrition maintained its horrible grip.

Yes, knowledge—knowing what's best for you and your baby—is power. But, as they leaned in to learn, the moms of the Palajunoj Valley, as well as the moms in India, Uganda, and Chicago, would discover one other valuable lesson: knowledge, absent the economic or physical ability to put it into action, can also be a burden.

THE MOTHERS IN Susy's nutrition program thanked her effusively for the weekly lessons. But the more they learned, the more they wondered: Can I afford to do all this? It was a nagging thought that accompanied Dianet on her walk back up the hill to her home after the cream of potato soup lesson. And now another group of moms discussed the dilemma with Susy at a meeting in a decrepit preschool building in Llanos del Pinal, a neighboring village of Chuicavioc under the Santa Maria volcano.

It had been a morning of fun interactive learning that began when Susy emptied her bag of nutrition tricks. Out tumbled pieces of Velcro cloth shaped like food: apples, peaches, pears, beans, potatoes, lettuce, cauliflower, pasta, bread, tortillas, chickens, cows, fish, cakes, pies, candy. She then taped a cardboard bowl to a wall—the bowl being the Guatemalan version of the American food pyramid—and began to fill it with the shapes. As she did, she explained the various food groups, the important nutrients in each, and how often they should be in the diets of the moms and children.

When her bowl was full, she turned the lesson over to the moms. They paired up, and Susy gave each team a cardboard bowl and a set of food stickers. It was up to them to shape a diverse diet as Susy quizzed them.

"Where do you get iron?" she asked.

"Meat. Green vegetables. Spinach. Beans." The women shouted out answers, each adding an ingredient. They worked diligently to fill their bowls with the right foods.

"Why do you need iron?" Susy asked.

"So we don't get anemic," volunteered Yolanda Chiche Perez. The other women applauded. Yolanda was twenty-eight years old, a mother of two.

She was breastfeeding her youngest, ten-month-old Andy, as she worked on the project. Yolanda had been taking notes throughout the morning.

Her partner for the exercise was her friend Maria Estella Lopez, who was twenty-five and due to deliver her second child any day. Maria Estella occupied two places in the 1,000 days. She had stopped breastfeeding her first child, one-and-a-half-year-old daughter Yesica Marisol, a month earlier. She was worried about Yesica, who was small, quiet, not eating well, clearly not thriving. Had she done something wrong as a mother? Her concern and hope that Yesica would improve, and that this next child would be healthier, had inspired her to join the Primeros Pasos nutrition rehabilitation course.

Susy quickened the pace. "Where do you get fiber?" she asked. "Where do you get vitamins?"

"Fruits and vegetables." The women added fruits and vegetables to their pots.

"Protein, where?" Susy demanded.

"Meat, milk, eggs, beans," came the answers.

"Yes," Susy triumphantly proclaimed. "You need to eat all these things, not just the food that gives us energy, so your children are healthy and big. They need this already in the womb. Your child won't benefit much if you just eat a tortilla, but a tortilla with beans, vegetable stew."

Susy inspected the bowls. She smiled and applauded. "I like your work, you paid attention."

The women applauded themselves. They now had the knowledge. They had learned well. Then they applauded Susy.

"Thank you for all you are teaching us," Yolanda said enthusiastically. Then she turned somber. Something had been bothering her as she filled the bowl. "We now know the foods to eat so our children can be healthy, but often we can't afford them."

Boom. Reality crashed the gathering, sadness barged into the fun. Yolanda said she had moved the chicken and cow shapes into her bowl, but at her home, meat was a very rare treat. "It's expensive and hard to come by," she said. "Some of us grow vegetables, but you need seed, land. It's costly for seeds and labor."

Yolanda worked several days a week in fields rented by her uncles, cleaning and bagging carrots and onions. The vegetables were grown to be sold; even Yolanda had to buy them, mainly the "ugly ones," those with funny shapes, deemed not worthy for the market.

"People don't give you anything here," Maria Estella added. She and her husband had very little land; they worked in fields owned by others.

Other women jumped into the conversation. Most of them lived with their in-laws; they didn't have their own land. "My husband doesn't earn enough, and the job he has is about to end," said Gabriela Chiche, who was twenty years old and five months pregnant with her first child. Her husband was a mason's assistant; he traveled the valley looking for any construction sites where he might find work for a couple of weeks. Gabriela didn't have a job. She had never been to school. She signed in for Susy's class by leaving a thumbprint on the paper. Their household income might be 300 quetzales a week (about $40), a bit more if her husband found steady work on a construction site.

"It all goes to food. And soap," she said.

It wasn't enough, even by the government's own healthy food bowl standard. The government estimated that the monthly cost for sufficiently nutritious food for a family of four was about Q3,000. Few families in the valley could afford that, or even come close.

All the women said their family's food money was allocated by their husbands. Gabriela shopped once a week, usually on Saturdays, at the large outdoor market near the bus terminus in Quetzaltenango. She recited a recent shopping list of necessities: a couple of pounds of sugar, one pound of noodles, one pound of rice, one bottle of cooking oil, three balls of soap, one head of cauliflower, one pound of tomatoes, one pound of green beans, a dozen bananas, fifteen eggs, and corn, of course, both the kernels and already ground flour, about ten pounds total.

"That's it," she said.

Saturday would also be meat day, if there was any money left over for a pound of chicken or beef. There rarely was.

Gabriela's mention of eggs prompted complaints from the other women of wild price variations; their neighbors in the village might charge Q3 for an egg, while at the market in the big city it would go for one and a quarter. Carrots also suffered price volatility, swinging between Q6 and Q15 for a dozen. "That's more than 1 quetzal a carrot!" Gabriela said. She sounded offended. The price of apples, too, stirred the ire.

"Apples, so expensive. Why?" protested Maria Estella.

None of the women had fruit in their houses at the time.

"Vegetables are sometimes very expensive, even though we see them every day in the fields," Maria Estella said. "And the fruit that comes from the coast is too expensive to buy. Our children want fruit, but we don't have any."

Everyone had corn, or corn flour. It was on all the moms' shopping lists, ten to twelve pounds to get them through the week. The women were unanimous about the ubiquity of tortillas. They described their daily menus: rare was a meal without tortillas, two to four per person.

Although they had all shouted "Milk" to Susy's calcium prompting when filling their cardboard bowls, it was an infrequent visitor to their houses. Fresh milk was Q7 a liter, powdered milk was 10. And so milk wasn't a high priority on anyone's shopping list. Instead, they relied on the Guatemalan-made Incaparina, a nutrient-fortified powder originally concocted by the Institute of Nutrition of Central America and Panama (INCAP) in the 1950s. An early version of Incaparina was the fortified porridge-like mixture given to pregnant mothers and their young children in the INCAP study in eastern Guatemala in the early 1970s; now, Primeros Pasos distributed it to the moms participating in the nutrition classes.

"We know it's important to drink milk for our bones, and that it's especially important for our children," said Yolanda, overcome by frustration. She knew what was best to do—it was there in her notes, and in her cardboard bowl—but so often she couldn't afford it. "I hardly ever buy milk, or cornflakes. My husband doesn't make enough." Her husband drove a bus throughout the valley four days a week, earning about Q450 per week.

And sometimes other expenses would pop up, eroding the food budget. "The children get sick, they need medicine, we need to buy clothes," Yolanda said. A month earlier, her son Andy had to have surgery to correct a urinary problem. The surgery was free at the government hospital in Xela, but the examinations cost up to Q100.

Even if their houses were well-stocked with all the commodities in Susy's food bowl, the moms would be last in line to eat them, behind their husbands and children, as is the social custom. "Sometimes," Yolanda noted, "my daughter says she wants milk, so I buy a little bit for her."

The lesson over for the day, Yolanda wrapped Andy on her back with a red blanket. She thanked Susy with a hug. It was fun moving the food shapes into the bowl. If only she could do the same at home with real vegetables and meats and fruits and dairy products. She tucked her notes into her apron and trudged back home, stooped with the burden of her knowledge.

THE LAMENTS OF the women of the Palajunoj Valley were common in the 1,000 days; their burden was shared by women around the world.

"I'm trying to eat more vegetables and fruit, like we are learning. But they are too expensive," Sushma told me when I visited her house in Rampur Khas late one morning. She had been up early, working in the mint fields before the sun began its merciless midday reign. Back at her one-room house, she was still working, stoking a fire in the clay stove just off the veranda. Beans and rice were on the boil. In between stirring, she fashioned *chapati*, a local flatbread, from wheat flour. These were the main features of most meals. Sushma cooked once a day, preparing both lunch and dinner at the same time. There would be no green vegetables or fruit this day. The day before, she'd cooked up potatoes and green leaves from the squash vines that grew beside the house. Her two-year-old daughter, Khushboo, ate what Sushma, her husband, and their older son ate. Sushma had stopped breastfeeding Khushboo after fifteen months, when she became pregnant again. Khushboo was now drinking water pumped from the communal well, like the rest of the family. They didn't own a cow.

Hearing our conversation, Mohana, the next-door neighbor, dropped by. She complained that the price of lentils was rising. Lentils were a main ingredient of *dal*, a common dish. Any increase in the price of lentils would be a significant economic and nutritional hardship; lentils were rich in protein, folic acid, iron, magnesium, zinc, and fiber.

Like the other pregnant women and new moms, Sushma and Mohana received a weekly ration of a fortified food powder, *panjiri*, from the local *anganwadi*, a government health worker. (The *anganwadi* also provided iron and folic-acid tablets for the pregnant moms.) The *panjiri* was a mixture of wheat (34 percent), sugar (25 percent), soya (18 percent), rice (12 percent), maize (5 percent), vegetable oil (5 percent), and assorted vitamins and minerals (1 percent). Pregnant and breastfeeding mothers were to consume 150 grams a day, which would provide 13 grams of protein and 400 calories. They could mix it with milk or water for a thick drink, or add it to porridge or rice pudding; sometimes Sushma just straight up ate the powder, which had a sweet taste. The *panjiri*—provided by the Uttar Pradesh government and the World Food Program—was meant to be consumed by the mothers, to give them added energy and nutrients while pregnant and breastfeeding. But Sushma and Mohana, and all the other moms I met, shared their *panjiri* ration with their families. Sometimes there wasn't even any left over for them. Though they shared their nutrients, it was rare for the women of Rampur Khas to eat at the same time as their husbands and children. Often, I saw the mothers eating by themselves, squatting in a lonely corner of the veranda, after the rest of the family had finished. They were scraping together whatever food remained. "First they give to the husband and children, and then they take," said Gayatri of the Community Empowerment Lab.

Gayatri had been making the rounds of the Saksham villages for three years. She had noticed many barriers between the knowledge she imparted and the ability of the moms to act on it. "The socioeconomic situation in our country is a big factor," she said with an unusual weariness in her youthful voice. Most of the families in the Shivgarh villages were of the lowest castes. The men were day laborers, scrounging work where they could, sometimes far from home, earning about 100 rupees a day (about $1.60), if they got paid at all. That meant even basic nourishment was a luxury purchase. Fortunately, the climate in this area of Uttar Pradesh fostered three harvests a year: rice was followed by wheat, which was followed by mint. The families that didn't have their own land worked for other landholders and were paid with a portion of their harvest. So they usually had some rice or wheat in the house, and the mint harvest provided a bit more income. In addition, the government's public food distribution system provided heavily subsidized rations to the poorest citizens. But what was distributed was largely more rice, wheat, and maize—energy and calories, but few nutrients. There were no fruits or vegetables in the public distribution because an adequate cooling and storage system that could prevent spoilage had yet to be developed. And the system was rife with inefficiency, favoritism, and corruption, leaving many poor, marginalized families excluded from the distribution rolls while wealthier, better-connected families received rations. Only a few of the families I met were receiving the subsidized food, even though their poverty certainly would have made them eligible.

Gayatri recognized that she was delivering a discordant message when she talked to the moms about diversifying their diets with more nutritious foods. It was more fantasy than reality. She winced at the frustration Seema and Sanju expressed when she checked up on them in the neighboring village of Barjor Khera. They had married brothers, lived side by side, shared a veranda, and now were expecting babies at the same time. For Seema, who was thirty years old, it would be her third child; for Sanju, twenty, her first. They met with us on the shared stoop between their houses.

"Now I'm aware of nutritious foods, thanks to Saksham. But I have difficulty in buying them," Seema said. "We know to take milk, beans, vegetables, be diverse in our diet. That's important. We know we should eat fruit, and maybe we do once a week when they are ripe. Banana, mango, grapes, oranges. But otherwise we can't afford them on the market."

The family's one cow lounged a few feet away, munching on straw. It was still too young to be producing milk. They also had a bull, good for fieldwork but useless on the nutrient front. So milk—an essential ingredient, Seema knew—was a luxury purchase. Water straight from the well would have to do, but that water—untreated—was often risky to drink, being a prime source of bacteria and parasites. Very few families in Shivgarh, or in all of Uttar Pradesh, purified the water in any way to make it safer. No one in Barjor Khera or in Rampur Khas or in any of the villages in rural Shivgarh had indoor toilets; even outhouses were rare. India accounted for about 60 percent of the incidence of open defecation in the world. Human waste seeped into the groundwater, which trickled into the wells. In the rural areas of Uttar Pradesh, more than three-quarters of the households had no toilet facilities. This resulted in a high prevalence of water-borne diseases like diarrhea, which then carried away whatever vital micronutrients that could make it into the body.

"I know milk is beneficial for me and my children, but I can't afford it," Seema said. She, too, was doubly in the 1,000 days; her second-oldest child, a son named Abhay, was eighteen months old. She had weaned him off breastmilk several months earlier when she realized she was pregnant again. It was a local belief that pregnancy spoiled the breastmilk. Abhay was eating rice and water from a tin cup. Seema wished she could give him fruit every day. She remembered one meeting with Saksham when the women of Barjor Khera had talked about the benefits of eating apples. Now Seema asked Gayatri, "Do you know how expensive apples are?"

Yes, Gayatri knew. They weren't in season, and the price could be as high as 150 rupees for one kilogram (2.2 pounds). Seema's husband chased 100-rupee-a-day manual labor jobs. A kilo of apples would eat up one and a half days of wages.

Gayatri also knew that even if the moms could afford apples, it was unlikely there would be a bite left for them, after the apples were grabbed by the husbands and children. "The children don't understand, they are demanding," Gayatri told me. "So there is very little for the mothers."

What no one here knew was that the nutrition affordability gap was widening all across India. As Seema and Sanju spoke on their stoop, the International Food Policy Research Institute (IFPRI) in Washington, DC, was preparing its annual *Global Food Policy Report* of 2013. It would chronicle how quickly food prices in India were rising, "especially for high-nutrient foods," confirming what the moms here were experiencing. IFPRI's food price index for India had been climbing steadily, going from a base of 100 in 2007 to nearly 160 by the middle of 2013. India's vegetable price index spiked even more dramatically in 2013, nearly tripling in the course of one year.

Rising prices for high-nutrient foods, deep poverty that made those foods unattainable for so many mothers, abysmal sanitation, family hierarchies that relegated girls and women to the bottom rung, especially when it came to eating—these were all barriers to acting on the knowledge they had gained about the 1,000 days. It was little wonder, then, that 90 percent of adolescent Indian girls were anemic, a prime indicator of malnutrition as they approached childbearing years. Pregnant women in India were generally far less healthy than moms-to-be in sub-Saharan

Africa. A study led by Princeton development economist Diane Coffey found that 42 percent of Indian women were underweight when they began pregnancy compared with 16 percent of African women. Coffey also noted that Indian women end pregnancy weighing less than African women do at the beginning of their pregnancies.

This relationship had become known as the Indian or South Asian enigma—the women were less healthy and their children were much smaller than would be expected given the relative wealth of India and Africa. Indians presumed they were better off—far better off—than Africans. India's overall economic growth and its flood of college graduates, high-tech advances, and lofty ambitions on the world stage fostered this pretension. After all, India was preparing to launch a mission to Mars.

Never mind that its mothers and children were among the most malnourished on Earth.

ACROSS MUCH OF Africa, the weight and health of moms fluctuated according to the farming seasons, which in turn were governed by the rains. If the rains came in a timely and full manner, the crops would steadily grow. Then, at harvest time, there would be food aplenty in both houses and markets. The moms and their children would eat well. But if the rains sputtered or failed, harder times were certain.

The size of the harvest dictated the length of the annual hunger season, which begins when the food from the previous harvest runs out and ends when the next harvest comes in. Nearly every farm family in northern Uganda, and throughout most of sub-Saharan Africa, experienced some kind of hunger season; the only variable was how long it would endure. Depending on the bounty of the previous harvest, the hunger season could stretch from a couple of weeks to several months or longer. In this period of profound deprivation, families rationed their food, and meals dwindled from three a day to two, to maybe just one, even none on some days. Men, women, and children would watch themselves shrink; their clothes would hang limply on their bodies, and they would cinch their belts a hole or two tighter.

For unborn babies, the hunger season could be a period of epigenetic change. Researchers at the London School of Hygiene and Tropical Medicine studying diets in rural Gambia compiled evidence that the season when a child is born can have a profound effect on lifelong health. They found that Gambian children born during the hunger season were up to ten times more likely to die prematurely in young adulthood. The "highly plausible" cause, according to the researchers: "Nutrition related epigenetic regulation in the early embryo."

In northern Uganda, anemia was rampant throughout the year, as was malaria; it was a debilitating, sometimes deadly, one-two punch. Both posed grave threats to pregnant women and their unborn children. Malaria accounted for nearly one-third of all deaths of children under five in Uganda. But to be pregnant during the hunger season, or to be breast-feeding a newborn then, was particularly precarious.

When I first met the moms of Ongica and Barjwinya, the hunger season was approaching. Food stocks in the houses were dwindling, prices in the markets were rising, stress levels were climbing. But hope that the season of want might not stretch too long had also arrived with the first rains. The pace of work in the fields accelerated as the farmers, mostly women, hustled to prepare for the planting.

Susan had scheduled her nutrition meeting at the Ongica clinic for midafternoon despite the heat; the mornings, when the temperatures were cooler, were reserved for work in the fields. As she finished the lesson, Susan beseeched the pregnant moms not to work too hard. Don't spend all day in the fields. Take time for yourself and the baby. "To give birth to a future president you need rest," she said.

Laughter rippled across the veranda. Susan knew her timing wasn't good. This advice was even harder to follow than her instruction to diversify diets. Pregnancy during the time of planting wasn't compatible with rest. Another vast chasm opened between the knowledge of what was best to do and what was actually doable given the reality of their lives.

With the arrival of the rains, the top priority was getting the crops planted in the fields. The most frequent sight during the growing season was of a woman bent over hacking at the ground. Many of them carried babies, wrapped in blankets, on their backs.

Esther's pregnant silhouette was a lonely-looking figure in her fields. She and her husband, Tonny, lived on his family's homestead; they had built a sturdy brick bungalow right beside the gravel road that led to

Susan's clinic. Tonny, who hoped to become a successful businessman, was off studying accounting at Uganda Commercial College, so on most days Esther toiled by herself, tending to the peanuts, millet, cassava, maize, peas, and kale. The task at hand was to get the high-iron beans in the ground, so they might be ready to eat when the baby was born. This involved bending over a short-handled hoe, turning the soil, dropping in the seeds, covering them with soil. She planted the beans beside her cassava bushes. Next up would be planting a quarter acre of sweet-potato vines. For that, she would be on her knees, forming the soil into hundreds of mounds and embedding the vines. Her diversified fields were Susan's lecture come to life.

Harriet, too, did most of the farming alone. Her husband, Moses, daily ascended the rocky hill on the horizon and broke stones into pebbles for the construction companies in Lira. On some days, especially during the planting, Moses came down from the hill early to help; he recognized how important the beans and orange sweet potatoes were to his family's health. The traditional white sweet potatoes had been widely considered a marginal crop, the last line of defense against famine; they would stay in the ground until needed. But over the past year, since the introduction of the vitamin A–rich orange variety, sweet potatoes—along with the high-iron beans—had become a daily staple, present in most meals along with pigeon peas, maize, and cassava.

"I see improvement in our children. They aren't in the hospital as much," Moses said. "And my wife is feeling better this pregnancy. She doesn't fall asleep as much. She has more energy to work in the field."

Brenda's husband, Dennis, also appreciated his wife's energy during this pregnancy. Having lost their first child, they were more cautious, but there was no getting around the need to tend to the crops. Brenda and the other pregnant moms were in a race with nature: the rains had arrived, and the babies were on their way.

As the weeks went on and the time for giving birth drew near, the rains dissipated. The dry spell came at the worst possible time, for the beans needed rain as they flowered, and the corn needed continued rain to flourish. Sitting under a tree outside their one-room mud-brick hut, Brenda and Dennis listened to a transistor radio attached to an old car battery. The spirited, carefree African music gave way to the news. And worries. Possible drought was looming.

Brenda knew what she needed to eat—she was planting it in her fields a short walk from her house—but would the weather cooperate so she could do so?

IN CHICAGO, JESSICA joined in on the global refrain: "Have you seen the price of apples?" she asked Patricia.

Expensive apples, again. Shivgarh, the Palajunoj Valley, Chicago. Moms in the United States were as sensitive to nutrient-rich food prices as were women in India and Guatemala. Poverty trumped knowledge in the wealthiest country in the world, too.

Patricia and her fellow doulas were sympathetic to the sighs and the rolling eyes of the moms they counseled with nutrition advice. They heard the same response as Susy and Gayatri: Thanks for the information, but how can we afford it?

"You're right," Patricia would say. She herself had flinched at paying $2 for oranges.

As was the case in India, the cost of nutritious food had been on a steady rise in the United States. In the previous decade, the price of fruits and vegetables had increased by about 16 percent, according to the US Department of Agriculture. Over the same time period, prices for sugar and sweets had decreased by more than 7 percent. One of the forces tipping these trends was the nature of the US food system, particularly agricultural subsidies designed to encourage high production of staple crops. Over the years, crops such as corn, wheat, and soybeans have received the bulk of farm subsidies, while fruit and vegetable growers have received a much smaller share. Greater production of fruits and vegetables would normally mean lower prices.

A raft of cultural counterweights also undermined the power of nutrition knowledge. Jessica and Quintana both lived near the Pulaski corridor, a fast-food highway lined on both sides of the street with an array of hamburger joints, pizza parlors, chili emporiums, sandwich shops, ice-cream stands, taco restaurants, and chicken shacks. There is a White Castle directly across the street from Jessica's high school.

"I often see my moms eating McDonald's or Burger King," Patricia told me. "I ask them, 'Do you at least pick the healthy options?' The mom says, and we hear this often, 'The salads are more than $5. The cheeseburger is $1. What's the choice?'" If nutrition wasn't convenient, it also wasn't hip. The pull of pop culture often overwhelmed her nutrition advice. Fingers stained with red seasoning became cool—and the sure sign of a Flamin' Hot Cheetos addict. A group of Minneapolis students called Y.N.RichKids, as part of a Beats & Rhymes after-school youth program, produced a rap video hailing the virtues of Flamin' Hots and a tortilla snack called Takis (coated with salsa and seasonings for various heat intensities, like Fuego and Nitro), with lyrics like these:

> Hot Cheetos and Takis
> Hot Cheetos and Takis
> I can't get enough of these Hot Cheetos and Takis
> Got my fingers stained red and I cannot get them off me
> You can catch me and my crew eating Hot Cheetos and Takis

The video went viral, with more than 11 million views.

Patricia, whose rap went from one mom to another, savored small victories. Like the time one of her moms saw kiwis at a WIC store and bought them with her coupons. She thanked Patricia for the kiwi introduction. Patricia had brought the vitamin C–rich fruit to one of their meetings and encouraged the mom to touch it and taste it. It seemed to her at first as strange as a moon rock. Now she knew better and couldn't get enough of those kiwis.

A FEW BLOCKS from the Charles Hayes Family Investment Center, at Ounce of Prevention's Educare school, moments of nutritional victory over cultural habits were greatly celebrated. The Educare school, which enrolled children as young as six weeks, was a model of the mayor's vision of starting education as soon as possible after birth. It was also part of the mayor's call for urban gardeners. On green stretches bordering the school's parking lot, all manner of vegetables flourished: cherry tomatoes, corn, carrots, collard greens, pumpkins, peas, beans. There was a plot for each classroom. The produce wouldn't be prepared for school meals, but

sent home with the pupils. Harvest time would become a teaching moment for the parents as well as the children.

"Don't be afraid of fresh vegetables," Educare's Erika Waller told a
group of parents. "We know it's much easier to open up a can or get some
fries out of the freezer than it is to peel a potato." Before the gardens,
moms would congregate while picking up their children and talk about
making deep-fried Twinkies. Now, they sipped water infused with herbs
from the gardens while swapping recipes for homemade salsa with fresh
tomatoes and onions. One harvest yielded a bumper crop of eggplant.
The parents kept asking: What's an eggplant? What do we do with it?
So Educare had an eggplant symposium. "And then they asked for more
eggplant," Erika told me. "It was a revelation. They also learned you can
pretty much grow this food anywhere and everywhere."

It was growing in a most unusual place on the North Side of Chicago—the former basketball courts of the old Cabrini Green housing
project, which had rivaled the Robert Taylor Homes for notoriety. At the
corner of Chicago Avenue and North Hudson, kids once played hoops
day and night, nurturing ambitions of becoming professional basketball
players, as depicted in the documentary *Hoop Dreams*. Now, with the
housing mostly torn down, kids rooted around in the dirt that covered
the old courts, nurturing kale and carrots and onions and squash and
learning how to grow up healthy. Cornstalks reached for the sky in the
shadow of Chicago's iconic skyscrapers. Hoop dreams had given way to
hoop houses—miniature greenhouses for year-round vegetables.

The Chicago Lights Urban Farm, an outreach of the Fourth Presbyte-
rian Church near Chicago's Gold Coast, was intended to break up a food
desert, introduce green space to an asphalt maze, and teach new eating
habits to residents as nutrition camps replaced basketball camps. The
goal was to change behaviors, just like in India, Guatemala, and Uganda.
When one child in the summer Farm Camp, part of the Children Achieving Maximum Potential program, celebrated his seventh birthday, he
asked not for cake, but for kale.

But here, too, the burden of newfound nutrition knowledge weighed
heavily on the neighborhood. Everyone knew fresh vegetables were
available there, but not everyone could easily access them. Invisible terri-
torial gang lines were still treacherous to cross. Chicago Lights organizers

posted signs on the chain-link fence surrounding the garden exhorting neighborliness: "Plant." "Thrive." "Share." But the signs didn't deter old behaviors. One cold January day, shots rang out beyond the corner with the "Share" sign. It was Chicago's first murder of 2013.

In mid-February, a few weeks after that shooting, President Barack Obama returned to his old neighborhood on the South Side to decry the city's violence, and one killing in particular. A group of local high school students, members of a band majorette team, had just performed at the president's second inauguration festivities. Upon their return to Chicago, one of the students, Hadiya Pendleton, who was about Jessica's age, was randomly shot and killed in a park not far from the Obama family house. She was with friends when a stray bullet hit her in the back, becoming one of forty-four homicide victims in the city that month.

Uganda had its hunger season; Chicago had its season of violence. It had once normally flared in the summer months, when temperatures and tempers rose. But now the season of violence was rolling year round. The Chicago Tribune's crime tracker project kept count: In 2012, Chicago endured more than 500 murders, 443 with a firearm, and 65 of those victims were children. And the pace hadn't slowed in 2013. Hadiya's murder—random, senseless, shocking, futile—demanded outrage.

"In too many neighborhoods today," said President Obama, his anger simmering, "it can feel like for a lot of young people the future only extends to the next street corner or the outskirts of town; that no matter how much you work or how hard you try, your destiny was determined the moment you were born. There are entire neighborhoods where young people, they don't see an example of somebody succeeding."

Greatness? Who could dream of greatness here?

The president wondered that himself. Mothers needed to feel safe raising their children; children needed to get off to a better start in life. "In America, your destiny shouldn't be determined by where you live, where you were born," he continued. "It should be determined by how big you're willing to dream, how much effort and sweat and tears you're willing to put into realizing that dream. . . . Those parents supporting kids—that's the single most important thing. Unconditional love for your child—that makes a difference."

It was imperative, he said, that society "give a child the kind of foundation that allows them to say, 'My future, I can make it what I want.' And we've got to make sure that every child has that."

A couple of months later, Jessica would learn she was pregnant, having conceived around the time President Obama was talking about a good start in life. She desperately wanted to dream big things for her child. But as her pregnancy went on, so did the violence in Chicago, mainly on the South Side. Gang fights, random shootings, more innocent children dying in parks or on their front porches. On some weekends, the death toll reached double digits. Jessica lived on the west end of Seventy-Ninth Street. On the eastern end, closer to Lake Michigan, the violence was so bad that the city's newspapers began referring to Seventy-Ninth Street as "Murderers' Row." Chicago's homicide numbers stacked up as the summer steamed on: 47 in May, 46 in June, 48 in July, 49 in August, 44 in September. A trip to the grocery store was a risky proposition. A walk in the park was folly.

Violence became a major barrier for Jessica as she attempted to use her knowledge about the first 1,000 days of her child's life.

"Are you exercising like we talked about?" Patricia asked her during one of their meetings that summer.

"I *was*," Jessica said.

Her mother had seen some men with guns on their neighborhood streets—which looked benign enough, with sidewalks and trees—and stopped Jessica's walks. Confined to her mother's brick bungalow, Jessica yearned for an escape from this opportunity desert. Her knowledge of what to do had now become a burden. "I know I should be doing more," she told Patricia.

All Jessica wanted was to give her baby the best start in life, to safely navigate the 1,000 days. Instead, she worried: What kind of world am I bringing my child into?

Jessica opened her diary and poured out her heart to the child in her womb:

> *Are you cozy in my tummy? Can you feel the warmth of my hands in there? I can't wait to see you, to hold you in my arms and love you forever.*

Jessica wanted her baby always to be safe. But how?

> *You do not need to join any gangs . . . to be important or known.*
> *Want to be known? Want to be important? Then finish school, go*
> *to college. Join activities as in debate, or anything that interests*
> *you that will be great on a school record. Join sports. Please stay*
> *off the streets. By getting excellent grades, staying involved in*
> *school will get you to become known. How? Teacher will talk*
> *about your excellent behavior and colleges will want to accept*
> *you and from there you'll be known as an achiever, not a quitter.*
> *Don't give up on what you believe in. The struggle will always be*
> *there, it's the achievement your trying to get too.*
>
> *Love, Mommy.*
> *PS: forever my baby.*

chapter six

IT'S A . . .

JESSICA HOPED SHE WAS CARRYING A GIRL, AND SO DID MARCO. Still, until they knew for sure, they hedged their bets; they pondered both boy and girl names and they browsed unisex outfits in the baby stores at the mall. Jessica also captured the suspense in her letters to her child. At fifteen weeks, as she listened to a song called "Stomach Tied in Knots" by Sleeping with Sirens, Jessica began her journal entry with a generic "Dear Sailor."

> *You are my sailor, okay? Why? Because I'm Sailor Jess. And your dad is Captain Marco. So your my little sailor. . . . Your father and I talk endlessly about you. We do not know your gender but your grandmother believes you are a girl and of course so does your father. And what do you think about that? Hmm. I feel like your a boy but then a girl. I think I'll stick with you being my little sailor.*

At her next checkup, during the ultrasound, Jessica asked the doctor and was told, "It's a girl." She was so happy she drew a picture of the ultrasound image of her daughter for her art class in high school. And she began her next journal entry more intimately: "My little Alitzel, Oh how I love you dear. I love you more than anything my little girl."

Jessica had several ultrasounds during her pregnancy. The first one confirmed that she was indeed pregnant; the second revealed that she was expecting a girl. The others assured her that her pregnancy was going well. She prized each image:

> *I saw your face, my cutie pie. You look like your daddy but once your here we'll see who you look like.*

After her last ultrasound, three weeks before the due date, Jessica wrote:

> *I had an appointment and I got sent to get an ultrasound to check if you were okay and Ali, I swear, I'll never forget how clear I saw your precious face. With the biggest cheeks and tiny nose. It was too perfect.*

The excitement and wonder of seeing a picture of their baby in the womb was singular to the moms in the Americas. In Chicago, Quintana also was delighted to see that she was having a girl. Her son and first child, Alex, studied the image and declared his excitement at having a sister. Quintana had already settled on a name, ShaLawn, which she used in her byline, her *nom de plume*.

In Guatemala, ultrasounds were rarer. Most of the women in the Palajunoj Valley went to Primeros Pasos every two months for their prenatal checkups. That was more convenient and less expensive than making a trip to the city, but at the time there was no ultrasound machine at the clinic. Only when they went to the regional government hospital in Quetzaltenango did they get an ultrasound, which did not happen often, and sometimes not until they were ready to deliver. Once during her pregnancy Dianet Coyoy did take the thirty-minute bus ride into the city for a checkup. She received an ultrasound, which revealed she was carrying a girl. Dianet rejoiced, but her celebration was tempered when she returned home to find her joyous news greeted with skepticism. "No, no, not a girl," she was told more than once by family members. "No, your belly is low. It will be a boy." The ultrasound was wrong, they told her.

IN BOTH ONGICA and Shivgarh, there were no pictures, no wonders, no excitement, no ultrasounds. "No power, no power." That was the constant refrain Harriet in Uganda heard when she went to the regional hospital in Lira for a checkup several weeks before her due date. She had suddenly been feeling listless and dizzy; a nurse at the Ongica clinic, where there is no ultrasound machine, suspected she had high blood pressure and referred her to the hospital for a routine fetal scan to make sure the baby was well. But as Harriet learned, the mere presence of a machine didn't necessarily benefit her. The facility needed electricity to run the ultrasound and a technician to fix it when it broke down, which was often. Neither was available the day Harriet showed up. She returned home, no wiser or healthier.

Harriet's malaise deepened. Try as she might, she couldn't work in the fields without getting tired and needing a rest, even though the sweet-potato harvest had just begun. This wasn't like her; she was always a hard worker. Now she was weak and had lost her appetite. She had battled malaria a few months earlier; maybe, she worried, she was having a relapse. Her legs were swelling and the headaches were becoming more persistent. She went to the clinic and was again referred to the regional hospital in Lira. She hitched a ride on the back of a motorcycle and rode sidesaddle for the twenty-minute journey. There, a doctor told her she was anemic and had high blood pressure; noting a risk of preeclampsia, the doctor checked her in for bed rest. It was now three weeks before Harriet was due. The doctor and nurses expected her to have a normal delivery. Still, they offered her the opportunity to have an ultrasound. This time, the power was fine. But there was another problem. The cost was 15,000 Ugandan shillings, or about $7. It would take several days of work crushing stones at the quarry to cover that. Harriet and her husband agreed it was too expensive. Again, poverty played the trump card. Harriet pleaded with a nurse, but she was told they would do a scan for free only if there was an emergency. "No money, no scan," she was told. Instead, the nurse listened through an old-fashioned fetal scope and heard a heartbeat. She believed neither Harriet nor the baby were in any imminent danger.

IN THE RURAL areas of India, it was rare that an ultrasound would even be offered. When I asked a gathering of moms and moms-to-be in Shivgarh if any of them had received an ultrasound, or would expect to, there was initial silence. Then muffled laughter. And then animated chatter. For them, it was a silly question. "It's generally prohibited," one woman coldly explained. The information, particularly if it showed a girl, could be used for an abortion, she said. "No, no ultrasounds." Rather than bringing the joy that Jessica and Quintana and Dianet experienced, an image of a girl in the womb here could lead to great tragedy. Official statistics put the annual number of abortions in India at several hundred thousand, but maternal and child health advocates believed the actual number was far higher, for many of the abortions happened in unauthorized facilities. National census figures had revealed a steady decline over the previous decade in the number of girls compared to boys up to age six. Domestic and international organizations advocating access to safe abortions estimated that a woman died every two hours from an unsafe abortion in India.

BEYOND THE EXPERIENCE of seeing an image of your child, ultrasounds are also valuable in assessing the health of babies and mothers. Quintana, already at risk of preeclampsia from high blood pressure, worried that the stress from her job—during her pregnancy, she was the only teacher in her office visiting classes on Chicago's South Side—was also affecting her baby. So Quintana saw her doctor nearly every week, especially in the third trimester, to make sure everything was okay with her and the child. Jessica, too, would head to her doctor at any sign of worry. She complained that one teacher at her high school wouldn't make a special allowance for her to bring a water bottle into class, so she battled dehydration at times. One time she feared that the baby had stopped moving; an ultrasound eased her concern.

In Uganda, India, and Guatemala, the women mainly worried alone, and their maladies remained a mystery. In India, Sanju's doctor sent her to a city hospital an hour away from her home for an ultrasound, but she didn't understand why it was necessary. She returned home still wondering. She later told me that no one had explained to her whether they had spotted any complications—or if they did, this woman with no education had not comprehended what they had said. Sanju doubted that the machine even worked. She certainly wasn't given an image.

Few of the moms in India and Uganda complied with the World Health Organization (WHO) recommendation of going to at least four prenatal-care visits with trained health workers. The distances to a clinic or hospital were too far, the travel too time consuming and costly, the medicines too expensive, the trained health workers too rare. The WHO had determined that four visits were the minimum needed to get a tetanus vaccination and proper screening and treatment for infections and any other potential problems. But, according to the WHO's own research during the period 2006–2013, barely half of all pregnant women in the world made the minimum four visits; in low-income countries, it was only slightly more than a third. In Uttar Pradesh, one of India's poorest states, just one-quarter of pregnant women went to any prenatal checkups. In Uganda, a government study revealed that although 95 percent of pregnant women attended their first prenatal visit, to confirm a pregnancy, only 48 percent completed the four visits—and most of those who did lived in urban areas. This meant they also missed out on the distribution of iron and folic-acid tablets and malaria pills. Only one in two women who visited a clinic were warned about pregnancy complications. (Even in the United States, not all pregnant women met the WHO standards; one study revealed that 6 percent of women received no or late prenatal care, and that most of the women who fell into this category were African American or Latina.)

Once they did reach a clinic or hospital for a prenatal checkup, mothers in the developing world would often find scarce staffing and appalling infrastructure conditions. Officials at the WHO and the United Nations Children's Fund themselves seemed shocked at the overall wretchedness of conditions revealed in their first multi-country review of water, sanitation, and hygiene services in health-care facilities. They called the findings "alarming." Reviewing data from 54 low- and middle-income countries representing more than 66,000 health-care facilities, the report concluded that 38 percent of these facilities lacked access to an improved water source, 19 percent didn't provide sanitation, and 35 percent didn't have soap and water for handwashing. It is hardly surprising then that functioning ultrasound equipment wasn't high on many priority lists.

The consequences of these deficiencies can be fatal, as infections can quickly spread in such conditions. The report said sepsis and other severe infections are major killers, one of the leading causes of maternal and infant deaths. The risks associated with sepsis are thirty-four times greater in low-resource settings. The impact is particularly pronounced for newborns. Poor hygiene during and after umbilical cord cutting—unclean hands, a dirty blade, filthy cloth—produce untold numbers of cord site infections. In many places, moms must bring their own blades, soap, and cloth—if they can afford them or even access them—and sometimes their own water. In facilities without toilets, women in labor need to walk outside to relieve themselves.

"The health consequences of poor water, sanitation and hygiene services are enormous. I can think of no other environmental determinant that causes such profound, debilitating and dehumanizing misery," said Margaret Chan, WHO director general, at the release of the damning report.

These conditions compromised the ability to provide basic, routine services such as child delivery and hindered the effort to prevent and control infections. As did a lack of staffing: more than 50 countries had fewer than the minimum 23 doctors, nurses, or midwives per 10,000 people deemed necessary by the WHO and other international organizations to achieve an 80 percent coverage rate for prenatal care and deliveries by skilled birth attendants. A report by Save the Children, *Surviving the First Day*, noted that sub-Saharan Africa had only 11 doctors, nurses, or midwives per 10,000 people, and that South Asia had only about 14.

All these deficiencies add up to one of the world's great inequalities. According to the World Bank, child mortality is about fifteen times greater in lower-income countries than in rich-world countries, and maternal mortality is nearly thirty times higher. Almost all of those deaths are preventable.

IN UGANDA, THIS inequality was laid bare in the innocuously titled, but remarkably frank, *Situation Analysis of Children in Uganda* prepared by the government and UNICEF. It confessed: "The main constraints to good quality health service provision include understaffing and absenteeism; inequitable geographical distribution of health facilities; poor logistics including frequent stock-outs of drugs and other essential supplies." It acknowledged "weak monitoring systems to prevent absenteeism and corruption," as well as budget constraints.

Then followed a list of lamentable statistics and admissions:

Less than a quarter of health facilities in Uganda had all the essential equipment and supplies for basic prenatal care. Although the percentage of births assisted by a skilled attendant had risen to 58 percent, only 2 percent of women received a postnatal checkup within the first hour after delivery, and only one-third in the first two days—and this is mostly in urban areas. Basic emergency obstetric and newborn care services were available in only 15 percent of facilities providing prenatal care, while neonatal resuscitation was available in only about half. Only 29 percent of prenatal sites provided elimination of mother-to-child transmission of HIV services. Over 80 percent of doctors and 60 percent of nurses were located in hospitals that mainly served urban populations. The top-level health posts in rural areas were staffed with only two or three midwives. One-third of the patients who needed sexual and reproductive health and family services, or HIV/AIDS support services, were unable to access them, mainly because more than half of the health facilities didn't have any staff members trained in family planning guidelines. Items for infection control were available in only one-third of health facilities offering prenatal services. Iron and folic-acid tablets were not universally available."Although the government abolished user fees for most health services in government facilities in 2001, many patients were still being charged and, because of medicine shortages, were forced to go to private pharmacies and pay even higher prices. The government's health spending as a percentage of the total budget had declined to 8.6 percent from 9.6 percent in 2003, considerably lower than the 15 percent target set by a summit of African heads of state. As a result, Ugandans bore most of the costs for maternal and child health care, with about two-thirds of costs covered by reaching into their own pockets, which weren't very deep.

Government spending on maternal and child health was 11 percent of the total health budget even though children under five accounted for about 20 percent of the country's population.

THESE STATISTICS AND the woeful state of rural health care in Uganda came to life at the Ongica clinic where midwife Susan Ejang worked and where most of the women in Barjwinya and Ongica came for prenatal checkups and delivery. The sparse infrastructure was scary at the best of times.

Susan gave me a tour. The entry hallway of the maternity ward was festooned with posters of family-planning and health advice: "A planned generation is a happy generation," said one. "You won't give your children half a meal. So don't give them half a dose of diarrhea treatment," said another. When a mom-to-be first arrived in labor, she would be admitted to a small room with one bed and a table. There was a conical tin device called a fetal scope to listen for the baby's heartbeat. With no ultrasound, the midwife would calculate the weeks of pregnancy by measuring the mom's belly with the width of two fingers, estimating the position of the baby by touch.

As labor progressed, the mom would be ushered through a gray door where "Delivery Room" was scrawled in white chalk. Inside were two metal-frame beds, one with a wobbly leg. The space between the beds was wide enough for just one person to move about. The brown mattresses were wrapped in crinkly clear plastic. If there happened to be a third or fourth woman about to give birth at the same time—and it did happen—they would sit on the floor until a bed became free. The walls were a dingy white, the floor a scuffed brown, the curtains a faded blue. The windows were open to ventilate the room with whatever breeze happened by. Lizards scampered in and out of the windows, often heading to the ceiling to feast on spiders and other bugs. A wasp had taken up residence in one corner. The gray door was also left open to help with air circulation, which constituted the only way to cool the building on sweltering days and sticky, humid nights.

A blue plastic barrel stood on a metal tripod in one of the corners. It was filled with water, unpurified, from the borehole well just outside;

the clinic staff pumped the water into buckets and carried them into the delivery room. On the wall above the barrel, Susan had posted a hand-written sign:

NOTICE: This is to caution all those who conduct delivery in this room always to supervise the delivery and keep instruments clean. NEVER!! attempt to remove anything from here. Thank you.

There wasn't much in the room to begin with—a box of latex gloves, a stethoscope, another fetal scope. Whatever equipment was in the clinic had to stay; if anything went missing, replacements would be expensive and a long time coming. Someone borrowed the flashlight one night and it never came back. The blood pressure machine had broken eight months earlier and a new one had yet to arrive; Susan dusted off an old manual pump and restored it to action. The resuscitation equipment, in case of infant breathing difficulty, consisted of a bag and hand pump that forced air into the nose.

Moms were encouraged to bring their own sheets, towels, toilet paper, and suturing material, and a malaria net if they had a good one. Also, it would be good if they could bring a jerrican filled with water (in case the borehole wasn't working) and two basins to hold water for the post-birth cleaning. Oh, and liquid soap to clean the floor; the government supplied some every couple of months, but it was never enough.

The government did provide a "Mama Kit" for each birth. Inside the little packages were the essentials for delivery: cotton, gauze, surgical gloves, a bar of soap, a plastic sheet, a blade to cut the umbilical cord, and a string to tie it off. The Mama Kits were stored in a wooden cabinet because they were valuable commodities. On average, about twenty-five babies were delivered here every month, but if the numbers spiked in any given month they might run out of Mama Kits. Then, someone from the mother's family was dispatched to buy a kit from a pharmacy; the cost was about $7. As a backup, in case they didn't return in time or there was no money for the kit, Susan told the moms it was a good idea to at least bring a clean blade with them for the umbilical cord. She emphasized the word "clean" to cut down the risk of infection, a major danger. One mom-to-be had once thanked her for that advice, for she had been planning to bring the knife she commonly used in the field and to cut vegetables at home; instead, she had bought a new blade.

A single bare lightbulb dangled from the ceiling of the delivery room. The electricity was provided by solar panels on the roof. But even on a bright, sunny day, the power rendered by those panels would last only a few hours beyond sundown. At about ten or eleven at night, the light would begin flickering and then go dark. That's when Susan would improvise. With the flashlight missing, the backup plan to illuminate a birth would be a lantern or candles. But more often than not the lantern would be low on kerosene and the candle drawer empty; in any case, the wind coming through the windows would blow out a candle, making that an impractical option. On those dark nights, Susan would turn to the light of last resort: the dull glow of her cellphone. As one young mom-to-be paced outside on the veranda, hoping her baby would arrive before nightfall, Susan demonstrated birth by cellphone light:

Squatting at the end of the delivery bed, she held the cellphone between her teeth and stretched out her arms in position to receive a baby. All the while, she said, she would be muttering a prayer for dear God to keep the phone battery and a speck of light alive.

Just as Susan squatted with the phone in her mouth, the pacing pregnant mom returned to the delivery room. Horrified by what she saw, she turned on her heels and continued pacing outside. Susan chuckled and then asked me if I knew where she could get used cellphones. She wanted to build up a reserve of spares; the phones were easily ruined, she said, by saliva, falling into blood, or being dropped on the floor.

Next, Susan showed off the post-delivery room. There were four beds with plastic mattresses and no sheets. Sometimes, moms outnumbered the beds three to one, for this after-birth recovery room doubled as the malaria treatment room. Here, pregnant women with severe cases of malaria would be put on IV drips with quinine dextrose. Malaria was the most common killer in Uganda.

"We're lacking everything," Susan told me. "Space, beds, mosquito nets, equipment." Indeed, it seemed the only commodity in surplus were mosquitoes; they buzzed about throughout the clinic, undeterred by a few old and mangy nets hanging beside the beds.

If Susan and her clinic colleagues encountered any birth complication beyond their ability to treat, or believed a mom needed further examination, like Harriet, they referred the patient to the main hospital in Lira, about eight miles away. The hospital had a small fleet of ambulances available for emergencies, but the fee from Ongica would be 35,000 Ugandan shillings, or about $14. Before asking for the pickup location, the ambulance driver would ask if the money was in hand. Most often the answer was no, so the driver returned to his nap. Then, instead of the back of an ambulance, the laboring mom would ride to the hospital on the back of a motorcycle, wincing over every bump.

CONDITIONS WERE NO less rugged, or scary, at the Shivgarh hospital in India. It was a squat, two-story building painted a stomach-turning pink; it looked as if someone had poured a bottle of Pepto-Bismol on it. Soothing it wasn't. In the maternity wing on the ground floor—a sharp right turn inside the front door—a poster from the National Rural Health Mission shouted:

> Don't have your daughters married off before 18. It's a punishable offense. First give them education and then give them away in marriage.

It was sound advice, but curiously located. Of the moms rushing in to deliver their babies, a high percentage were no more than eighteen years old themselves. For them, this advice came too late. Another sign, this one in the entrance courtyard just outside the maternity ward, was equally unheeded:

> Adopt male sterilization. One snip, one stitch. No pain. No weakness. All services are free. Good health. No worry.

A nurse would later tell me she didn't know of any vasectomies ever performed at the hospital.

A third sign was more positive:

Your aspiration is our endeavor. To provide you with hygiene, medicine and advice for behavior change. Stay safe mother and child.

Beneath that sign some of the medication for mothers, folic-acid tablets, idled in large boxes. A label read: "Store in a cool, dry and dark place.
Protect from sunlight and moisture." The area was neither cool, nor dry,
nor dark. Sunlight streamed in. The temperature topped 100 degrees.
The humidity, in the pre-monsoon days, was heavy.

This was where the women of Rampur Khas and Barjor Khera would
give birth. Electricity was provided by solar panels and a backup generator, but there was an overall shortage of lights. The hallway between the
mothers' room and the delivery room was dark and gloomy. The mothers'
room, where women waited to give birth, and to which they returned
for recovery, had four metal beds with thin mattresses and washed-out
sheets. Four wasn't nearly enough to handle demand. Women often
waited in the hallway or outside.

The delivery room featured two short, narrow beds. One was covered
by a rubber sheet; a rubber pad was in position at the bottom of the mattress. Illumination duties were handled by a neon light hanging from the
ceiling and a single lightbulb on a wall above a clock, which was used to
record the time of birth. In a corner of the delivery room were elements
for caring for the newborn: a warming table with blankets, oxygen masks
and breathing pumps, a saline drip. There was no ultrasound machine; as
at the Ongica clinic, the nurses assessed the position of the baby by feel.
Women with complications, or in need of a Caesarean delivery, were sent
to a larger hospital about fifty miles away. A couple of ambulances waited
in the courtyard.

A nurse told me they delivered about 1,300 babies a year. Often there
weren't enough beds to handle the demand; it wasn't unusual for babies
to be born in the hallway or outside. The Indian government had made
a big push for women to deliver in hospitals or clinics. As an incentive,
moms received 1,400 rupees after the birth. But as the number of hospital births increased, there was no commensurate expansion of facilities,
especially in rural areas. So overcrowding was a widespread problem.
Still, the hospital offered more skilled attendants and emergency equipment than a mom would have with a home birth.

As we spoke in the delivery room, the nurse spotted a mouse scampering along the wall to the baby-care corner. The nurse recoiled and scurried herself—through the open door of the room. I wondered what would happen if the mouse appeared during a delivery. Would the attendants abandon their posts?

The recovery room served as a brief stop-over, for it was also overwhelmed by demand. Rather than wait for one of the beds to become free, moms often left with their babies an hour or two after giving birth, forgoing any postnatal exams.

THE INFRASTRUCTURE AT smaller rural clinics was even more rudimentary.

Shyamkali's village of Pure Baishan was several miles further from the Shivgarh hospital, so she was planning to deliver her baby at a smaller maternity post about fifteen minutes from her home by bicycle. It, too, was a pink building. A clunking generator provided electricity; the midwives had bought it themselves so they wouldn't have to work in the dark. There were two beds—one for waiting, one for delivering—separated by a cinderblock wall. A brown three-blade ceiling fan stirred the air in a slow, wobbly cadence. It hung from the ceiling by an exposed wire plugged into a rusted outlet. Two bare lightbulbs were attached to wall sockets. The pointy end of a nail randomly jutted from one wall, skewering anyone who got too close. The ceiling didn't inspire confidence; it was pocked with water stains, and the plaster was cracked and falling around the edges. Spiders—daddy longlegs—ambled across the ruins. Below, the concrete floor was covered with ragged, blood-stained blankets; that's where women sat while waiting for a spot on a bed, and where they often delivered when it was too crowded.

The only diagnostic equipment was a blood pressure machine that had been broken for two months; it idled in the corner while, as at the Ongica clinic, an old hand-operated gauge had been pressed back into action. A red plastic flashlight was perched on a ledge beside the delivery bed, ready for action should the generator conk out. The bed itself was a green plastic mattress. Dirty towels were rolled into a pillow. A red-orange rubber mat loitered at the foot of the mattress, waiting to receive the next baby.

HAD ANY OF the women of Shivgarh made the fifty-mile trek to the Uttar Pradesh capital of Lucknow, they would have marveled at a towering billboard in the city center. It featured a new mom in a flowing white robe cuddling her naked newborn, and this astonishing boast:

Sahara Hospital Introduces truly Painless Labour & Delivery services
- Offering a birthing experience of normal delivery without pain
- Managing skillfully all complicated pregnancies round the clock supported by skilled super specialists

Painless? Truly? The boast itself was an indication of the wide inequality in health care within India. The Sahara Hospital was a kind of Taj Mahal of the medical world. Patients entering the vast lobby were greeted by an imposing, elaborate statue of Mother India, wreathed in gold, one of her hands clutching the flag of India, the other commanding the reins of a chariot drawn by four roaring lions. To her left was the radiology ward, the first stop for all moms coming in for a prenatal checkup or delivery. Three ultrasound machines were on duty to check on the position and health of the baby. The first things parents saw when entering radiology was a sign, in Hindi:

Being examined to find out the sex of the fetus or giving information about it is punishable by law.

It was a warning to parents and to doctors, who could face jail time and a big fine for disclosing a baby's gender. Not that it stopped parents from finding out. A hospital administrator who was dispatched to show me around the Sahara said a doctor (not one at his hospital, of course) may use code words, like "Cancel the sweets," if it's a girl. He also said parents who were given a copy of the ultrasound (it's usually just an image of the head, sometimes more of the body) could fax or scan it to radiologists outside of India to see if they could determine the gender. It was medical globalization in reverse: while some X-rays from the United States and Europe were dispatched to India for examination, ultrasound images went the other way. After all, the Sahara administrator explained, it was just doctors *in India* who weren't allowed to identify the sex of the child.

From radiology, we took an elevator up to the maternity ward. Immediately we could hear a fetal heartbeat sound coming from one of the rooms; a fetal monitor was amplifying it. Here there was a mobile ultrasound machine that could be wheeled from room to room, and a fetal distress monitor. In the delivery room were two beds with thick mattresses and clean sheets, oxygen, a breathing resuscitator, a baby warmer, and all the essentials for delivery, including clean blades, clamps, and suturing material. The moms weren't required to bring anything with them; it was all here. A doctor was on duty around the clock, and the neonatal intensive-care unit was always staffed. Nearby was an operating theater with one bed. This was for the C-sections. Every month, the doctors performed forty to forty-five normal deliveries and fifty to sixty C-sections. Mothers with birth complications came here from miles around. There were ten beds on the ward, so mothers could stay for three days after delivery.

What about the painless boast?

"We give epidurals," the administrator said proudly. "Well, maybe there's 90 to 95 percent less pain."

He claimed the Sahara was the only hospital in the capital city and surrounding districts that used epidurals. "You need to have an anesthesiologist available," he said. "And we're the only maternity ward that does."

THE LARGEST HOSPITAL in Guatemala's western highlands was a state-run facility in the center of Quetzaltenango. On the surrounding streets were pharmacies, prosthetic device makers, and undertakers. The hospital didn't make any outlandish pain-free claims, but it did offer mellow surroundings of trees and flowers, an oasis of green amid the urban grime and clamor. Outside the front doors, swarms of people waited for an appointment or for visiting hours. The women of the Palajunoj Valley would push their way through the crowds when it was time for them to deliver.

The lobby was welcoming and clean, the hallways bright and wide. The maternity ward on the second floor was a cheery place. The walls were white with red and purple stripes. There were paintings of Smurfs and Mickey Mouse and the cartoon characters of *Monsters, Inc.* Winnie the Pooh, Eeyore, Tigger, and Piglet looked down at the newborns from the drapes of the observation room.

Most of the services and treatments were free, including the ultra-sounds. But this being a government hospital, dependent on the ministry of health budget, not all was well. There were sporadic shortages of medicine and vaccines, and the staffing of nurses and doctors was thin. And space was tight. There were forty-six beds in the maternity ward, but at times even that wasn't enough. On the busiest days, with as many as fifty to sixty women present, there was a constant rotation of moms in and out of the beds. Unless there was a need for extended care, no one stayed for long.

Unfortunately, many of the babies would be returning at some point in their young lives. The specialties of the hospital were delivering babies and treating children for malnutrition and parasitic infections.

HOLY CROSS HOSPITAL in Chicago, where about four hundred babies were born every year and where Jessica planned to deliver, offered all the comfort of a modern maternity ward. There were seven rooms outfitted in the LDRP model—labor, delivery, recovery, and postpartum care were all performed in the same room. Mothers didn't move from room to room, nor did the babies; the newborns roomed in with their moms. Each room was nearly bigger than the entire clinic where Shyamkali planned to have her baby. The rooms featured one bed with a nice foam mattress, clean white sheets, and a green bedspread; it could quickly be reconfigured to serve as the delivery bed. A computer monitor stood sentinel on a mobile tray, recording the vital signs of the mom and baby. Everything needed to administer an epidural was close at hand, as were an oxygen machine, a vacuum-assist delivery system, and a blanket warmer. A tier of drawers under the computer held gloves, suturing material, and blades and clamps for the umbilical cord. One of the walls slid open to reveal a cabinet containing all that a doctor might need, including a fetal monitor. The lights were bright, the air conditioning cool. A TV was propped up on the wall opposite the bed. A comfortable sofa chair welcomed overnight visitors. The moms in Shivgarh, Ongica, and the Palajunoj Valley couldn't even begin to imagine such luxury.

A full contingent of nurses was on twenty-four-hour duty, as was a neonatal specialist and an anesthesiologist. The room for Caesarean deliveries and labor emergencies was down the hall; an ultrasound stood ready to pinpoint any problems. The walls of the nursing station featured philosophical, inspirational writings: "Be the Change you wish to see in the World," and "All things grow better with love."

Below, in the emergency room, the chaos of the neighborhood was often in full roar; Holy Cross was one of Chicago's busiest hospitals for ambulance drop-offs. Many arrived from the scene of a crime.

As THE TIME for giving birth neared, anxieties escalated.

Throughout their pregnancies, Esther, Brenda, and Harriet held tight to their dreams of a healthy baby and successful child even as they saw the dreams of other mothers shatter. They learned how perilous the 1,000 days could be.

Word of tragedy traveled quickly through the villages of tiny huts. The bush telegraph, now enhanced with the proliferation of cellphones, was full of heartbreaking news. Reports of miscarriages were always tinged with a certain level of mystery: Was malaria to blame, an intestinal disease caused by bad water, abuse from a husband? And bulletins of stillbirths had the moms fretting up until their deliveries.

Grace Akullu, the community nutritionist for the World Vision–HarvestPlus food project, had worked beside the women in their fields and in their houses, instructing them in the ways of planting, harvesting, cooking, and eating the new sweet potatoes and high-iron beans. And she intimately shared their 1,000-day experience, for Grace herself was pregnant with her third child. She was the picture of health, full of laughter, energy, and life.

This had been a smooth pregnancy, she told everyone. Even as the anticipated delivery date came and passed, Grace felt fine, remained calm, and believed all was normal with the baby. Two weeks past the due date, she went for a checkup at a smaller private hospital in Lira. During the ultrasound exam, she heard the heartbeat; the baby was fine. Early the next morning, her contractions started. She returned to the same hospital and was sent for another ultrasound to prepare for birth.

The machine wasn't in operation; the radiologist needed to read the ultrasound wasn't in the building. He also worked at other clinics. Grace waited. And waited. The contractions quickened. Finally, after nearly an hour, the radiologist appeared and performed the ultrasound. There was no movement; he frantically guided the wand around Grace's belly, searching, praying to find something, but all was still. They listened for a heartbeat. Nothing. Still, Grace had to deliver the baby; she was in labor for several hours. Throughout, she prayed: "Please God don't take me, too. Save me for my other children." After the stillbirth, in her sorrow, Grace prayed again—this time in gratitude and praise that she had survived.

And she questioned the doctors and nurses: "How could this happen?" Grace was used to getting to the bottom of things in her job, and she always encouraged other women to speak up. But the answers she heard now were incomplete. Someone mentioned that perhaps the umbilical cord had wrapped around the baby's neck; no one seemed to know for sure.

ESTHER HAD BECOME increasingly nervous since enduring a bout of malaria five months into the pregnancy; she had learned about the heightened dangers that could come from a mosquito bite. Pregnant women were particularly susceptible to malaria, increasing the risk of illness, anemia, and death. In Africa, 30 million women living in malaria-endemic areas became pregnant each year, according to the WHO. For the unborn child, maternal malaria increased the risk of miscarriage, stillbirth, premature delivery, and low birth weight, which is a leading cause of child mortality. The WHO estimated that up to 200,000 newborn deaths each year were related to malaria in pregnancy. In Uganda, a government report said malaria was a factor in 36 percent of all maternal deaths and 31 percent of deaths of children under five. And those numbers were on the rise, as malaria was endemic, striking throughout the year. Esther walked to the clinic and got some anti-malaria medicine and a few tablets of Panadol pain reliever. She recovered quickly, and the baby, who was very active in her womb, seemed to be unaffected. That was certainly her fervent hope, but the nagging concern wouldn't vanish.

Esther was feeling strong, and still working in the fields; her husband, Tonny, had returned home from college to work beside her and help prepare for the birth. But with each passing day, Esther's anxiety increased a notch. She reached her due date, then passed it. Was everything all right? she wondered. She was comforted that the baby was still active. Esther loved to feel her baby move.

JESSICA ALSO LONGED for the movement of her child. At six months, she wrote to her daughter:

> Hia babes—why aren't you moving? I want to feel you move
> around to know your okay. I worry too much about you, about
> so many things, if your okay, do you have any birth defects, just
> everything baby. But I pray to St. Jude and Divino Nino and
> Nuestra Guadalupe and God to bless and take care of you.
> My Alitzel, I love you.

Six weeks later, Jessica's worry shot off the charts:

> Do you know last night I went to the hospital? I thought my water
> broke and I almost cried. I pretty much was tearing when I was
> talking to your dad. I was so nervous, so scared. I honestly was
> not ready for you, for the labor. We still need to buy your stroller,
> socks, bibs, etc. But even if I was unprepared, I was ready to go
> through everything to have you in my arms. Your dad was in
> shock, but at the end it was nothing. You still have 10 more weeks
> left my little princess. Mommy is waiting for you and of course
> your dad too. We all love you and are waiting for your arrival.
> 67 days left! Keep on moving around. Mommy loves that.

Jessica counted the days, which only made her more nervous. With three weeks to go, she wrote:

> I want you in my arms already!!! Your dad is so nervous and so
> am I. 22 more days baby. Love.

Later that night, Jessica was lying on her bed, texting Marco at his band practice, when her water did break. Two hours earlier, she had prank-called Marco, saying, "I think it's time." Now she was serious, talking about contractions and back pain. Marco could hear the difference in her voice. He left his bandmates and headed to Holy Cross. Jessica's mother drove her to the hospital, about ten minutes away from their house. It was after 10 p.m. when they arrived.

Then nothing. Night turned to day, morning to afternoon. The contractions started up again, this time more intensely. As a second night approached, Jessica began sweating with a fever. She hadn't slept. She was tired, weak. A nurse said that if she didn't deliver by 10 p.m., they would perform a Caesarean delivery. Jessica didn't want that. Her doula, Patricia, helped with breathing exercises. Jessica pushed, watching the clock, the hand ticking toward 10. Now she spoke directly to her daughter: Come on, Ali. It's time.

IT WAS ALSO well past sundown in northern Uganda, about 9 p.m., when Esther told Tonny her contractions had started. Tonny hustled to a neighbor who had a motorcycle. He hired the man to give Esther a ride to the clinic. She hopped on the back, riding side-saddle for the five-minute rush down the washboard dirt road. Tonny set out running, taking a shortcut through the fields to the clinic. Esther spent an uncomfortable night there; it was the middle of summer, and the open windows and door did little to cool the delivery room. She paced back and forth on the veranda, the same place where Susan had told her that her child could achieve great things.

Esther's labor stretched on through the next day. Why was it taking so long? Was the baby okay? Without an ultrasound, the birth attendant held a fetal scope to Esther's belly to listen for the baby's heartbeat. She heard it. Everything was fine, she said. The sun had set, darkness surrounded the clinic. The lights began to flicker.

IN THE PALAJUNOJ Valley, Dianet woke up in pain. It was a week before her due date, but her husband said she should go to the hospital; he believed the baby was ready to come. Dianet made her way down the hill from her parents' house and at the main road climbed on a bus for the ride to Quetzaltenango. She carried a bag with clothes for a baby girl, still believing that the original ultrasound image, and not her relatives, was correct. Dianet arrived at the hospital around 11 a.m. After a quick checkup, a nurse said it would be a while yet before the birth, and she encouraged Dianet to eat something and walk around. Everyone was confident it would be a routine birth. Dianet had lunch. After another checkup, the doctor suggested that she go home and wait. Dianet said she didn't have a car and would rather wait at the hospital. She resumed walking the corridors, strolling past Mickey and the Smurfs. Later in the afternoon, in preparation for birth, Dianet was sent for an ultrasound. Suddenly, the nurse didn't sound so confident. The exam spotted *meconium* (the baby's first stool) in the amniotic fluid. Dianet was told it was a sign of fetal distress and that it was a dangerous situation. If the baby inhaled the meconium, it could partially or completely block the baby's airways, and there was a risk of lung damage. The waiting was over. Dianet was prepped for an emergency Caesarean.

IT WAS NEAR midnight in Pure Baishan when Shyamkali rose from her *charpoy* to go to the clinic. Having already delivered four children, she felt no panic. She calmly grabbed a blanket, a towel, and a new blade for the umbilical cord. Her husband had gone to Delhi to find work, anything he could scrounge up. An elderly neighbor woman had been staying with Shyamkali, and she, too, stirred. She summoned a bicycle rickshaw, which was nothing more than an open-sided wagon hitched to the back of a bike. Shyamkali and her neighbor hopped on the wagon and set out on their midnight ride to the little pink clinic. The driver stood up from his seat to get more leverage, and for fifteen minutes he pedaled furiously over the potholes and ruts. At the clinic, Shyamkali encountered four other women waiting to deliver. She spread her blanket and towel on the concrete floor and gingerly sat down, hoping and praying that this one would be a boy.

PART TWO | BIRTH

chapter seven

THE MOST PERILOUS DAY

S HYAMKALI ARRIVED AT THE CLINIC JUST IN TIME. THE BABY WAS coming. There was still no bed free, so she remained on the floor. And there she gave birth.

She studied the faces of those who moved quickly to tend to the baby. They looked sad. "We're sorry," they said.

The baby was alive and seemingly well. Shyamkali heard the crying. Why, she wondered, were they apologizing?

"It's a girl," she was told. Such a pity, the midwife and the nurse said to each other and to the other moms waiting to deliver; this mother now had five girls.

Shyamkali ignored them. She loved this fifth daughter immediately and rejoiced at the birth. Her name would be Anshika, which means "to be a part of something." Part of a house full of girls, to be sure. Shyamkali put her daughter to her breast to keep her warm and give her the first milk, rich with nutrients and antibodies.

For one hour Shyamkali rested on the floor with her baby, but her mind was racing with worry. How would her husband greet the news? What would her neighbors in the village say? Already her elderly friend who had accompanied her to the clinic was adamant that she would have to try again for a boy; her husband, she said, would insist on it. Shyamkali was anxious to get home to her other daughters; she also didn't want to take up space that another mother might need. So she rose from the floor and swaddled Anshika to her chest. Then she climbed back on the wagon of the bicycle rickshaw. The driver began the strenuous pedaling, now with one more passenger on board. It was still pitch black outside and very humid. Shyamkali grimaced over every bump on the road, holding tight to her baby and to the cart so they wouldn't topple over. Just a few hours after leaving for the clinic, she was back home with Anshika.

IN QUETZALTENANGO, DIANET was wheeled to the operating room for a C-section. The doctor and nurses worked quickly, and soon Dianet was holding her baby, a girl she named Keytlin (pronounced Kaitlin). The earlier ultrasound had been correct. What surprised Dianet, so small herself, was that her daughter was so robust, more than seven pounds. Dianet breastfed immediately and bonded with her daughter while she recuperated in the hospital. Before heading home after three days, Dianet was told she needed to rest after the C-section and shouldn't do any strenuous work in the fields. She promised to be careful but knew she couldn't stay out of the fields long, for that was her family's business. At her parents' house, the family celebrated the first grandchild with much excitement. The baby was so strong and healthy! Maybe, they hoped, this next generation would be taller.

The same hopes arrived with the birth of Maria Estella's son, Jorge, who weighed in at nearly eight and a half pounds. Maria Estella had been a good student in Susy's classes, and now her son was so big compared to his older sister, who was already showing signs of stunting. Improvement might not need to wait for the next generation; perhaps change could come with the next child.

Gabriela, the youngest of Susy's pregnant moms, couldn't spare a thought for the future; she was shocked when a doctor at the Quetzaltenango hospital told her that her baby was slowly suffocating in the womb. An ultrasound revealed that the lungs weren't developing properly, the baby was squeezed too high up in the womb. A C-section was ordered, even though the birth would be more than a month premature. José Geovani weighed just four pounds, and was placed in an incubator for four days. Gabriela went home disconsolate that she couldn't take him with her. When José was removed from the incubator, mother and son were inseparable—literally. José was wrapped in a blue blanket on his mother's chest, and they stayed attached all day, like a kangaroo with her baby in the pouch. It was a practice spreading throughout the developing world—the same change Vishwajeet introduced in Shivgarh: KMC, kangaroo mother care.

IN CHICAGO, JESSICA pushed and kept watching the clock. She delivered, finally, nine minutes before the C-section deadline. After all the journal letters to her daughter, she was delighted to greet Alitzel in person. That face, the cheeks—just like the images. Jessica had imagined having an eight-pound baby. But because Alitzel arrived three weeks early, she was smaller: five pounds, thirteen ounces, nineteen inches. Any concern, however, was quickly overwhelmed by joy. "Having her in my arms after nine months, looking at her face . . . " she said dreamily to Patricia. Alitzel was placed on Jessica's chest; they began breastfeeding, but it was a struggle, as Alitzel had difficulty latching on. There was a lot of commotion in the room celebrating the birth. Jessica was exhausted from the lengthy labor. She dozed off to sleep.

Quintana also delivered early, by fifteen days. At Mercy Hospital, with its advanced maternity wing just west of Lake Michigan, an examination revealed she had elevated levels of protein in her urine along with high blood pressure, putting her and her baby at risk. The attendants first tried inducing labor, but then decided a C-section was necessary. ShaLawn was also born small; five pounds, nine ounces, and nineteen inches long. The baby was in no danger, but Quintana's condition was alarming. Her temperature had plummeted. Nurses scrambled to cover her with heated blankets. Steadily, her temperature rose back to normal. While Quintana recovered, she was separated from ShaLawn. After two days, they were reunited, ShaLawn on Quintana's chest, mother and child growing stronger together.

As the night advanced in northern Uganda, Esther prayed that her baby would finally arrive. Susan stood by with her cellphone light. It was around 10 p.m.—the lightbulb above the bed just a dull glow—when a boy, Rodgers Okello, was born. He was a healthy seven pounds. Esther immediately began breastfeeding. The next day they returned home to a great family celebration. Rodgers joined his great-grandmother, his paternal grandparents, and his parents—four generations living together in their cluster of little houses beside the dirt road.

When Brenda's time came to deliver, her baby didn't keep her waiting. Strong contractions began so quickly she told her husband, Dennis, that they might not make it to the Ongica health center in time to deliver. Dennis noted that the evening darkness was rapidly thickening, which would make any journey slower. So the gathering family members went into action for a home birth. One of the village children ran through the bush to summon a fixture of African life, a traditional birth attendant; she was an older woman who had delivered countless babies over the years before the rural clinics were built. She was happy to be needed this night. Dennis spread a reed mat over the dirt-and-dung floor of their little one-room house, beneath the thatch roof, and helped Brenda to the ground. Brenda was calm, for she had always known that a home delivery was a possibility. Actually, she thought, it might be better this way. After the death of their first child, her faith in hospitals and clinics had been sorely tested.

The birth attendant arrived and began deploying some of the elements of the Mama Kit that Brenda had prepared. She unfolded a plastic tarp beside the reed mat while Dennis ran to fetch water and cloth. His mother held the family flashlight. It wasn't long before a healthy son arrived, crying loudly. He was a big boy; the birth attendant could only estimate—about eight pounds, she thought—for there was no scale. The baby was immediately laid on Brenda's chest and began breastfeeding. His parents named him Aron, from the Bible.

Harriet was already in the Lira hospital when her contractions started. The midwife still expected Harriet to have a routine delivery. But when the time came, the first thing she saw was the baby's feet; it was a breech birth. The activity around Harriet's bed quickly became serious. A doctor appeared. It seemed to Harriet that the delivery was taking forever, as if the baby were stuck in mid-birth. The doctor managed to deliver the baby—a girl—and then handed her off to a nurse. The baby cried, weakly. She looked so small. A nurse weighed her—just four and a half pounds.

Then, a stunning announcement from the doctor: "There's another one."

Twins? It was a shock to everyone. Harriet had no idea. Neither did the midwife or the nurses. Of course not. There had been no ultrasound. They had heard a heartbeat through the fetal scope, but assumed it was just for one baby.

The second baby was delivered. Another struggle for Harriet. Another girl.

Silence.

Why wasn't the baby crying, Harriet wondered? She listened for a weak yelp, like the first one. Silence, still.

The baby was dead.

What happened? No one had an explanation. They told Harriet the baby had skin ulcerations on the bottom half of the body, a condition rarely seen at the hospital. They had no idea of the cause, or whether that was what had led to the stillbirth. Harriet and her husband, Moses, were left alone to speculate. Perhaps the baby had already been dead in the womb for a day or more, and the skin had begun to deteriorate. Maybe Harriet's bout of malaria had something to do with it. Was it birth asphyxia, the baby strangled by its umbilical cord? What they did know was that this second child weighed nearly six pounds. She was bigger and stronger than the first, which only compounded the agony and the mystery. Harriet and Moses named their surviving daughter Apio, which means the first girl of two. It was a name commonly given to the firstborn of twins. Her sister would have been called Acen, the second.

Harriet was heartbroken at the loss, but she still felt blessed that one baby had survived, and that she had, too.

THE FIRST DAY is the most perilous day of life. Each year, more than 1 million babies die on the day of their birth. It is the most sorrowful note in the sad statistical regression of child deaths: Three-quarters of all deaths of children under five happen in the first year of life (that's about

4.5 million infants annually). Two-thirds of those infant deaths occur in the first month (about 3 million), and two-thirds of the deaths in the first month are in the first week (about 2 million). Of the deaths in the first week, half occur on the first day. In addition, more than 2.5 million babies are stillborn every year, according to a report by the international humanitarian organization Save the Children. And nearly 300,000 mothers die each year during pregnancy or childbirth. What should be the happiest day of life often turns into the saddest for so many families.

These numbers are staggering, but they have dramatically improved over the past quarter century. In 1990, about 9 million children died in their first year of life, and nearly 5 million in the first month; maternal deaths numbered about 500,000. Still, the toll remains stubbornly high in undeveloped and still-developing countries, where poverty and lack of health-care infrastructure trump improvements on other fronts. The Save the Children study, *Surviving the First Day*, noted that the vast majority of first-day deaths are in the developing world and would be preventable in richer countries via interventions before, during, and immediately after birth. The primary causes of first-day death are complications during birth (such as asphyxia), prematurity, and infection and sepsis from poor hygiene or bad water.

The solutions are simple and inexpensive: ready and reliable access to water and soap, resuscitation devices to save babies who struggle to breathe at birth, antiseptic umbilical-cord cleansing to prevent infections, steroid injections for women in preterm labor to help develop the baby's lungs, injectable antibiotics to treat newborn sepsis and pneumonia. Save the Children estimated these common products cost between 13 cents and $6 each. But in poor countries, where health budgets are minuscule, these common treatments are often unavailable beyond large urban hospitals.

The highest percentage of first-day deaths is in sub-Saharan Africa, where the first-day mortality rate is 12 per 1,000 live births. That's a total of about 400,000 babies each year. The rate in South Asia is 11 per 1,000 live births, which, owing to the larger population, amounts to a larger number of annual deaths, nearly 425,000. Those two regions account for more than 80 percent of first-day deaths worldwide. This is the day when health-system failures, including poor nutrition, too few prenatal visits, absence of more advanced technology, power outages, medicine shortages, untrained staff, and sparse immediate postnatal care, as well as social deficits, such as low education levels among mothers and gender inequalities, take their greatest toll. In Uganda, for instance, Harriet had done all she could, following what she had learned about proper nutrition and hygiene, only to see it undermined by woeful infrastructure (faulty machines, lack of electricity), poverty (no money, no ultrasound), and general inefficiency (lack of specialized care).

Only 1 percent of the world's newborn deaths occur in the industrialized world. But even there, the first day is still the riskiest. According to the Save the Children report, the United States had by far the most first-day deaths among the richer countries—about 11,300 babies in 2011, or about 50 percent more than all the other industrialized countries combined. As leading causes, Save the Children cited poor nutrition among mothers, complications in mothers who were overweight or obese, diabetes and high blood pressure in mothers, difficulties encountered by premature and low-birth-weight babies, and the high number of adolescent moms. The preterm birthrate in the United States was one of the highest in the world; Save the Children's research found that 130 countries were doing better than the United States on this important measure.

The most perilous first days of all were in India. There, more than 300,000 babies died each year on the day they were born, accounting for nearly 30 percent of the global total of first-day deaths. About 20 percent of all child deaths in India were on the day of birth. It was also a dangerous day for the moms: India had more maternal deaths than any other country in the world, about 56,000 a year.

OF THE WOMEN I met on my first visit to Rampur Khas, two lost their babies on the first day. They both had stillbirths. They were the two youngest moms of the group, and the smallest: Meera, a couple inches shy of five feet; and Kiran, who entered her pregnancy so thin. Meera was doing her afternoon chores around the house when she felt a pain in her stomach. She went to the hospital, where a doctor gave her a quick checkup and said all was normal; the baby was coming. The next morning,

Meera gave birth and the baby was dead. How could that happen, she wondered, when she was feeling so healthy? Meera recalled that she had a bout of malaria during her pregnancy. Could that have caused the stillbirth? She asked, but didn't get much of an answer. "Fate," seemed to be the consensus. Meera left the hospital alone, her baby another of India's sorry statistics.

Kiran, too, was left with nothing but questions. She went into labor at home and was being cared for by her mother-in-law and other neighborhood women. They watched the timing of the contractions, waiting for the right time to go to the hospital. They waited and waited. After a couple of days, Kiran was taken to the hospital. On the fourth day of labor, her baby was born dead. Again, there were no explanations for the cause of death, though it was certain that both mother and baby were under prolonged stress. Some in Kiran's family blamed the hospital for its inability to detect the problem, but her mother-in-law was more sanguine, as if she had expected a tragic outcome all along: Kiran, she told me, "was too small" to deliver a baby.

Sushma and Mohana, both experienced moms, delivered their babies without incident, though the birth weights were low, which was all too common throughout rural India. Sushma had a boy, Sunny; Mohana had a daughter, Sarita. Both babies weighed about five pounds. The two sisters-in-law, Seema and Sanju, gave birth within two weeks of each other: Seema, a girl named Priyanshi; Sanju, a boy named Adarsh. Their babies each weighed less than six pounds. The birth attendants lightly cleaned the babies and handed them to the mothers to begin breastfeeding; it was a big departure from their earlier practice of aggressively scrubbing the babies with oil or mud and withholding the babies from their mothers until the moms expressed their first milk and colostrum. The hospital's new postnatal routine matched the Saksham principles. The moms practiced kangaroo mother care, with immediate skin-to-skin contact, and breastfed their babies the nutrient-rich first milk that they had once viewed as dirty waste.

None of the mothers stayed at the Shivgarh hospital long after birth; it was crowded and uncomfortable, and they were anxious to go home with their babies. Before they left, they stopped briefly in the dingy recovery room to meet with a woman from their community—the accredited social health assistant, or ASHA—who helped them fill out the forms to claim their 1,400-rupee incentive payments from the Indian government for having their babies in a hospital or clinic. The only splash of color in the room, on the far wall above one of the beds, caught their eyes. It was a poster from India's Rural Health Mission featuring a beaming mom snuggling her baby, and this bold, empowering message in Hindi:

In the First Hour, a mother can change the fate of her child.

Four simple drawings at the bottom of the poster illustrated how:

- To prevent infection, use a clean blade to cut the umbilical cord
- To provide warmth and avoid hypothermia, lightly swaddle the newborn and place on the mother's chest
- To boost the immune system, breastfeed immediately, for the first milk and colostrum are rich in antibodies
- To avoid complications, if the child appears ill quickly tell a doctor

The moms from Shivgarh recognized these principles from their meetings with the Community Empowerment Lab. The admonitions were straight from the lyrics of the songs they had sung. And now they were putting them into play. Here, as the first hour ticked on, was confirmation that they were doing all they could to give their children the best possible start in life.

ONE WAY TO make the first day less perilous is early initiation of breastfeeding. The World Health Organization and UNICEF have estimated that suboptimal breastfeeding leads to 800,000 newborn deaths every year due to a weak immune system. As UNICEF explained in a *Progress for Children* report: "Ideally, infants should be breastfed within one hour of birth, exclusively for the first six months of life, and continue to be breastfed up to 2 years of age and beyond. An infant who is not exclusively breastfed is at a substantially greater risk of death from diarrhea or pneumonia than one who is. Breastfeeding supports infants' immune systems."

This sentiment was seconded by the World Health Organization, the Centers for Disease Control and Prevention in the United States, and the American Academy of Pediatrics (AAP). The AAP in 2012 stated that, "given the documented short- and long-term medical and neuro-developmental advantages of breastfeeding, infant nutrition should be considered a public health issue not only a lifestyle choice." The *Surgeon General's Call to Action to Support Breastfeeding* acknowledged in 2011 that "the decision to breastfeed is a personal one," but added, "Given the importance of breastfeeding for the health and well-being of mothers and children, it is critical that we take action across the country to support breastfeeding."

The medical and scientific evidence shows that breastmilk provides all the energy, nutrients, and liquid that an infant needs for body and brain growth in the first six months of life. A raft of studies has found that the nutritional composition of a mother's milk adapts to her baby's needs according to the stage of development and the threats from bacteria and infections. The first milk, the colostrum, is full of vital antibodies and is essentially a child's first vaccination. Another Save the Children report, *Superfood for Babies: How Overcoming Barriers to Breastfeeding Will Save Children's Lives*, hailed it as "the most potent natural immune system booster."

Then, too, there are the more practical elements of breastfeeding: it is the cheapest and cleanest baby food available, eliminating the costs of formula milk and avoiding the risks of unclean water and other potentially impure liquids, and it fosters bonding between mother and child. Breastfeeding, concludes the Save the Children report, "is the closest thing there is to a 'silver bullet' in the fight against malnutrition and newborn deaths."

Yet, despite all this, less than half of all infants under six months of age worldwide are exclusively breastfed, with large disparities between regions. Global rates of exclusive breastfeeding have remained below 40 percent for the past two decades. The highest regional percentages were in eastern and southern Africa (56 percent) and South Asia (47 percent). Uganda's rate was 63 percent, India's had climbed past 60 percent, and Guatemala's was 50 percent. The US rate, while increasing, has for years been less than 20 percent for exclusive breastfeeding at six months.

Although the US government and the nation's humanitarian agencies have been at the forefront of the international breastfeeding campaign, the United States itself is the lone industrialized nation not to provide support for new mothers in the form of federally mandated paid maternity leave and guaranteed job retention. It also remains an exception in the American workplace that lactating mothers are afforded the time and space to pump their breastmilk, though more employers are making such provisions under the Affordable Care Act.

The Centers for Disease Control and Prevention *Breastfeeding Report Card* for 2013 revealed that about 77 percent of infants in the United States were breastfed at some time (mainly within the first hour after birth); at six months, nearly half were still breastfeeding to some extent, either exclusively (just over 16 percent) or in addition to formula or other liquids. There were wide racial and ethnic differences in the US breastfeeding rates. According to a study by the Center for Social Inclusion, about 45 percent of white infants, 46 percent of Latino/a infants, and 28 percent of African American infants were breastfeeding to some extent at six months. Among Latina mothers, the six-month breastfeeding rate fell to 32 percent for those mothers born in the United States.

Throughout the world, the reasons for not breastfeeding, or stopping exclusive breastfeeding, are many and varied, and not without controversy. Breastfeeding can at times be frustrating and painful. There may be medical reasons why a mother or baby can't breastfeed. Moms may worry that their breastmilk isn't sufficient for their baby, and reach for a formula supplement. And there are social barriers. Save the Children highlighted four of the social barriers in its *Superfood for Babies* report.

Community and cultural pressures—such as the practice in rural Uttar Pradesh of discarding the colostrum—topped Save the Children's list. From mothers in India and Uganda I heard about local traditions of feeding newborns all manner of liquids: sugar-sweetened water, animal milk, a taste of home-brewed beer or moonshine, a dollop of honey—all of which are difficult for a baby to digest and carry the risk of disease. Some mothers told me that local custom dictated that they stop breastfeeding when they became pregnant again. "Many women aren't free to make their own decisions about whether they will breastfeed, or for how long," Save the Children concluded. For example, a Save the Children survey in

Pakistan revealed that "only 44% of mothers considered themselves the prime decision-maker over how their children were fed"; husbands or mothers-in-law often called the shots. Conversely, in the United States, Patricia and her fellow doulas watched how mothers who decided *not* to continue breastfeeding, for whatever reason, were often made to feel as if they were being judged as bad moms, particularly in the raging debates occurring on social media platforms.

Save the Children cited the health worker shortage as a second social barrier. Chronic staffing problems meant that one-third of infants worldwide were "born without a skilled birth attendant present," which meant that new mothers were not being instructed and supported in breastfeeding during the important first hours following birth. Save the Children analyzed data in forty-four countries and found that women who had a skilled attendant present at birth were "twice as likely" as women without such help "to initiate breastfeeding within the first hour."

Lack of maternity legislation was third on the list. Many mothers stop exclusive breastfeeding when they return to work or school. A majority of poor countries (and the United States) have failed to meet the international standard of paid maternity leave recommended by the International Labor Organization: at least fourteen weeks with at least two-thirds pay, which would give working moms the opportunity to spend more time with their babies. National policies requiring employers to provide paid breaks and private places where women can breastfeed or express milk are also lacking worldwide.

Fourth, Save the Children described the big business barrier: "While there is a recognized need for certain infants to be formula-fed, there has long been concern that the marketing activities of some manufacturers has led to infant formula being used unnecessarily and improperly, ultimately putting children at risk." In 1981, the World Health Assembly adopted a set of standards known as the International Code of Marketing of Breast-Milk Substitutes that attempted to regulate marketing that could undermine breastfeeding, including advertising, distribution of free samples, and health claims on packaging. While almost all breast-milk-substitute manufacturers acknowledge that breastmilk is best, violations of the code pushing infant formula continue around the world.

The formula business has been booming globally, with nearly $45 billion in sales at stake and fierce competition for market share. New, lucrative markets are emerging in countries with a growing middle class where more women are joining the workforce. In those countries, formula feeding has been portrayed as modern and a sign of prosperity (as it was in the United States in the post–World War II years). UNICEF's China office has warned of a "hyper-aggressive push to get the emerging market hooked on infant formula." In response to widespread advertising, China's government was considering effectively banning the promotion of infant formula while it sought to increase the country's exclusive breastfeeding rate from about one-third to one-half. Save the Children interviewed mothers in China and found that 40 percent of them had been contacted directly by representatives of baby-food companies while in the hospital or after returning home; 40 percent of those interviewed also said they had received free formula samples from company representatives or health workers—all in apparent contradiction of the World Health Assembly's Code of Marketing.

Clearly, contrary to the assertion of the maternity ward sign in the Shivgarh hospital, many forces loom that can dislodge the breastfeeding decision from the hands of a new mother.

JESSICA WOKE FROM her nap to find Alitzel sleeping beside her and thought it was time to feed her daughter. She pushed the buzzer to summon a nurse to help with breastfeeding, but no one came. She buzzed again; no response. Then she noticed a bottle with water and a little packet of Enfamil infant formula powder on the table beside her bed. Jessica tried breastfeeding again, holding Alitzel in different positions, but again, with no guidance, she struggled to get her baby to latch on. Frustrated, Jessica reached for the bottle and mixed the formula. Alitzel took to the bottle. Jessica later learned that Alitzel had been bottle-fed by a nurse while she was sleeping. And now, it seemed, she preferred it.

"I was disappointed. I didn't want formula," Jessica told me several days after the birth.

But formula is what she got. When she left the hospital, Jessica was given a bag filled with gifts for mom and baby: diapers, shampoo, a pacifier, bottles, samples of Enfamil to last several days, and coupons for future purchases. Enfamil, a product of Mead Johnson Nutrition Company, a leading formula brand, also distributed to moms a booklet called *Nourishing Milestones: Your Essential Feeding Guide*. It begins, "Breastfeeding is a wonderful way to nourish your baby while you create a loving bond." There follows a description of the nutrients in breastmilk, some advice on feeding frequency, and the basics of pumping and storing milk. Then comes a passage on how to wean the baby off breastmilk, and finally, a section on it all being the mother's choice: "If you're thinking about formula-feeding, it's good to learn about your options so you can make a choice you feel good about, especially if you've been breastfeeding. And when you find out more about Enfamil, you'll see why it's an excellent choice if you plan to formula-feed." Enfamil formulas "are closer than ever to breast milk," it claims, and it's the "#1 brand recommended by pediatricians."

Jessica felt the choice was made for her by the time she woke up at the hospital. Patricia, her doula, was studying to become a certified lactation consultant, and she had been encouraging Jessica throughout her pregnancy to breastfeed. Jessica was initially ambivalent, but then she came to believe that breastfeeding would be part of doing what was best for her daughter. She heard that Holy Cross didn't have a particularly good track record when it came to breastfeeding. Indeed, two years earlier, the Chicago public radio station WBEZ had broadcast a report noting that Holy Cross had the lowest newborn breastfeeding rate in the city, just 10 percent. Jessica thought about switching to a hospital that had a better reputation for breastfeeding. But then her water broke and she was off to Holy Cross.

In their bedroom at home, Marco sat in a chair while feeding six-day-old Alitzel from a bottle. The samples from the hospital had run out, so Marco bought a new twenty-two-ounce can of Enfamil Newborn formula, "with key nutrients patterned after breast milk," according to the label. It had cost more than $20 at the store; Marco paid with his family's food-stamp card. He calculated they would be needing several cans a month, but he made just $9.25 an hour working at a pizza restaurant in the neighborhood. Jessica had also just started pumping her breastmilk, so throughout the day she and Marco fed Alitzel two ounces at a time, alternating between the breastmilk and formula. Jessica had waited for the hospital to provide a pump. It didn't, so her mom bought one at a pharmacy.

"We can try to breastfeed again," Patricia suggested.

"No, I want to pump," Jessica said, with a tone of weary resignation.

Patricia sighed. It was Jessica's decision. "We need more baby-friendly hospitals," Patricia said wistfully.

Holy Cross wasn't yet part of the international Baby-Friendly Hospital Initiative, which was launched by the World Health Organization and UNICEF in 1991 to recognize hospitals and birthing centers that placed breastfeeding at the core of their activities. To receive a Baby-Friendly designation, a facility needed to implement the initiative's "Ten Steps to Successful Breastfeeding" and comply with the International Code of Marketing of Breast-Milk Substitutes. Nearly 20,000 maternity facilities in 150 countries had received the designation, but at the time fewer than 200 were in the United States—and none in the city of Chicago.

The "Ten Steps" are:

1. Have a written breastfeeding policy that is routinely communicated to all health care staff.
2. Train all health care staff in the skills necessary to implement this policy.
3. Inform all pregnant women about the benefits and management of breastfeeding.
4. Help mothers initiate breastfeeding within one hour of birth.
5. Show mothers how to breastfeed and how to maintain lactation, even if they are separated from their infants.
6. Give infants no food or drink other than breast-milk, unless medically indicated.
7. Practice rooming in—allow mothers and infants to remain together 24 hours a day.
8. Encourage breastfeeding on demand.
9. Give no pacifiers or artificial nipples to breastfeeding infants.
10. Foster the establishment of breastfeeding support groups and refer mothers to them on discharge from the hospital or birth center.

Also, to comply with the Code of Marketing, Baby-Friendly hospitals couldn't accept any free formula from the companies. This is where many hospitals struggled. Purchasing formula would be expensive; they needed a certain supply for mothers who couldn't breastfeed or decided not to. Additionally, the training of staff was a steep expense—in time and money—for hospitals on tight budgets.

Holy Cross, after the WBEZ report, had begun the process to become certified under the Baby-Friendly Hospital Initiative, but that effort was disrupted with a change in the hospital's ownership. An administrator I spoke with said she would like to restart the certification process. "It's an awesome thing," she said. Many of the moms who come to deliver at Holy Cross are "walk-ins," she noted, meaning they didn't go through the hospital's prenatal program and didn't have any breastfeeding education. And some nurses, she added, defaulted to the bottle too soon. Success, she said, would depend on behavior change for both the moms and the staff. "Should the nurses be more proactive?" she asked. "Yes. That's part of the initiative."

At Mercy Hospital, Quintana began breastfeeding as soon as possible after recovering from delivery. For the first two days, ShaLawn had formula milk and some breastmilk that Quintana was able to pump. Quintana had experience with breastfeeding with her son, and now she had help from Mercy's lactation consultants. Mercy, one of Chicago's busiest maternity centers with about 2,400 births a year, was hoping to become the first Baby-Friendly-certified hospital in the city; the municipal effort was being spearheaded by the Consortium to Lower Obesity in Chicago Children. Mercy's maternity staff was receiving breastfeeding and kangaroo-care training, and moms and babies were "rooming-in" together after birth. And Mercy had stopped sending formula home with the breastfeeding moms. Administrators at Mercy said it was important to change old habits. "The night nurses used to think, 'Mom's sleeping, so I'll give the baby a bottle.' That's a big no-no now," one told me. "When I do rounds and see a bottle at the bedside, I just scream."

AT HOME IN their bedroom, decorated with a Tinkerbell sticker and letters spelling out "ALITZEL," Marco finished feeding his daughter and patted her on the back. The burp wasn't coming.

"Bring her up to your shoulder, bring up the bubble," Patricia suggested. Marco moved Alitzel to his shoulder and continued patting on her pink blanket.

Jessica said Marco was holding her all wrong, then apologized. "I'm such a hypocrite, that's how I hold her," she said with a laugh. Alitzel burped, and followed up with a series of hiccups. "That's normal," Patricia said. "You're doing great."

Marco handed Alitzel to Jessica. He studied the Enfamil can and the promotional material. He read about growth, brain development, and the nutrients that replicated mother's milk. It sounded attractive. But Jessica was determined to provide as much of her milk as possible.

She pumped for several weeks, but by the time she went back to school to resume her junior year, at the beginning of 2014, her milk stopped. Alitzel would be on formula full time. Jessica often told me she wished she had breastfed; she thought it might have helped Alitzel gain length and weight faster and helped herself lose weight after giving birth.

As Jessica settled back into school in early 2014, Mead Johnson Nutrition executives spoke at a conference of investment analysts in New York City and outlined how growth in their Enfamil formula business depended on lower breastfeeding rates, higher birthrates, and more women around the world moving into the labor force—where moms working full time in jobs without accommodations to breastfeed, or paid leave to stay at home with the baby, might be more inclined to use formula.

"Our growth trajectory is built on the premise that economic growth in emerging markets drives job creation, attracts women into the workforce, thereby creating dual-income families who increasingly have the ability to spend on premium nutrition products. It's a very simple story," said Kasper Jakobsen, Mead Johnson president and CEO, according to transcripts of the conference provided by Thomson Reuters StreetEvents. The move of its infant formula into emerging markets like Brazil and China was to compensate for slower growth in the United States due to increasing breastfeeding rates and women leaving the workforce during the recession (which would potentially give new moms more time to breastfeed). For instance, about business prospects in Brazil, Jakobsen noted optimistically, "Female participation in the workforce has only recently exceeded 50%, which speaks to the potential for the country."

(At the same conference the next year, Jakobsen would bemoan rising US breastfeeding rates as he explained the one factor dragging on growth in the $4 billion American market: "We continue to see breastfeeding rates in the U.S. climb through 2014. Now we'll be watching very closely as we go through 2015 to see whether the improvement in unemployment trends will cause this trend to abate somewhat. It's our hope and expectation that that will be the case. But, through 2014, it remained on the rise.")

IN GUATEMALA, BREASTFEEDING rates were on the rise as hospitals embraced the Baby-Friendly Initiative. "Breastfeeding, breastfeeding, breastfeeding. That's what we teach," Yesica Bethancourt, the head of nutrition and food services and the Committee of Maternal Lactation at the government hospital in Quetzaltenango, told me. She and two other nutritionists shared a small, cramped office in the basement, beside the hospital's kitchen.

The hospital was working through the stages to earn the Baby-Friendly certification, but Yesica was concerned that the staff was too small and the budget too low to complete the process. Still, she proudly told me that 90 percent of mothers were breastfeeding when they left the hospital with their babies—and none of them were going home with free formula samples. She believed that getting each mother and newborn to begin practicing kangaroo care in the delivery room right after birth increased the breastfeeding rate. "The mothers who worry about breastfeeding and have difficulty are those who are separated from their babies right after birth. Those with kangaroo care have less difficulty. They are very enthusiastic," she told me. "In general, the women in Guatemala want to breastfeed. Especially those in the rural areas. For them, formula is too expensive."

The hospital staff had an unlikely ally in their breastfeeding campaign: the country's most popular marimba band, Internacionales Conejos (the International Rabbits). Working on lyrics with Save the Children's Guatemala office, the Rabbits provided a jaunty soundtrack to the 1,000 days

with their hit song "Dale Pecho" (Give the Breast). It was an ode to the
virtues of breastfeeding, and an anthem to the potential greatness of the
nation's children:

> For all the mothers, some advice from the
>   International Rabbits . . .
> So that your kids grow up healthy
> Give, give, the breast to the child
> Only breastmilk is good
> Give, give, the breast to the child
> If you want them to be an engineer
> Give, give, them their food
>
> If you want them to be a good teacher
> Give, give, them their food
> For an abundant harvest
> Give them the breast
> Because from the time the child is born,
> You should give them breastmilk
>
> Listen mama, for up to six months
> you should only give them breastmilk.

On the hospital maternity ward in Quetzaltenango, as the nurses
went from room to room encouraging breastfeeding, they had another
secret weapon on their side. It was unobtrusively stationed in the hallway, inside a large silver pot of tea. This was no ordinary green or black
tea. This was a special herbal concoction laced with *ixbut*, a plant long
cherished by the indigenous populations for one special quality: it was
said to stimulate the flow of breastmilk. Whenever I looked, there was a
line of new moms at the teapot waiting for a drink.

chapter eight

LOTTERY OF BIRTH

S HYAMKALI WAS BACK ON THE FLOOR, THIS TIME THE HARDENED mud-and-dung floor of her little house. She sat in the open doorway of the only room, facing an interior yard that was supposed to be the second room of the house but wasn't yet finished. The walls were incomplete, as was the ceiling. Two dung fires laced with incense smoldered, one at the entrance to the house and one beside the door of the interior room. There, in a haze of smoke, I found Shyamkali the day after she gave birth, sitting cross-legged, looking smaller than ever. Anshika slept on a thatch mat behind her.

Upon returning from the clinic, mother and daughter had gone into confinement in accordance with an ancient purification ritual meant to protect the child from evil spirits. For the first two weeks of her life, Anshika would be alone in this room with her mother. The baby would breastfeed, and Shyamkali would drink water and eat rice as well as whatever her neighbors and older daughters might bring her. No one else could enter the room, aside from the local health worker. The rest of the family would sleep outside. The men of the community had plugged all the holes in the mud-brick walls of the room with green plastic bags, so no evil—not to mention air—could squeeze in. Without ventilation, the room was stifling—the outside temperature scraped 100—and pungent. The smoke from the dung fires was meant to purify anyone and anything—people, cats, rodents—walking past the house or the confinement room, but it also stung the eyes and nostrils and throat, including mine as I stood outside the confinement room, in the open, unfinished part of the house, to speak with Shyamkali. This would be the only air Anshika would breathe for two weeks, though indoor smoke was a major culprit in respiratory problems, lung disease, and early death throughout the developing world where open fires inside living quarters were used for cooking, warmth, and light.

Shyamkali didn't seem worried about the confinement or bothered by the smoke. Her main concern was the reaction of her husband, Rajender, to Anshika's birth. She hadn't spoken with him yet, as he was away in Delhi, seeking work, though she knew he had heard the news from the neighbor woman who had accompanied her to the hospital, and she feared he was angry at her for having another daughter. He had canceled plans to come back home and celebrate; those plans were contingent on the arrival of a son. Shyamkali also fretted over what his response would be to her wish that this be their last child.

Little Anshika, conceived to be a boy, was born into a world of discrimination and the attendant inequality and injustice. Discrimination is particularly virulent in India, where it begins in the 1,000 days based on gender, place of birth, caste, and the economic circumstances of the family. Differences in the allocation of resources such as food and health care not only within Indian society but within families has led to girls having higher rates of stunting and lower levels of education than boys. More girls died before the age of five—73 per 1,000 girls compared to 64 per 1,000 boys—even though there were considerably fewer girls to begin with. Newspaper headlines of rape and abuse of women, and the callous response of some men, were common. At the time Anshika was born, consciences were still convulsing over the horrible bus rape in New Delhi several months earlier. A young woman had gone to see a movie with a male friend. After leaving the cinema, she and her friend hailed a private bus, where they encountered a pack of men who set upon the woman. The male friend fought, but to little avail. The men raped and beat the woman and tossed her from the bus. Her injuries were so severe that she died within weeks. A cry arose in some quarters for a reckoning within the country's culture—but not in all quarters. Attorneys for the men blamed the woman, saying she shouldn't have been going out at night.

JUST A FEW hours after Anshika's birth, Poonam Muttreja walked onto a stage in Kuala Lumpur, Malaysia. Poonam, the executive director of the Population Foundation of India and a longtime campaigner for gender equality in her country, joined a panel discussion at the Women Deliver Conference, a huge international gathering of maternal and infant health advocates. She began her talk with a story about a middle-class family with two daughters in New Delhi.

"The mother is pregnant for the third time, and everybody is praying for a boy to be born," she began. "As chromosomes would have it, the third child is a girl. The same wonderful and loving mother who was congratulated at the birth of her first two children is scorned. And the traditional Indian sweets that the aunt distributes to mark the birth of a child are returned. 'What is there to celebrate in the birth of a third child?' they say."

Time goes on, the third girl turns six years old and begins school. Poonam continued, "Her parents sadly do not have the resources to educate her and her sisters equally. So her sisters go a private school in a private school bus, while the third daughter goes to a government school in a crowded public bus. At the age of six, she could have internalized that her gender puts her at a disadvantage, and that she doesn't deserve better. Let me tell you, she decided, not only she, but all girls, all women, deserve better."

The mother in her story, Poonam explained, was "brought up to believe that she must produce one son at least, if not more, an heir for the family." And indeed, she said, "the mother goes on to have a fourth pregnancy and produces a son. In the hope of having sons, women continue to have children they can ill afford. It is not only about access to family planning and contraceptives, but rather, it's about women's empowerment. We need to look more closely at why people do sex selection, why there is a strong preference for sons. Women and men, yes, men, are also robbed of the freedom to make the choice and decide on the size and composition of their families. . . . This was a middle class family. Think of a girl born into a poor family, first, second, or third girl. She is likely to not be literate, [to] be undernourished, have multiple pregnancies, and risk dying in a childbirth."

Poonam paused, stopped the story, and proposed a major cultural shift, through the vehicle of what she called a "Y Chromosome Campaign." "The majority of women and men do not know that it is the Y chromosome of the man that determines the sex of the child," she said. "We need . . . a growing movement of men who acknowledge this, who assume responsibility, and who stand alongside women who speak against sex selection, who condemn discrimination of mothers who have daughters." Men, she insisted, needed to be a part of the discourse. "It is just as much a men's issue; it is a societal issue, it is a moral issue, it is an ethical issue. It is about social justice and human dignity. . . . Yes, enlist men who will speak up against violence and any form of discrimination. Yes, design programs to include men and women to eliminate violence. And yes, engage men and women as responsible partners and parents."

Poonam looked out into the audience and powerfully delivered her story's conclusion:

"Fifty years later, the six-year-old daughter is asking you to join the Y Chromosome Campaign."

She was asking for herself, for Anshika, for all the daughters of India.

GIRL OR BOY, rich or poor, urban or rural—they were all tickets in the lottery of birth.

Despite decades of progress in reducing global child mortality rates and the prevalence of illness, one constant stubbornly remained: babies from the families with the lowest incomes and in the most remote areas were still the ones most likely to die or struggle to thrive. Malnutrition and hunger were worse in the countries with the widest gaps between rich and poor and the ones where ethnic or religious minorities had faced generations of discrimination.

In 2013, it still mattered greatly where and when you were born and into what circumstances. Factoids from Save the Children's *Surviving the First Day* report include the following:

WHILE DOZENS OF countries—mostly middle-income countries in Eastern Europe and Latin America—have halved newborn mortality in the last decade, countries in sub-Saharan Africa, on average, have seen no statistically significant change. Without dramatic change in the trajectory for Africa, it is estimated that it will take over 150 years for an African newborn to have the same chance of survival as one born in Europe or North America. Progress in South Asia, while significant, has also lagged behind the rest of the world.

AS A WHOLE, the developed world has seen a 2.7 percent reduction per year in newborn mortality. This is twice the reduction seen in sub-Saharan Africa . . . and 50 percent higher than that seen in South Asia . . . from 1990 to 2011.

A MOTHER IN sub-Saharan Africa . . . is 30 times more likely than a mother in an industrialized country to lose a newborn baby at some point in her life. On average, 1 in 6 African mothers is likely to lose a newborn baby—a commonplace but largely untold tale of grief.

AN ANALYSIS OF 50 developing countries found babies born to mothers in the poorest fifth of the population were on average 40 percent more likely to die in infancy compared to those in the richest fifth. A similar analysis of 38 countries in Africa and Asia found babies born in rural areas were 20 percent more likely to die compared to those in urban areas.

BABIES BORN TO the poorest mothers [in India and several other countries] die at twice the rate of babies born to the richest mothers.

In rural India, another lottery factor was involved: the season in which a child was born. The *Global Nutrition Report* highlighted a study showing that Indian children born in the cooler, drier, post-harvest season (October to February) were less likely to be stunted than those born at other times of the year. After the harvest, there was more food in the house and less disease afoot. Stunting rates were highest in April through August, when temperatures soared, rains fell, malaria reigned, water-borne disease rampaged, and the agricultural demands on women increased. Other studies in Asia and Africa have similarly matched hot, wet, intense fieldwork seasons with lower body mass among pregnant and lactating women and low birth weight among babies.

PERHAPS SUSHMA'S BABY, Sunny, had ushered in some changing fortunes in the lottery of birth, for he was born on the day of the first Nutrition for Growth Summit, held amid much fanfare in London. Governments, philanthropists, business executives, and development specialists from around the world pledged greater investments, particularly in the 1,000 days, to overcome these many equality gaps. Might that change Sunny's life and the destiny of other infants around the world?

And maybe Sanju's son, Adarsh, and Seema's daughter, Priyanshi, had also drawn good lottery tickets. For they were born just as India was hoping to put its new National Food Security Act into action. The act, which had just been passed by parliament, was meant to narrow India's vast poverty and hunger chasm by significantly expanding the existing Public Distribution System, one of the largest social safety net programs in the world. Under the act, more than 800 million people—two-thirds of India's population—would be entitled to five kilograms of rice, wheat, or coarse cereals per person per month at the highly subsidized price of 1 to 3 rupees per kilogram—the equivalent of just a couple of cents in the United States. The legislation, often referred to as a "right to food act," was hotly debated in parliament, on editorial pages, and in nightly verbal jousts on television.

The passage of the act should have been very good news for the families of Shivgarh, but no one I spoke with had even heard about it, despite all the public clamor. Very few people here had televisions, so they hadn't seen the roiling debates. And since most were illiterate, or had minimal education, they hadn't read the miles of editorials in the newspapers. Still, they were precisely the people the act was supposed to help. When I explained it to them, they all thought it sounded like a very good idea.

There had always been a great disconnect between the fine words about ending hunger and actually doing so in the desperately poor villages. Even before the act, only a few of the families I met were receiving the subsidized rations of wheat, rice, maize, and cooking oil available under the existing public food distribution scheme. Only Mohana's family received a full monthly package of two kilograms of sugar, fifteen kilograms of rice, twenty kilograms of wheat, and two and a half liters of cooking oil, for which they paid less than three dollars. Between their two families, sisters-in-law Sanju and Seema received only the cooking oil, even though they surely were poor enough to qualify for a full ration. Which families got how much was up to village councils, and particularly the elected leaders; cronyism and corruption often influenced these decisions, as well as discrimination against the lowest castes. In every village I visited, I heard complaints that some wealthier families received full rations while some of the poorest got nothing. Moms were told they could only apply when a new village leader was elected; others were ridiculously instructed to go to the wealthier families themselves and ask if they would give them their rations, though to do so would be to risk ridicule, humiliation, and a beating.

The new act was meant to correct that: to reach those at the bottom of the hunger and poverty gap. Might Sanju and Seema soon be welcoming more food equality, and a better start in life, for their new babies? They shrugged in concert. "I hope," said Sanju. "What else can we do?"

IT WAS A grand irony that the women of Shivgarh shared few of the benefits from India's emergence as a food and economic power in recent decades, for they lived in the Rae Bareli district, the longtime political base of the Nehru-Gandhi family dynasty. Indira Gandhi was representing the constituency in the 1960s when she became India's first female prime minister and an international symbol of women's empowerment.

And yet there had been scant improvement since then in the everyday status of women and children.

Despite the high-tech innovations in the country, the manual labor of Indian women remained medieval. They still tilled the soil the old-fashioned way, fetched firewood and water, cooked over open fires, scrubbed pots and pans clean with ash from the fire in lieu of soap, and slathered new layers of cow dung on floors and walls. During the rice harvest of 2013, I found the new moms of Shivgarh doing double duty, bringing their babies with them to the fields so they could continue caring for them and breastfeeding. Once a mom arrived in the field, she spread a blanket on the ground for the baby. Then she gathered up some sheaths of rice stalks and arranged them in a crescent-shaped row to shade the baby from the sun and provide a break from the wind. She didn't tarry over the child, for she needed to join the other workers, who were swinging bundles of rice over their heads and slamming them down hard on a wooden table to knock loose the kernels. *Whoosh, slam.* The work went on for hours. If the baby cried, mom would stop her work to sit with the child and breastfeed. Then it was back to harvesting. The breaks were short, for her pay—one-eighth of the amount of rice she harvested—was contingent on her productivity. The more time a mother spent with her child, the less rice she would take home to feed her family.

The rice harvest coincided with Diwali, the annual festival of lights. One thing Diwali illuminated besides the homes, businesses, and public spaces of India were the divisions in Indian society. On the first day of the festival, called Dhanteras, Indians honored Lakshmi, the Hindu Goddess of Wealth. Jewelry stores did big business as the better-off bought gold and silver. Those of more modest means bought utensils, such as cutlery or pots and pans. The poor bought some candies or biscuits, if anything. "I don't think we'll buy anything," Sushma told me. "We can't afford it." Mohana said the same.

Shyamkali smiled wanly and shook her head. "Nothing."

On the high day of Diwali, firecrackers cackled and lit up the evening sky, particularly over the cities. Lamps and candles brightened streets, sidewalks, and houses to show the way for Lakshmi, who, it was believed, would visit and bestow prosperity and well-being for the coming year. But the poor villages of Shivgarh remained fairly silent and dark. Those families who could afford candles set them alight at their doorstep. Shyamkali had none. How would Lakshmi, and wealth and good health, even know where she lived?

For her and her community, Diwali wouldn't be much different from the rest of the year. The moms wore the same saris, colorful but simple, not elaborately detailed like the saris draping women in the cities and higher society. They wore bracelets, earrings, nose studs, and rings on fingers and toes, but there was far more plastic and tin than gold or silver. The mothers' sacrifice for their families extended from food and nutrients to every facet of life.

IN NORTHERN UGANDA, Harriet Ogwal was up in the hills, breaking rocks into gravel. As midday approached, I spotted her walking through the scrub trees and plots of vegetables. She was barefoot, wearing a dirty blue skirt and a tattered T-shirt, and carrying a hammer. It was a crude homemade tool—a round stone bound to a thick stick. She had been using it to chip away at the boulders in the quarry where her husband, Moses, worked on most days. Harriet was trying to earn extra money to care for the family. Now she was returning to their small homestead to start the cooking before heading back up the hill.

It had only been a few months since Apio had been born. Harriet said she still often felt dizzy and needed to rest frequently. She confessed that she wasn't the best worker. At the health post, she was told her high blood pressure persisted, and she was adamantly advised to stop working. Harriet scoffed. How could she? For a day of breaking stones, she could earn about $2. That, in turn, would pay for her purchases of high-iron beans on the market, which were going for about 25 cents a cup. Her family would consume about 20 cups of beans each week. The rains had begun, so tomorrow, Harriet said, she would be back in the field, planting the beans.

The deprivations of mothers in Uganda, and across Africa, were driving a "vicious circle of poverty" that spun from one generation to another, according to the *Situation Analysis of Children in Uganda* report. The government and UNICEF noted in the study that, "of all inequalities, gender is of specific concern." The researchers found that about 35 percent of girls were dropping out of school because of early marriage, and 23 percent because of pregnancy. Over 15 percent of Uganda's married women had been married by the age of fifteen, and nearly half by eighteen. Teenage pregnancy rates varied according to the lottery of birth: 34 percent of teenage girls from the poorest households and 24 percent of rural girls became mothers, compared with 16 percent of girls from wealthier households and 21 percent of urban teenagers. Family planning and sexual and reproductive health services were limited, particularly in rural areas. Gender-based violence, said the report, was a pervasive problem, "with about 6 in 10 women agreeing that wife beating is justified if the woman doesn't comply with culturally expected gender roles." An official of one organization working on women's rights in northern Uganda told me of a case where a husband put his wife up as collateral for a loan. And when the husband couldn't pay, the lender actually took the wife, only returning her after the community protested.

GUATEMALA HAS HAD the highest rate of gender-based violence in Latin America in recent years. According to the Women's Justice Initiative, which works to empower women to overcome inequalities, nearly half of Guatemalan women are victims of violence during their lifetime. The violence is both physical and economic; in most families, women have no control over finances, and frequently their husbands don't give them enough money to properly nourish their children or themselves. Women also have little say over family size. Conceiving a boy is often seen as a top priority. Child marriage is common, and 20 percent of babies born in Guatemala are to mothers younger than twenty years old.

In the United States, Alitzel and ShaLawn were born into a particularly stubborn inequality: In 2013, a woman working full time earned, on average, 78 cents for every dollar a man earned. The president's Council of Economic Advisers noted that this gender pay gap had narrowed between the 1970s and 1990s, but had remained between 76 and 78 cents since 2001. In addition, the pay gap widened beyond wages when workers' full compensation packages were considered. Women were less likely to have health insurance from their employer, retirement savings plans, or access to paid leave. And as President Obama would underscore in his 2015 State of the Union Address: "Today, we're the only advanced country on Earth that doesn't guarantee paid sick leave or paid maternity leave to our workers. Forty-three million workers have no paid sick leave. Forty-three million. Think about that."

And think about this: the only other country—out of 185 surveyed by the International Labor Organization—with no law to provide some kind of paid maternity leave was Papua New Guinea.

AS THE MOMS in each of the countries held their newborns, I asked them about their aspirations for their children. Education was the unanimous wish. Every mom—and the dads, too—hoped her child would do well in school. On the South Side of Chicago, in northern Uganda, in the Palajunoj Valley, and in the villages of Shivgarh, education was seen as the trump card to the lottery of birth. For many of the moms, this was an aspiration for their children to achieve something they hadn't had the chance to achieve.

For Jessica in Chicago, education was her top goal for both Alitzel and for herself. Marco had dropped out of high school to work and contribute to the support of his daughter, and, for a few moments, Jessica, too, had thought about leaving school. But what kind of example would that set? How could she encourage Alitzel to keep going—"to be known as an achiever, not a quitter," as she wrote in her journal—if she herself gave up? With Alitzel in her arms, Jessica determined to finish high school and also set her sights on college—for herself and her daughter. "I'm looking forward to going back to school. Not just to give my daughter an example, but for myself," she told me. "I don't want to be forty and regretting it."

Harriet in Uganda, for Apio: "I hope she will be educated so she can be a nurse or a doctor. Then there will be someone in the hospital to help me and others, so that no other mother loses her daughter, and no other girl loses her sister."

Dianet in Guatemala, for Keytlin: "I want her to get a good education, to have a career, whatever career she chooses. So that when she grows up and has children, she won't want for anything. She can buy food and clothes for her children, pay for their education, have a good life, have a job that allows her to travel and live in a different country with more opportunities."

Shyamkali in Shivgarh, for Anshika: "I wish for her a good education and a good marriage. I'm not expecting a rich man, but a good man who will take care of her. If she is educated, she will get a good man."

Mohana, for Sarita: "School is a good thing. I hope she is educated. But that is up to fate."

"No, no," said her husband. "Not just fate. I want the baby to be well-educated and to get a good government job." He smiled broadly, proudly. "Then her father will be famous for having an educated daughter!"

Midwife Susan Ejang leads a nutrition class on the veranda of the Ongica clinic in northern Uganda. With proper nutrition and care in the first 1,000 days, she told the moms, "your child can achieve great things."

Harriet breastfeeds one-month-old Apio, whose name means the "first of twin girls." Her sister was stillborn.

Harriet playing with Apio, who had just turned one and was beginning to walk.

Brenda with two-month-old Aron. Her smile is a sign she is beginning to recover from the sorrow she had carried after losing her first child.

Brenda cooking up a nutritious lunch of orange sweet potatoes, high-iron beans, and local greens.

Aron, fifteen months old, loves his orange sweet potatoes.

Esther and Rodgers in the vegetable fields on his second birthday. He is one of the new generation of biofortified babies in Africa.

Jessica, five months pregnant, with boyfriend Marco, after meeting with her doula at the Ounce of Prevention center on Chicago's South Side.

Jessica with ten-month-old daughter Alitzel at their home in Chicago.

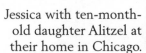

Quintana reading *With My Brother* with one-year-old ShaLawn at her house in Chicago. During her Ounce of Prevention home visitations, Quintana learned that words are nutrients for her baby's brain.

Quintana with ShaLawn, who is about eighteen months old, at an Ounce of Prevention mother-and-child party.

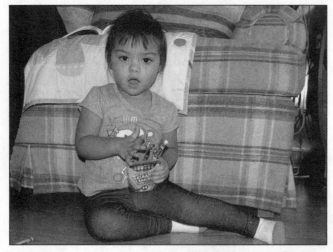

Alitzel with her crayons, shortly before turning two.

Jessica, Marco, and Alitzel at Alitzel's second birthday party, a festive Little Mermaid–themed gathering with family and friends.

Maria Estella (right), nine months pregnant, and Yolanda have fun filling up the food bowl at a Primeros Pasos nutrition class, but the women worried that, beyond the classroom, they couldn't afford to put their knowledge into action.

Maria Estella measures her five-month-old son, Jorge. Weighing more than eight pounds at birth, Jorge continued his robust growth, giving his mother hope that he could beat the odds of rural Guatemala, where the majority of children are stunted.

The valleys of Guatemala, beneath the dormant volcanos, yield a cornucopia of nutrient-rich vegetables. But at harvest time, trucks arrive and haul away most of the bounty for export markets, including the United States.

Griselda and her sixteen-month-old daughter, Sucely. Born with a clubfoot, Sucely wasn't yet walking and instead crawled around on ground shared with the family's chickens, sheep, dogs, and horses. She was constantly battling intestinal illnesses.

Dianet with Keytlin at a Primeros Pasos meeting. A month before her second birthday, Keytlin was more active and mentally sharper than most of the other children her age, even though she was lagging behind on the international growth chart.

Jorge and his sister, Yesica Marisol. Though they appear to be the same size, Jorge has just turned two and Yesica is nearly four.

During the Indian rice harvest, moms do double duty in the fields. They often bring their babies with them and use sheaths of rice stalks to build a protective sun-and-wind shelter for them.

Seema and Priyanshi, with Sanju and Adarsh. The children are twenty-one months old.

Shyamkali and five-month-old Anshika. Shyamkali had hoped to have at least one son, but declared that Anshika, her fifth daughter, would be their last child.

Shyamkali and her daughter Anshika in "confinement," one day after Anshika's birth. For two weeks, mother and child would be alone in this room of their house, surrounded by smoke from incense-laced dung fires—a traditional practice to ward off evil spirits.

On the day daughter Anshika turned two, her father, Rajender, hauled coal to fuel the local brickmaking kiln in 100-plus degree temperatures. Each fully loaded yoke weighed about 100 pounds.

Shyamkali and Rajender with their girls on Anshika's second birthday. Anshika laughs in her father's arms.

Sushma and her son Sunny, who had just turned two.

ALL PHOTOGRAPHS BY ANNE THUROW.
To view more photos of *The First 1,000 Days* journey, go to www.outrageandinspire.org.

PART THREE | THE FIRST YEAR

chapter nine

"THE CHILD IS NO LONGER HERE"

ALL OF SHIVGARH WAS BUSY WITH THE WHEAT HARVEST IN early 2014. Mohana had just returned from the fields and was sitting on the floor of her veranda, separating the chaff from a pile of wheat. She was wearing a dull green sari; one corner partially covered her face. On the *charpoy* beside her, a child slept, covered by a brown shawl. The figure looked too big to be Sarita, who would have been about six months old. And it looked too small, I thought, to be the next oldest child, three-year-old Lakshmi.

"How's the baby?" I asked Mohana, through a translator with the Community Empowerment Lab. Mohana didn't reply.

We tried again. "Where's the little one?"

Mohana looked up from the wheat. In Hindi, she said, "The child is no longer here."

"The child is finished," said Krishan, her husband, who had appeared carrying another bundle of wheat.

It was their way of explaining an unspeakable tragedy. Sarita had died.

Krishan joined his wife on the veranda; he sat on the edge of a second *charpoy*, one leg dangling over the side. All around them, everyone was

155

on the move. A certain buoyancy filled the Shivgarh villages—the store-rooms would soon be full. But on this veranda, a deep sadness prevailed. Together, Mohana and Krishan described what had happened to their daughter less than two months earlier, each relaying pieces of the ordeal. They spoke matter-of-factly; there was no crying, no hysteria.

Mohana said Sarita had been doing well. She was four months old, healthy and growing strong. She was always hungry, demanding ever more of Mohana's breastmilk. Mohana worried she might not be satisfying her daughter, so she began giving her a bit of cow's milk in a bottle as well. For two weeks this turbo-feeding continued. Sarita must really be growing, her parents thought.

Suddenly, things went in reverse. Sarita began vomiting all the milk. She couldn't keep anything down. She also developed diarrhea. She was breathing heavily and with difficulty. She coughed but couldn't clear the phlegm. She shivered, and no number of blankets would stop it. This was worse than what had afflicted Lakshmi two years earlier. After several days, as the illness increased in severity, Mohana and Krishan took Sarita to a private clinic. At the government regional hospital, they reckoned, they would have to wait in line only to get a cursory checkup. And whatever medicine would be prescribed likely wouldn't be available. The doctor who had treated Lakshmi was too far away. At the nearby private clinic, at least Sarita would get attention. It would be expensive, about 500 to 600 rupees for each visit and the medicine. Hedging their hope in modern treatments, they also went to the local healer with his traditional cures. And all the time they worried: Had they waited too long to seek help?

There was no clear diagnosis at the clinic. The doctor prescribed medicine to bring down the fever and to fight the cough. The traditional healer ran some feathers over Sarita and applied herbal treatment. Both of them told the parents the stomach illness would run its course.

Mohana and Krishan brought Sarita home and gave her the medicine prescribed by the doctor. The shivers continued. She began to turn blue around the lips and eyes. Sarita never recovered.

"The doctor said when her stomach is empty of the disease, the sickness will be finished, and the child with be fine," Krishan said. "Instead, the baby was finished."

Two months later, the parents didn't remember the exact date when their daughter died. "It was a Monday," said Krishan. All that remained were the empty medicine bottles. They were still where Mohana had kept them when Sarita was sick, in a little nook chiseled into the wall by the front door, like a shrine to their daughter. Krishan reached for the medicine and handed it to me. The labels were macabre. A white baby wrapped in a green blanket peered out from the label of one bottle; a teddy bear was pictured on the second. Inside the first there had been sixty milliliters of a paracetamol suspension; inside the second, the same quantity of Tedykoff.

A pain reliever and a cough syrup. For all of Sarita's wrenching symptoms, that was all that had been prescribed to cure her; or at least, it was all her parents could afford.

Her parents believed she had died of "cold fever," hypothermia, the catch-all evil blamed for almost every unexplained infant death in the rural communities of Shivgarh. It was the coldest time of the year in northern India, and babies were the most vulnerable. It didn't seem to be a virus, since no one else in the family got sick. The child under the shawl on the *charpoy* was Lakshmi, who didn't fall ill with her sister. She was small for her age, but full of big smiles. And Sushma's children on the other side of the wall remained healthy. The reality was that Sarita could have died from any number of child killers in India: diarrhea from bad water and poor sanitation, intestinal infection from spoiled milk, pneumonia, even hypothermia—or from a combination of those ills. Still, in the narrow passageways between the brick and thatch houses of Rampur Khas, whispers spread, particularly among the men, that Mohana was a bad mother; that she had waited too long to seek treatment for her daughter. Nonsense, said her friends, other women, who tried to stifle that talk with a dose of fatalism—these things just happen; it's the way things are. "*Dehat*," they said, using a Hindi expression for "rural, backwards." It was usually accompanied by a shrug, as if to say, "Look where we are. What do you expect?"

Sarita's death was a tragedy, but not a rarity in the rural villages of Shivgarh. I mentioned her passing to Vishwajeet at the Community Empowerment Lab. He winced in sorrow. "Unfortunately, children will still die," he said. "We're just trying to lower the odds that they will."

AT ABOUT THE same time, in rural northern Uganda, Brenda was terrified that she could lose her son, Aron. He had just turned six months
old, and he was beginning to eat solid foods, including corn porridge,
mashed sweet potatoes, and beans, and to drink cow's milk, water, and
tea in addition to his mother's milk. He was big, about eighteen pounds,
and he was active, crawling all over the place. Brenda had been so proud
and eager to have others see her son's development that she had recently
taken him to her family's homestead, about ten miles away. There had
been great celebration over the healthy boy.

While they visited, her family heard that an elderly neighbor had
fallen sick with dysentery. Everyone knew that one incident of a water-
borne disease could quickly turn into an epidemic. And it did. Soon, much
of the community was violently ill. Brenda's sister was the first in her
family to get sick, shortly after they heard about the outbreak. The next
day it was Brenda and Aron. Brenda feared something was wrong when
her energetic boy suddenly became listless. In short order, Aron shivered
with fever and his eyes swelled. Diarrhea was followed by dehydration.
Brenda herself was suffering the same symptoms, and not for the first
time in her life. She understood how dangerous this could be, especially
for an infant.

Brenda's initial concern quickly escalated into panic. Could it be
happening again? Was her second child dying, too? Her father, Sylvester,
rushed to get the family bike; his wife, carrying Aron, climbed on the
back. Sylvester pedaled frantically over the rough dirt roads to get to
the nearest clinic. The grandparents spent the night keeping watch over
Aron.

As Brenda recalled the ordeal for me—back home now with her husband's family—she began to cry. Two months had passed, but the fear
was still raw. Brenda covered her face with her hands and turned away.
She sobbed mightily, her shoulders heaving.

She sat on the stoop of the cooking hut, beneath the overhang of the
thatch roof. Her husband, Dennis, lounged several feet away in a chair
outside their one-room house. He seemed preoccupied with fixing a
shoe, or maybe it was just something to do while lost in thought as his
wife spoke. Dennis never said a word; nor did he move to comfort his
wife.

At the clinic, the nurses quickly treated Aron's diarrhea with zinc tablets and rehydrated him with liquids. They had a lot of experience dealing with dysentery and diarrhea. They prescribed some antibiotics that cost about $2.50, which Aron's grandfather purchased at a private store, as the clinic was out of the drugs. The medicine worked; within a few days, Aron was back to his active self.

As Brenda talked about Aron's recovery, a calm returned. She spoke softly but analytically, focusing the blame. Brenda believed the dysentery outbreak began at the community well about one kilometer from her parents' house. It was an old hand-dug well called *Olorogweng*, meaning "rolled stones," a description of how the local residents had built it: rolling away stones to uncover the flow of an underground spring. The water accumulated in a dirt hollow. It was in the middle of a field surrounded by tall grass, thick bushes, and trees, and was used by both humans and animals for drinking. Animals grazed in the area and also urinated and pooped; so did the people who came to collect water. The waste would seep into the groundwater and also run off into the water hollow.

When I first saw the well, the water was a greenish color. Women and children arrived carrying empty jerricans on their heads and in their hands. They would collect the water from the ground in a basin, and then, using a funnel shaped out of a plastic soda bottle, pour the water from the basin into the jerricans. Back at home, the standard method of purification was to filter the water by pouring it over a thin piece of cloth. The cloth caught the larger particles of dirt; the water that passed through was collected in a pot and considered ready for drinking and washing. It really wasn't safe to drink, but it was marginally cleaner than when it came out of the ground. Some families additionally boiled the water before drinking. Some drank it straight from the source, unfiltered in any way.

The well had been a source of water-borne disease throughout the years. Diarrhea was an all-too-common illness in the area. One bout of diarrhea just set the stage for another, as one sick person drew water from the well and potentially soiled it for others.

Several years earlier, an international relief organization had constructed a borehole about another kilometer away, just beside the main dirt road. They had used a pipe to channel the water to the surface, and poured some concrete to form a cleaner perimeter. This well served a couple of villages and often had a waiting line, as people came from miles around to fetch the water. Because *Olorogweng* was closer and more convenient to use, it remained a prime source of water for Brenda's family and her neighbors, despite the greater health risk.

While Aron's physical health steadily improved after he received treatment, Brenda's mental state only worsened. She blamed herself for Aron's illness; she felt she should have been more careful with what he ate and drank. And when she returned home, Dennis's family piled on another load of guilt. They had already scolded her for the death of the first child. Now this, a close call with little Aron. Her mother-in-law wouldn't let up; two months later, she was still at it. As Brenda spoke about the *Olorogweng* well, her mother-in-law, who was listening closely to our conversation, interrupted. "This is what happens when you take your child to your side," she harangued. "The baby was fine when you left."

Again, Brenda broke down in tears. The guilt was enormous. The verdict, she felt, was in: she was a bad mother.

Not that Dennis's family maintained a pristine homestead. Throughout this family drama, Aron, wearing just a red and blue shirt and no pants, sat on a plastic grain storage bag, which was spread out on the dirt under a tree. A brown calf was tethered to a bush five feet away, and a gray calf and a brown cow grazed on the brush a few feet beyond that. Cow patties were everywhere. So were chickens and roosters scratching and pecking and pooping in the dirt all around Aron.

A week earlier, Aron had broken out in a rash and had a fever. Brenda had taken him to the Ongica clinic. The nurses said no testing was necessary; they could tell just by looking at Aron that he had malaria. They prescribed the standard treatment: the antimalarial medication Coartem. And they recommended he sleep under insecticide-treated bed nets.

Why didn't they already have malaria nets? I asked.

Now Dennis spoke. Too expensive, he said; each net would cost about 10,000 shillings. The government's free bed net distribution program hadn't arrived in their area yet, and he doubted it ever would. Dennis explained that the family's meager income came from the sale of any surplus crops, and from beer they brewed themselves. In great detail, he described how they mixed cassava and sorghum with molasses left over from the local sugar factory. They boiled it in a metal barrel and then let it ferment for two weeks in a hole in the ground lined with banana leaves. Dennis gestured in the direction of a small grove of banana trees; there, a new batch was on the boil.

How much was the malaria medication? I wondered.

"12,000 shillings," Dennis said.

The treatment was more expensive than the prevention.

UNCLEAN WATER, POOR sanitation, and lousy hygiene—and the burden of diseases that result—combine with poor nutrition as the leading causes of mortality and stunting in the 1,000 days. Diarrhea killed about 600,000 children in 2013, according to UNICEF and WHO. Other intestinal diseases, such as environmental enteropathy, caused by chronic exposure to fecal bacteria, contribute to stunting by diverting energy toward fighting infection and away from growth. As do intestinal parasites and worms, which are spread by unsanitary conditions. As do aflatoxins, which arise when various foods, including corn and peanuts, are spoiled with a fungus, whether by climate, through poor harvesting techniques, or from bad storage methods.

There has been considerable progress on the WASH (water, sanitation, hygiene) front in recent decades. Globally, about 2.6 billion people have gained access to an improved drinking water source since 1990, and about 2 billion people have begun using improved sanitation facilities during that time. But behind these global improvements (reported in a 2015 study by UNICEF and the World Health Organization entitled *25 Years Progress on Sanitation and Drinking Water*), huge disparities remain. Access to clean water and improved sanitation varies widely in the developing world. The report estimated that more than 660 million people worldwide still used unimproved drinking-water sources, including unprotected wells and springs similar to *Olorogweng* or surface water from rivers and lakes. And more than 2 billion people either still used unimproved sanitation facilities, such as uncovered latrines, or defecated in the open. Most of these cases of poor water and sanitation were in sub-Saharan Africa and South Asia.

In Uganda, 30 percent of children were without access to safe water in 2013, according to the *Situation Analysis of Children in Uganda* prepared by the Ugandan government and UNICEF. But "access" didn't mean turning a tap on a nearby faucet. Nearly two-thirds were at least a thirty-minute round-trip walk from a safe water source, and more than one-third were sixty minutes away. The greatest distances were in the Northern region, with three-quarters of the children at least thirty minutes away from safe drinking water. About 70 percent of Uganda's rural population used some type of latrine, but there were large disparities across the country. The proportion of children with no toilet at home in the Northern region was seven times greater than in the Central region. The most troubling statistic was that only 8 percent of Uganda's population had a handwashing facility at home with readily available soap and water. This data matched my observations: moms merely poured water over their children's hands before meals, if they used any water at all.

One result of this poor access to safe water and improved sanitation was that one-quarter of Uganda's children suffered severe diarrhea or dysentery. Diarrhea sapped vital micronutrients out of the body and left children weaker and more vulnerable to other diseases and infections, particularly malaria. Diarrhea and malaria formed the most deadly combination against children in Uganda.

The government had declared its ambitions to improve conditions for its children. The ministry of health in the capital city of Kampala is filled with posters and slogans trumpeting good intentions. "Hurry Up! 2.6 billion people want to use the toilet," shouted a sign on the door of a ministry bathroom, referring to all those around the world without improved facilities. "Hands washed with soap and water are hands to be proud of," proclaimed another. In a ministry conference room, two wall posters hailed investments in WASH programs as important not only for good health but also for economic growth. They were part of the GDP for GDP campaign: Good Domestic Practices for Gross Domestic Product. "Invest in Waste," instructed one of the posters, which went on to say that latrine construction and sanitation innovations—turning waste into fuel or fertilizer, for instance—were good for jobs, productivity, education, tourism, health, and human dignity. The other poster bluntly asked, "Will You Help Turn Shit Into Gold?"

It was beside these admonitions in the conference room that I met with Sarah Opendi, the minister of state for health. She acknowledged her frustration with the country's modest progress on the WASH front; there were too many scattershot initiatives that hadn't amounted to much. She said that Uganda's membership in Scaling Up Nutrition finally pushed the government to engage all of its ministries in initiatives concerned with the 1,000 days.

"For quite a long time, the issues of nutrition have been in the hands of the ministry of health," she told me. "We'd say, 'Here's the nutritious food to eat,' but we weren't the ministry that produced food." That was the ministry of agriculture.

"We'd say, 'Drink safe water,' but we didn't drill wells." That was the ministry of public works.

"We'd say, 'New moms should have six months of maternity leave,' but we had no mandate to authorize that." That would be the ministry of gender.

"We had the messages, but we didn't have the means to implement them," the minister lamented. "The political will is there, but it hasn't been transformed into more resources."

Indeed, the government's *Situation Analysis of Children* noted that insufficient funding "remains a major roadblock to the roll-out of large-scale sanitation programs."

AFTER THE DYSENTERY outbreak, Brenda's neighbors complained to local government officials, despaired at the inaction, and then took matters into their own hands. "We've protested to health workers before about this well," Brenda's father, Sylvester, told me. "They say, 'Yes, we're coming. We're coming.' But they never came." As he spoke, the Dire Straits sang from a transistor radio sitting on the ground at the center of the family homestead. "Especially during elections, they promise to cement the well, put in a pipe for the water," Sylvester grumbled. "They keep on lying and lying."

The community itself formed a work crew that cut back the grass and bushes around the well. They dug a deeper hole for the springwater. They spread the word that families should keep their cows and goats away from the water, and that people shouldn't defecate in the area. In the meantime, the improved well beside the road—with a pipe set in concrete—was out of operation. The pipe had broken, and the water stopped flowing. The community took up a collection to repair the well, but it wasn't enough.

Another election was coming up in several months. "We'll try again to talk to the politicians about our well. I'll say my grandson got sick from the bad water," Sylvester said. "Maybe this time they'll listen." He shrugged and chuckled at the seeming folly of his intentions. He sounded like a man who had given up.

Back at the ministry of health, a senior nutrition officer, Agnes Chandia, bemoaned the fact that only about 60 percent of Ugandans used toilets, despite the ministry's exhortations to do so. "We talk about toilet use all the time," she said. But even in places where toilets had been built by the government, people didn't use them. There were superstitions against pregnant women using toilets (the baby might fall in) and against using the same toilet as your in-laws—a big taboo. And people complained that outhouses were too small and smelly compared with the great outdoors, or too obvious: "I've had men tell me, 'If I walk to the toilet, everyone will know what I am doing,'" said Chandia.

She laughed. "People have all sorts of reasons."

PEOPLE ALSO HAVE their reasons for avoiding toilets in India, where more than 50 percent of the population defecates in the open, which represents about 60 percent of the global incidence of open defecation. Indoor plumbing is extremely rare in rural India. A survey of the sanitation behavior of more than 20,000 people in rural northern India, including Uttar Pradesh, by the Research Institute for Compassionate Economics (the report was called *Sanitation Quality, Use, Access and Trends*, or, appropriately, SQUAT), found that "open defecation is not only socially acceptable in parts of rural north India, it is seen as a wholesome activity that promotes physical health. When performed in conjunction with other daily rituals, it is seen to promote the purity of the body."

This attitude was reflected in high rates of open defecation despite latrine ownership; SQUAT revealed that even among households that owned a latrine, 40 percent had at least one member who regularly defecated in the open.

One seventy-two-year-old man, a retired army officer of a lower caste who owned a latrine, told SQUAT researchers: "I don't want to go inside the latrine. . . . [O]ne benefit of going out in the open is that one can have some exercise and the second is that all the impurities of one's breath get out. But if one eats and drinks and goes to the latrine in the house one would not live long."

A twenty-two-year-old man, a high-caste Hindu, also praised open defecation: "One can stretch the body, one can go out for a walk. You can also prevent yourself from getting diseases. If a latrine is in the house, bad smells will come, germs will grow. Latrines in the house are like . . . hell. The environment becomes completely polluted."

The SQUAT survey noted that "latrines are seen as a luxury item for use by weak people—the old, infirm, young women and children. Healthy, strong decision makers typically prefer open defecation."

This should all be cautionary advice for the Swachh Bharat (Clean India) Mission of Prime Minister Narendra Modi, who set a goal of building a toilet for every household in India by 2019, thus, theoretically, ending open defecation.

For years the Indian government had followed a *Field of Dreams* philosophy to building toilets for the rural population: if we build it, they will go. In fact, SQUAT found just the opposite: people living in households with a latrine built with government support were more than twice as likely to defecate in the open as people living in households with a latrine they constructed themselves. Those who built their own latrines generally had greater awareness of the health benefits and were more motivated to use it. Also, households that built their own latrines often chose more expensive ones costing upward of $300, with a larger pit that might last a family for a generation. The toilet pits built by the government for half the cost would be about one-fifth the size; these smaller pits would need to be manually cleaned every three to five years. And that, noted SQUAT, would be a task considered dirty and degrading and associated with untouchability. This was a main reason why decades of spending on rural sanitation programs in India hadn't made much progress compared with projects in other developing countries, such as neighboring Bangladesh, where construction of simple, inexpensive toilets has greatly lowered open defecation rates. This shift has coincided with a fairly rapid decline in stunting in Bangladesh.

SQUAT's conclusion: Launching a large-scale program to build latrines without an equally large-scale campaign to promote latrine use and educate the population on the health benefits of latrines would likely create a lot of waste itself. The rejection rate of the government-built toilets would be high.

IN EARLY 2014, a new advocate for toilets appeared in India, someone who could spearhead a behavior-change campaign. She was six years old. Her name was Raya. She was the newest Muppet, debuting in *Sesame Street*'s Cleaner, Healthier, Happier campaign in India, Bangladesh, and Nigeria. She was introduced at the Reinvent the Toilet fair in Delhi with this message: Stay clean when using the toilet. With her sidekick Elmo, Raya would talk about handwashing and wearing sandals when visiting the latrine.

Sushma hadn't heard of Raya, or *Sesame Street*. Houses without a toilet usually didn't have a television. Sunny, wearing only a black T-shirt, was sleeping in a reed bassinet hanging low from the roof of her veranda. Although he wasn't walking yet, he was getting in the habit of open defecation. The bassinet was lined with a large vinyl banner, once an advertisement for a beauty parlor in Lucknow. It had been hanging above a street somewhere, a male model's face flapping in the wind, when a storm dragged it back to earth. Sushma's husband came across it and brought it home. Sushma had an ideal use for it. Sunny didn't wear diapers; none of the babies in rural Shivgarh did, because they were far too expensive. Rather, he would begin the day wearing little shorts until he peed in them. Sushma would remove them, give them a bit of a scrub, and then hang them out to dry. Sunny would be bottomless until his pants dried. Then the cycle would repeat. While his pants were drying, Sunny would pee on the plastic banner, right onto the hipster hairdo of the model. Sushma laughed. "It's easy to clean," she said.

I looked around her little homestead for a toilet. There certainly wasn't one in the house; it was far too small, and no one had indoor plumbing. Nor was there a latrine beside the house or behind any of the bushes. I asked Sushma if she used a latrine. She shook her head and pointed to the field beyond her house. There was a row of trees at the far end. That's where she and her family would go.

Was it safe? I asked. Was she ever afraid, especially at night?

"We're used to it," she said. "It's what we all do."

AS SEEMA AND Sanju sat on the stoop between their houses, they looked across a narrow alleyway at the unfinished shell of a latrine. It was just three sides made of brick. There was no roof, and no door in the front. I could see a mild dent in the dirt floor, but there was no hole. Some workers paid by the government had come by and started construction, but they never came back. So the would-be latrine stood as a monument to futility.

Seema's daughter and Sanju's son were both about seven months old. "Our children have been sickly," Seema told me. "They have frequent fever. They catch colds. They pee in their clothes and then lie in wet clothes and get cold."

"My son often has an upset stomach," Sanju said. "I give him medicine. And diarrhea. Sometimes it takes two or three days to be cured. Sometimes he vomits." The doctor told her that her son had been exposed to chill winds, which caused his ill health.

"It's nothing worrisome," Seema said. "Just that it keeps happening."

The medicine prescribed for both children was paracetamol and a cough medicine called RidCold. "It's the medicine they give us for everything," Seema said.

I measured both children. Their frequent illnesses already had them falling behind the international growth standards for their age. Seema's daughter, Priyanshi, was twenty-five inches, which put her a couple of inches behind the rate for girls. Sanju's son, Adarsh, was half an inch shorter than his cousin. At seven months, he was the length of a four-month-old boy on the international growth chart.

A cow and her calf lounged in an open stall right next to where we were sitting. Wasps and bees buzzed around. And there were flies, too; many, many flies. They sat on the cow dung and flew over to the children.

Sanju was pregnant again, so she stopped breastfeeding Adarsh, as was the local custom. Instead, Adarsh clamored for his bottle. Sanju filled it with buffalo milk thinned with water, and screwed on a yellow top and nipple. Adarsh held it while he drank and then dropped it in the dirt. It rolled across the ground. Seema's older son picked up the bottle by the nipple and eventually dropped it back in the dirt. It rolled over to Priyanshi, who picked it up and put it in her mouth. Seema was just beginning to wean Priyanshi from exclusive breastfeeding. Both mothers gave their children biscuits—the Parle G brand, "G for Genius"—after soaking them in water straight from the well in front of the house. The milk bottle eventually made it back to Sanju, who handed it to Adarsh without cleaning it.

The moms also gave their children amulets, leather pouches filled with the spices cardamom, cloves, and hing, which they wore around their necks. And they had smeared charcoal around the children's eyes to ward off eye infection and evil spirits.

A fire had been made from the chaff of the wheat. The smoke was intended to keep away mosquitoes—and malaria. But it had no effect on rodents. A mouse scampered past the children and under the door of the house.

Anil, Sanju's husband, stepped out of the house to join us. He worked construction jobs, wherever and whenever he could find them.

I asked him if he would ever finish off the latrine. "I could," he said, "but we'll need some money first."

Would he use it once it was complete?

"It sounds like a good idea, I suppose," he answered without conviction. "But it's probably better for use by the children and women and the elderly."

IN GUATEMALA, SUSY preached that cleanliness was next to godliness, or at least next to good nutrition in the 1,000 days. When she visited the moms at their homes, she posted a ten-point WASH checklist in the most prominent place in the house, which often was beneath a portrait of Jesus:

- Always wash raw food like fruit and vegetables with water and Cloro (a mild form of Clorox bleach).

- Boil your drinking water and water used for preparing food.
- Wash hands before eating, while preparing food, after using the latrine and after changing the child's diapers.
- Make sure food is properly cooked. Chicken, meat and seafood can be contaminated with germs and must be cooked thoroughly.
- Keep raw food separate from cooked food.
- Immediately eat the food once it is cooked.
- Refrigerate leftover food or store in a safe place.
- Reheat leftover food before eating.
- Food must be well covered and kept out of reach of flies, cockroaches, rats and other animals.
- Wash all kitchen utensils and disinfect all surfaces with Cloro.

Griselda Mendoza posted the list on the front of a cabinet in her bedroom, which she shared with her husband and baby daughter, Sucely. It was one room of a common house occupied by her husband's family. Griselda also tucked a diploma from the Primeros Pasos nutrition project inside the frame of a mirror. It certified Griselda as "a healthy mother" and praised her "outstanding participation in the development of proper healthy habits to improve the health of the family and the community." It was the only diploma she had ever received; she had left primary school after several years.

Griselda's room was tidy, but beyond that was a 1,000 days' nightmare. The common yard, which was mainly barren soil, was home to a menagerie of animals: chickens, dogs, sheep, goats, and horses. There was poop all over the place. None of the animals looked healthy. The dogs were mangy and skinny and flea-ridden. Those dogs, along with the chickens and sheep, occasionally entered the house. It was in this barnyard mess that Sucely was beginning to crawl.

Susy praised Griselda for keeping clean conditions in her room, but scolded her for allowing Sucely to play in such a dirty environment outside. Sucely's face and clothes—even her pink hat, embroidered with a kitten and the word "Health"—were smudged with dirt. Susy realized that care of the household wasn't totally in Griselda's control, so she also spoke with Griselda's in-laws and implored them to keep the animals separate from the living quarters, saying the health of their children depended on it. Tests at the clinic showed that Sucely already had parasites when she was just two months old. So it wasn't surprising when Griselda reported that Sucely had been battling diarrhea and stomach problems. Susy measured and weighed the baby. The readings indicated that Sucely was falling behind the standard norms and was on the path to being stunted. An older girl, also smudged from head to toe, toddled over and tugged at Susy's dress. She was tiny, with delicate features, and she wanted to be measured as well. She was Sucely's cousin, Darlyn, who was being cared for by the family. Griselda said Darlyn was born with fetal alcohol syndrome; her mother had been a heavy drinker and died when Darlyn was a baby. Darlyn smiled and stood straight and still for Susy during the measurement; she was severely stunted, barely thirty inches tall at three years old. Susy shook her head; it was impossible for any child to recuperate and thrive in such unhygienic conditions.

"You must clean up. Sweep the yard, wash the clothes, use soap on hands and face," Susy told Griselda and the other adults. "You can see what is happening to your children."

AT THE SAME time, researchers from universities and institutions in the United States, the United Kingdom, and Zimbabwe were releasing a novel study called "Hygiene Behaviors, Geophagy and Fecal Bacteria," also known as the chicken poop paper. Geophagy is the practice of eating dirt and other soil components like chalk or clay.

The researchers observed infants and caregivers in rural Zimbabwe and recorded what the children put into their mouths. A number of the infants, while crawling on cow-dung-smeared floors or bare soil and on chicken feces in the yard, actively ingested the soil and feces, or licked stones from the soil, resulting in contamination with *Escherichia coli* bacteria. The researchers found that about half of the caregivers had *E. coli* on their hands. Handwashing with soap for the infants or adults was uncommon.

Focus group discussions confirmed that babies ate soil and either fresh or dried chicken feces. Some mothers told the researchers that in-laws or village elders advised soil eating, believing it was good for the baby's intestines and that it treated stomach illness, despite what the study showed: "Active exploratory ingestion of soil and chicken feces had the greatest risk of fecal bacteria exposure in terms of high microbial load. Crawling on bare highly contaminated soils and kitchen floors exposes infants and young children to low but frequent dosages of fecal bacteria for most [or] part of their active developmental stage. . . . Ingestion of fecal bacteria may cause environmental enteropathy, the major pathway associated with poor growth in early life."

Environmental enteropathy, found throughout the developing world, is a chronic inflammatory disease of the small intestine most likely caused by poor sanitation and recurrent fecal ingestion. When people develop this disease, the absorption and immune functions of their intestines are compromised, leading to an inability to properly absorb micronutrients and oral vaccines. In essence, it undermines nutritional interventions, leading to an absence of nutrients, including zinc, which are critical for the growth of the body and brain development. This study and others pointed to environmental enteropathy as a major culprit in stunting, and this finding, in turn, has prompted new interventions for the first 1,000 days.

The authors of the Zimbabwe study noted that existing WASH projects, such as those involving handwashing, water treatment, and improved sanitation, need to be extended to interventions designed to keep animals away from family living areas and prevent contamination from fecal bacteria. "Existing WASH interventions are failing to protect infants and young children from ingesting soil and feces at a critical growth and development state," the researchers said.

Growing awareness that bacteria and parasites could undermine nutrition was already leading to some changes in community health-care practices. In several places, I saw deworming medicine distributed in tandem with treatment of micronutrient deficiencies. In the Karamoja region of eastern Uganda, at mobile clinics operated by the government and the Irish humanitarian agency Concern Worldwide, children lined up for their twice-yearly dose of vitamin A. After they opened their mouths and tilted back their heads so that health workers could deposit a few drops of the valuable liquid from a tiny red capsule, children were directed to another line to get their twice-yearly dose of deworming tablets. The organizations that distributed the medicines, such as Vitamin Angels and the Micronutrient Initiative, put together this one-two combination when they realized that the vitamin A they'd been providing wasn't being adequately absorbed by bodies riddled with bacteria or parasites.

Primeros Pasos workers did the same when children came to their clinic. "People here live and die with parasites," lab technician Irma Yolanda Mezariegos told me. "It's one of the reasons that Guatemala has such a malnutrition problem, and stunting. The children just stay short and small." She would know. For hours every day she stared through a microscope, examining stool samples of the children of the Palajunoj Valley. She invited me to take a look and pointed out the squiggly parasites. "So tiny, but so dangerous," she said.

That morning, kindergarteners from the Tierra Colorada Baja primary school came for their annual checkups as part of the clinic's Healthy Schools program, which involved ten schools in the valley. Sixteen children, mainly five and six years old, brought stool samples to be tested. Irma collected the samples and retreated to her microscope. Meanwhile, the children were weighed and measured, and then were ushered into a classroom at the back of the clinic for a dose of nutrition and hygiene education. Lucy Alvarado, then the director of the Primeros Pasos children's health education program, stood in front of a wall covered with posters. One was entitled "Comidas Buenas," another "Comidas Malas": Good Foods, Bad Foods.

She pointed to the pictures of processed foods like chips and candy and artificially sweetened products on the "Comidas Malas" poster. "If you eat too much of these, you'll stay small," she said. "You don't want to stay small, do you?"

"No," came a chorus in reply.

"You all want to be big and strong?"

"Yes!"

"Then you have to eat these foods," Lucy said, pointing to the "Comidas Buenas" poster, featuring pictures of fruits, vegetables, meats, and dairy products. "You've seen cars on the road. What do they need to run?" she asked.

"Wheels," said one boy.

"Well, yes," Lucy said. "What else?"

The children pondered. "Gas," one finally blurted.

"Yes! Fuel. And what if the car runs out of fuel?"

"The car stops," a girl shouted.

Lucy smiled at the connection. "Good foods are the energy, the fuel, for us. What if we don't have energy?"

"You fall down," was the unanimous reply.

Lucy opened up a simple picture book and told a story about a girl named Marequita, who always played in the dirt and didn't wash up afterward. She drank dirty water from the river. She ate carrots straight out of the ground without washing off the dirt. She didn't wear shoes, brush her teeth, or use a toilet. Her friends teased her, calling her "the dirty one." But worse, Marequita got worms in her stomach.

Lucy turned to a page with cartoon-like drawings of worms and other parasites. One is named Valentin. (Before the class, Lucy had checked with the teachers to make sure none of the children were named Marequita or Valentin, to avoid subsequent teasing.) "Marequita ate bread with dirty hands and Valentin came into her stomach," Lucy said. "Valentin eats the food that you need. You may be eating good foods, but Valentin is eating them once he gets into your stomach. Valentin gets the benefits of the vitamins and nutrients, not you. Valentin grows, you don't."

Marequita gets a stomachache. She gets a fever. She is sick in bed.

"Have you ever had a stomachache, a fever, been sick in bed?" Lucy asked.

"Yes. Yes. Yes," the children replied.

Marequita visits the doctor, who finds her parasites. She is given the medicine to fight the worms.

"Who has taken pills?" Lucy asked.

All hands shot up.

Marequita learns to wash her hands and that she must boil water before drinking it. She promises to wear shoes and use the toilet. She becomes known as "the clean one."

"So what do you need to do?" Lucy asked.

"Wash Hands. Use soap."

"When?"

"Before eating. After using the toilet."

The class walked outside to a water tap. The pupils practiced washing their hands with soap, and their wrists and arms as well.

With clean hands, they enjoyed a snack: a bread roll; no Valentins here. And they clutched their takeaways for the day: a toothbrush and soap. Those whose samples indicated they needed it would be given medicine.

As the children lined up on the veranda to return to school, Irma, the lab tech, announced the results of her testing. "A big success!" she said grandly. "Only fourteen have parasites."

Only fourteen? That's success?

"Absolutely," Irma said. "On most days, it would be fifteen out of sixteen, or sixteen of sixteen."

chapter ten

"THIS CHILD IS BRILLIANT"

IT WAS LUNCHTIME IN UGANDA. BRENDA HAD BEEN PONDERING the menu while she swept the dirt yard of the family homestead. She didn't go to a pantry, or open a cupboard or refrigerator, or run to a store or a fast-food restaurant. She grabbed a pan and walked five minutes to her field. She carefully stepped between some green, leafy vines and knelt on the ground. Pawing at the soil, she quickly hit pay dirt: a sweet potato, rust-colored, oblong, nearly twice the size of her hand. She carefully lifted it from the hole, dusted it off, and put it in the pan. Then she turned to another cluster of vines, dug into the soil, and pulled out another sweet potato. Then another, and another, until her pan was full. She rose to her feet, balanced the pan on her head, and returned home.

In the cooking hut, Brenda scooped up a bowl of water from a larger barrel. She washed the dirt off the sweet potatoes and plopped them into another pot filled with water. A wood fire was already smoldering. She cleared space in the ashes for the pot of potatoes. An hour later, Aron was eating his lunch: boiled orange-flesh sweet potatoes, brimming with vitamin A. Brenda mashed one potato and cut another into chunks. Aron reached out his right hand and grabbed one of the larger pieces and took a big bite.

Aron's encounters with dysentery and malaria had interrupted his growth, Brenda said. But now he was thriving again, eating robustly. He was approaching nine months and was nearly twenty-eight inches tall, which was close to on-schedule according to the international growth chart. His mother said he especially liked the orange sweet potatoes. "He can't get enough," Brenda said. And she credited them with Aron's swift recoveries and his growth, for she had begun feeding him the potatoes shortly before his illness. And she herself had eaten them during her pregnancy and while breastfeeding.

It wasn't all a coincidence, or a mother's wishful thinking. The HarvestPlus program that had brought the orange sweet potatoes and the high-iron beans to Uganda and Mozambique and other countries had been evaluating the impact of the crops. Its findings, and research by others, matched Brenda's observations: eating orange sweet potatoes reduced the incidence and duration of diarrhea in children. For children under three, the likelihood of developing diarrhea was reduced by more than 50 percent, and the duration of diarrhea was shortened by more than 25 percent.

That was good news for both Brenda and Howarth "Howdy" Bouis, the director of HarvestPlus, who for decades had been on a single-minded mission to improve nutrition through crops with higher levels of key vitamins and minerals. In Aron's case, the orange sweet potatoes couldn't prevent the water-borne illness that swept through an entire community, but they seemed to aid his recovery. "We like to say that the statistical result dovetails with stories the mothers tell about how their children seem healthier switching to the orange sweet potato," Howdy told me. "You might be a skeptic, but when you hear the stories of better health of the children, healthier pregnancies, and you hear them often enough, and then you see the science, you start to believe."

THE RUGGED AND decidedly low-tech fields in which Brenda and Esther and thousands of other farmers in Uganda grew crops were on the cutting edge of the new cooperation between agriculture and nutrition that was playing out in the 1,000 days. It had become known as "biofortification"—the breeding process of highlighting certain nutrients in staple foods that are consumed daily: vitamin A in orange sweet potatoes, cassava, and corn; iron in beans and pearl millet; zinc in rice and wheat. Plant breeders at both international institutes and labs in various countries in the developing world screen thousands of different types of crop seed stored in global seed banks to discover varieties with naturally high amounts of micronutrients. These are used to breed new high-yielding biofortified crop varieties that are also disease and pest resistant and adaptable to climate changes. The breeding is accomplished through conventional techniques—it doesn't add anything new to the crops (as is the case in genetically modified seeds); it simply brings out nutrient traits already present.

It would seem to be a program ripe for fast-tracking in the battle against malnutrition and stunting. But the route from Howdy's initial research to the breeding labs to deployment in the field—a three-decade odyssey—has been fraught with the illogical divisions that had grown between agriculture and nutrition.

Before biofortification, the main weapons against "hidden hunger" had been mineral and vitamin supplements and commercially fortified processed foods, both for pregnant moms and for infants aged six months and up as they began eating solid foods. Billions of dollars are spent annually to distribute these products throughout the world, particularly to its remotest corners. But even with these efforts, the supply of the supplements is inconsistent. Delivery is burdensome; budgets are always tight. Even when the supplements are available, those in pill form are often be taken with water, which is usually unclean, triggering other health problems. And follow-up care to assure adherence to a regime of supplements is sporadic, at best. As a result of these barriers, hidden hunger stubbornly persists: nearly 200 million children under the age of five in the developing world still suffer from vitamin A deficiency, which not only damages immune systems, turning common diseases such as measles and malaria into fatal ones, but also constitutes the leading cause of preventable blindness in children. And approximately half of all children and pregnant women in the developing world continue to suffer from iron deficiency anemia, which leads to stunting in children and is a primary cause of maternal deaths.

Ah, but what if we could get plants to do some of the nutrient-supplementing work for us? That was the question that first stirred Howdy Bouis in the 1980s and has taken over his life ever since. It was what brought him to the sweet-potato fields of northern Uganda, the details of his crusade unfolding as we made our way along the Nile River Valley.

Howdy was a young economist at the International Food Policy Research Institute (IFPRI), exploring the diets of poor households in Asia, when he became especially interested in how nutrient intakes were influenced by food prices and household incomes. The conventional wisdom among economists had been that a lack of energy (calories) was the primary dietary factor limiting better nutrition in developing countries. But in his research Howdy was finding something different: mineral and vitamin deficiencies, not lack of calories, were the leading constraints to better nutrition and, in turn, to healthy and economically productive lives. He found that people basically ate the same amount of staple foods—rice, wheat, corn, beans, and potatoes—no matter the household income. But where income did matter was in the purchase of the more expensive non-staple foods that were packed with vitamins and minerals, particularly fruits, vegetables, and meats. Since the poor couldn't regularly afford these non-staples and the nutrients they contained, Howdy wondered if the nutrients could be increased in the staple foods that were the basis of the everyday diets of the poor. It would, he thought, be akin to putting fluoride in the water systems of developed countries.

Howdy's theory was supported by some colleagues at IFPRI who encouraged him to continue his research into nutrient deficiency. But he encountered a wave of skepticism when he first took his idea to breeders at the Consultative Group on International Agricultural Research (CGIAR), a consortium of crop centers around the world that had been established to help increase the productivity of smallholder farmers. Government funding for agricultural research was on a sharp decline, and based on previous experience at some of the CGIAR centers, it was assumed that Howdy's proposal would present a tradeoff between high yields and higher mineral and vitamin content. The consensus held that crop yields would decrease if you increased nutrient content. And that was anathema to farmers and the agriculture industry; they would never adopt a less-productive, less-profitable crop variety just because it was more nutritious. Howdy's challenge to conventional wisdom—and his requests for funding to test his theory—was roundly rebuffed. He was dismissed as a heretic. Leave improving nutrition to the nutritionists and dieticians, he was told. The job of breeders was to increase yields and, as a result, increase farmers' incomes.

An introvert despite his gregarious nickname, Howdy was an unlikely disruptor. But there was a stubbornness beneath his easygoing and un-assuming nature. He pressed on, barnstorming with his idea. The head-winds only increased. Despairing that his quest was folly—that he was a modern-day Don Quixote tilting at windmills—he arrived at the Plant, Soil and Nutrition Laboratory at Cornell University in upstate New York in June 1993. It was a US Department of Agriculture lab, and was more focused on the productivity of American farmers than on nutrition in the developing world. Howdy gave a thirty-minute presentation and ex-pected to be shown the door, as usual. But then one scientist at the end of the long conference table stood up and said, "That's fabulous! Plants also need the nutrients to grow. It's a win-win."

What? Howdy was stunned. The enthusiastic voice belonged to Ross Welch, a plant nutritionist and soil scientist who was part of an interdisci-plinary group of scientists at Cornell studying the notion that plants need minerals and nutrients for their growth just as humans do. Welch told Howdy about research showing that wheat seeds with a higher zinc con-tent were more vigorous and produced greater yields than standard wheat seeds. This was just what Howdy had been longing to hear: breeding for high mineral content could result in both better harvests *and* improved hu-man nutrition. Welch mentioned another scientist, Robin Graham, a plant nutritionist in Australia, who had been tilting at the same windmills, trying to forge a link between agriculture and nutrition. Soon, the three men were strategizing for days on end at Cornell and the University of Adelaide.

Individually, they were loners shouting into the wind. Howdy was an economist who had no credibility with plant scientists, and Welch and Graham were plant scientists who had no standing with economists. Now they were three kindred spirits clamoring together. They barged into conference after conference, assaulting the conventional wisdom. Separately they had made little headway in convincing the skeptics, but together they made sense. A handful of breeders at the CGIAR centers acknowledged the potential of their theory; a few national development agencies kicked in some funding, first the Danes, then the Americans and Norwegians; and the work began. It was the encouragement Howdy needed. He pushed the idea of biofortification as a new frontier in the fight against hunger. The funding flow thickened, with the Asian Development Bank, the World Bank, and the Bill & Melinda Gates Foundation jumping on board. Then came the Copenhagen Consensus and the argument for increased investment in micronutrients, articles in *The Lancet* calling for "nutrition-sensitive agriculture," and the food crisis of 2007–2008, which upped the urgency of their work. Howdy found more fertile ground for his project, which he began calling HarvestPlus. The question around biofortification was no longer "Why?" but "Why not?"

The breeding pace quickened, involving scientists around the world in trials of higher-nutrient varieties of rice, maize, millet, wheat, cassava, and beans. Now Howdy worried that things were going almost too fast. He favored conservative estimates as to when the crops and the research would be in. But the funders were pushing to get the crops into the hands of smallholder farmers in Africa and Asia. Rich-world governments, including Canada and the United Kingdom, were calling; they wanted to put biofortification into their development aid action strategies. How soon could he deliver?

By 2011, nearly three decades after Howdy began his mission, biofortified crops rich in iron, zinc, and vitamin A were growing in several countries. They would soon enter the diets of 1.5 million households. Howdy set a goal of reaching 50 million people.

IN THE SUMMER of 2012, Howdy Bouis, the man who had been chased out of so many rooms, received a fancy invitation to take a seat at a very prestigious table. Before the closing ceremony of the 2012 London Olympics, British prime minister David Cameron convened a nutrition summit aimed at knocking back childhood stunting, which was cast as an affront to the Olympic ideals of swifter, higher, stronger. "It is really important that while the eyes of the world are on Britain and we are going to put on this fantastic show for the Olympics, that we remember people in other parts of the world who, far from being excited about the Olympics, are actually worried about their next meal and whether they are getting enough to eat," the prime minister said when he announced the summit. The event, he proclaimed, would challenge the international community to raise the level of political commitment, create new partnerships, and develop new products and services to tackle the global problem of undernutrition and stunting.

Howdy was asked to speak about the potential of biofortification. It would be brief—about three minutes—but this time his words went not into the wind but into the record. "After 10 years of investment, biofortification is one new agricultural tool that is now ready for widespread scale-up in Africa and Asia," Howdy told the gathering. "Biofortification . . . provides a comparatively cost-effective and sustainable means of delivering more minerals and vitamins to the poor, especially in rural areas. A one-time investment in plant breeding can yield micronutrient-rich plants for farmers to grow for years to come. It is this multiplier aspect of agricultural research across time and geography that makes it so cost-effective." He concluded: "Only if we are willing to involve agriculture, will we win the battle against hidden hunger. One community. One farmer. One seed at a time."

Howdy spoke, and people listened. The Olympic nutrition summit resulted in substantially higher long-term funding for HarvestPlus, precisely what was needed for implementing agricultural projects requiring long gestation periods to succeed. After the summit, the UK government's foreign development department gave HarvestPlus an additional three-year grant approaching $50 million. And other donors followed suit, jumping in to either add to past funding or start new contributions.

What Howdy now needed were success stories on the ground, real-life testimony that would keep the momentum going. The vitamin A–enriched orange sweet potatoes, developed in conjunction with the International Potato Center, were first deployed in Mozambique, and then in Uganda. With the introduction of the high-iron beans, Uganda became the first country with two crops simultaneously in the ground along with a national ambition to get them to all corners of the country so everyone could eat them. And it was in Uganda where anecdotal evidence was accumulating in conjunction with the scientific evidence.

I once mentioned to Ross Welch at Cornell some of the things I was hearing in Uganda about the impact of the high-nutrient crops. Tears welled in his eyes. "You so dearly want to see some impact," he told me as we visited the room where he and Howdy first met twenty years earlier. "To see that it isn't all for naught, that it's helping people." To see that they were right.

Howdy, too, was moved by the testimonials of farmers, and by Brenda's story about how the crops were helping her son, Aron. He arrived in northern Uganda eager to hear more.

"THIS CHILD IS brilliant," Harriet Okaka told Howdy, gesturing to her son Abraham, who was approaching his second birthday. She wasn't bragging, just observing. "I can tell, just by looking at him. The way he plays, the way he is."

Abraham was her sixth child. "He was walking earlier than the others," she said. From the time he was crawling, Abraham would see an animal and motion for it to come. When he heard music, he clapped and danced. "These are indications that his brain is developing well," Harriet said.

A mother knows. Especially this one. Harriet, thirty-three, was a teenager when she and other girls were abducted by the forces of Joseph Kony. They were forcibly marched to Sudan for training as child soldiers. On a return to Uganda, Harriet was able to escape during a break in the marching. She fled through the bush and eventually settled just up the road from the Ongica health clinic, not far from Esther and Brenda. Harriet married and had children, and she dedicated her life to making sure they would have healthy and safe childhoods. She kept a keen watch over their development.

Now she had a story for Howdy:

Harriet was finishing up her first HarvestPlus training session in the art of planting orange sweet potatoes and high-iron beans when she went into labor. She told Grace Akullu, the World Vision nutritionist who was leading the training, that she might not be able to attend the second session. That evening, she gave birth to Abraham. A month later, with Abraham perched on her back, Harriet eagerly planted the sweet potatoes and beans. The harvest coincided with the time she was beginning to supplement Abraham's breastfeeding with complementary foods. She fed him a mashed-up combination of orange sweet potatoes and high-iron beans for his first solid food. Abraham, she told Howdy, was a true child of biofortification. "It's been good for his development," she told Howdy in her soft, humble voice. He hadn't battled sickness as her other children did, especially her second youngest, Isaac.

Here Harriet's story became even more remarkable. When he was four, Isaac suddenly fell gravely ill. He was losing weight, he was fainting, and his skin was rough. Harriet took him to the nearby clinic, which performed tests. None of the nurses knew what was wrong. She took him to the regional hospital in Lira. More tests. Again, bafflement among the doctors. Isaac was so thin, so weak, Harriet was terrified that he would die. It was what everyone was expecting, the nurses, doctors, neighbors. Surely, people whispered, this child wouldn't survive. At wit's end, Harriet turned to the new food. It was a last resort. "I just kept feeding him the beans and the orange sweet potatoes," she said. "And he got better."

Now she profusely thanked Howdy. She told him that word of Isaac's miracle recovery spread throughout the neighboring villages. People see Isaac once again wearing the chartreuse uniform shirt of the Good Luck Nursery School. They see Abraham, lively and healthy. And they ask, "Mother, what have you done?" She tells them about the new crops. Everyone wants them, and she tries to meet the demand. The first year, right after Abraham was born, Harriet planted a quarter-acre of high-iron beans and a small plot of orange sweet potatoes. The next year, she rented an additional two acres, not only to increase the harvest for her family to eat, but also to share with her neighbors. She gives them bean seeds and sweet-potato vines so they can plant their own. She delivers the crops to the local schools. "If my children are healthy, then the neighbor children must also be healthy," she told Howdy. She proudly announced that she had become known as the "orange sweet-potato lady" and the "high-iron bean lady," depending on the season. Howdy beamed.

THE HIGH-NUTRIENT CROPS were themselves breeding local legends. They were making their way into songs and oral histories. In neighboring Rwanda, where 700,000 farmers were growing and eating the high-iron beans, the beans had their own music video with cameos from some of the country's top rap, rhythm and blues, and Afro-pop musicians. "We are bringing good news for all Rwandans that will change their lives once they start listening to the song, because it raises their knowledge about the benefits of growing and eating these high-iron beans," said King James, an R&B artist. Added rapper Riderman, "We came together to make sure that we say goodbye to malnutrition."

While a video about Flamin' Hot Cheetos that hailed junk food went viral in the United States, their song, called "Better Nutrition from High Iron Beans," swept through the hills of Rwanda:

> A meal without beans in Rwanda
> Is just like a meal without food.
> High-iron beans
> They should be eaten at every meal.
> Delicious and full of nutrients
> So tasty you'll be missing out if you don't eat them.
> Young children who eat beans without iron
> They are always worn out and fatigued
> And suffer from memory issues.
> Those who eat high-iron beans are strong
> They don't forget or get tired
> Their future is bright because they are strong and healthy
> With enough blood in their bodies.
> These beans can make your blood stronger
> For children and pregnant women
> These beans should always be part of their daily meals.

HOWDY ACKNOWLEDGED THAT biofortified crops likely wouldn't satisfy all the daily nutrient needs of consumers—perhaps from 25 percent upward to nearly 100 percent, depending on the food and the nutrient. However—here he deployed an archery metaphor popular in the nutrition realm—biofortification is one of the arrows in our quiver.

That quiver had been filling up over the past several decades as fortification efforts—including new innovations such as the "Lucky Iron Fish" and "Project Spammy"—grew. Fortification began in the United States and elsewhere in the 1920s, when iodine was added to salt to reduce endemic goiter, an enlargement of the thyroid gland. Over the next several years, the incidence of goiter in the United States declined dramatically. Now, more than 120 countries fortify salt with iodine, both to prevent goiter and to aid cognitive development. Next came the fortification of milk with vitamin D in the 1930s to prevent rickets. Milk was chosen because it was a staple food for children as well as for pregnant and lactating mothers. In the following decade, thiamin, niacin, riboflavin, and iron were added to flour and other grain products. Most recently, folic acid was added to that list.

In addition to these efforts, vitamin and nutrient supplementation have accelerated around the world. Most national health systems distribute iron and folic-acid tablets to pregnant women; vitamin A is also widely distributed. Still, these nutrients often don't reach some of the most remote areas. So organizations like Vitamin Angels in California and the Micronutrient Initiative in Canada step into the breach. Vitamin Angels was founded by entrepreneur Howard Schiffer, who was spurred into humanitarian action by an earthquake in Southern California in 1994. When he asked relief workers how he could help, he learned that two tiny red capsules of high-dose vitamin A each year could significantly reduce child mortality and prevent childhood blindness. In 2013, rallying corporate partners for funding, and working with nearly three hundred organizations in the field, Vitamin Angels was able to reach about 30 million children in forty-five countries, including the United States, with vitamin A, at a cost of just twenty-five cents per child per year. Along with Vitamin Angels donations, I have seen the Micronutrient Initiative label on bottles of vitamin A capsules as well as zinc, iron, and folic-acid tablets in clinics from the Himalayan foothills in Nepal to the savannahs of East Africa. Alongside these supplements there will also most likely be packets of albendazole, a deworming treatment to kill parasites that block the absorption of the micronutrients.

The Global Alliance for Improved Nutrition (GAIN) spearheads fortification efforts of products ranging from milk and cookies to porridge and cooking oil in a number of developing countries. In Rajasthan, India, for example, 10 women in a remote village own and operate a factory delivering 30 metric tons of a flour enriched with vitamins and minerals daily to 6,000 children under age three and nearly 3,000 pregnant and breastfeeding mothers. The factory—established by GAIN, the World Food Program, the Indian government, and the Shitalamata Self-Help Group—produces a wheat and sugar concoction called Raj Nutrimix. The state government buys the product and then distributes it as "take-home rations" through three community centers. The next step has been to educate mothers on how to best cook and consume the product, along with promoting the nutritional value.

Do-it-yourself fortification is also gaining traction. DSM, a Dutch-based vitamin and nutrition products company, has been in the forefront of home fortification with micronutrient powders. These powders contain more than a dozen vitamins and minerals, including iron, vitamin A, and zinc, and are specifically designed for the 1,000 days. The powders are generally packaged in single-dose sachets of one gram and are added to foods prepared at home just before consumption. They can be sprinkled over soups, noodles, porridge and stews—almost anything that is cooked at home. Importantly, the powder doesn't change the taste, color, or texture of foods to which it is added. The Sprinkles Global Health Initiative also notes that the sachets are easy to use, since they don't require special measuring utensils and can be given at any mealtime during the day, and you don't have to be literate to learn how to use them. Since 2000, micronutrient powders have reached 14 million children under five in twenty-two countries. Still, expansion hasn't been that simple; some efforts have been tripped up by cultural misunderstandings. At an early distribution of sachets at a refugee camp for Somalis in Kenya, would-be beneficiaries initially shunned the product. The outer packaging depicted a man, woman, and child, creating the impression that "the white man only wants us to have one child," as some refugees reported. Also, the material of the sachet was aluminum foil, like the wrappers for condoms. Suspicion and gossip spread throughout the camp: Was the powder fortified with nutrients, or with some kind of sinister birth-control dust?

UNDERSTANDING LOCAL BELIEFS was certainly important for students from the University of Guelph in Canada as they set out to attack the iron-deficient anemia problem in Cambodia. They came across research showing that cooking in a cast-iron pot increased the iron content of food. So they decided to create an iron ingot made from melted-down metal. They shaped their invention like a fish, which is a symbol of good luck in Cambodia. As luck would have it, the shape also released iron at the right concentration to help women and children stave off anemia. The instructions are simple: Cook the fish in boiling water or soup for ten minutes; while the water is boiling, tiny amounts of iron leech off of the fish. Add lemon juice or anything acidic to help with the absorption of the iron. Remove the fish ingot from the pot and add other ingredients, such as rice, meat, and vegetables. If used correctly every day, the Lucky Iron Fish, which is three inches long and weighs about 7 ounces, can provide up to 90 percent of a family's daily iron needs for up to five years, according to a project evaluation. The fish, which is present in about 2,500 households in Cambodia, reeled in a $500,000 award from Grand Challenges Canada to scale up the project in Cambodia and beyond.

IN GUATEMALA, PROJECT Spammy has gotten plenty of smiles, at least from those who know it comes from the folks at Hormel Foods Corporation, the purveyors of the much-joked-about yet popular—more than 8 billion cans sold since 1937—precooked pork product known as SPAM. Spammy is a turkey spread fortified with a range of nutrients generally deficient in the Guatemalan diet, chiefly vitamins D and B12, zinc, iron, and animal-based protein, which are all important in cognitive development, particularly in the 1,000 days. Project Spammy is a not-for-profit initiative intended to attack childhood malnutrition; Hormel distributes about 3 million cans a year to 8,300 families through the humanitarian organization Caritas. During the distributions, Caritas workers teach families how to mix Spammy into traditional diets, which has resulted in the emergence of Spammy rice and beans, Spammy lambada, Spammy tortillas, Spammy chuchito, Spammy nachos, and Spammy burritos.

In 2011, Hormel received a US Department of Agriculture grant to study Spammy's effectiveness in a twenty-week school feeding program. The teachers reported a significant reduction in school absences due to illness during the course of the program; the science revealed increases of vitamins D and B12 levels in the treatment group; and testing showed cognitive development gains among the students.

At a Spammy distribution in the hills above Guatemala City, mothers lined up for their monthly ration of twenty-four cans. While they waited, they watched a cooking demonstration of how to mix Spammy with other foods—eggs, onions, beans, chili, noodles, rice. "You can mix it with every food, every meal," explained one of the Caritas workers. She turned to me and added, "Eating out of a can isn't part of our culture. That's why it's important to show how Spammy can be integrated with our usual foods." The moms also spoke of how Spammy had helped their children grow and develop. I followed one mom to her house, a one-room hovel with a rugged dirt floor and corrugated walls. Two of her three youngest children had been manifestly malnourished. They were very small for their ages; they had lost patches of hair. Seven-year-old Lusbi was rail thin; her two-year-old sister, Dulce, was just a shade over two feet tall. Only the youngest, eight-month-old Luis Claudio, was thriving—he already weighed nearly as much as Dulce. Regina, their mother, began eating Spammy when she was pregnant with Luis, and Spammy was one of the first foods he ate at six months old. In recent months, Dulce finally began walking and talking; "Spammy" was one of her first words. And Lusbi's hair started coming back.

What's made the difference? "Spammy is the only thing new in our diet," Regina said. She revered her monthly ration; there were no Spammy jokes from this family.

GUATEMALA HAS ATTRACTED a swarm of research on the potential impact of new fortified products. The Mathile Institute in the United States has developed a nutrient-packed drink mix called Chispuditos, and Guatemala's ministry of health, the Secretariat for Food and Nutrition Security, and Humanitas Global in Washington, DC, have been fashioning a community nutrition engagement program that would incorporate the product. While surveying communities to find out why past nutrition programs haven't succeeded, they have discovered that the missing ingredients weren't just vitamins and minerals; the products also needed the acceptance of the children and their caregivers. And it was key for local influencers—fathers, grandmothers, midwives, traditional healers, church leaders, and mayors and other politicians—to become champions of good nutrition for building stronger families and communities.

Guatemala has also become a testing ground for transforming emergency nutrition treatments into products for everyday use, particularly in the 1,000 days. Most of the development is centered on fortified peanut-paste innovations that have emerged in the decade since a product called Plumpy'Nut was deployed to treat severely malnourished children in the Horn of Africa and elsewhere. Nutriset, the French maker of Plumpy'Nut, and an American nonprofit enterprise called Edesia have been introducing similar nutrient-rich peanut-spread products for pregnant and breastfeeding moms, and for infants once they begin eating solid foods, aimed at preventing stunting in the 1,000 days.

And in a factory in Guatemala City, on the campus of the Institute of Nutrition of Central America and Panama (INCAP), seventy-year-old machines are being cranked up to rejoin the battle against malnutrition that began there in the 1950s. Edward "Ted" Fischer, an anthropologist at Vanderbilt University, with funding from the Tennessee-based Shalom Foundation, had joined INCAP nutritionists to produce a ready-to-use supplementary food called Mani-Plus for children six to twenty-four months old. Designed by researchers specifically to fill holes in the Guatemalan diet, it is made of peanuts, sugar, powdered milk, vegetable oil, and a mix of nearly two dozen micronutrients.

It was in this factory where INCAP began developing the fortified drink powder called Incaparina (INCAP flour) in 1953. By 1965, the researchers had come up with the final formulation and were using it in a study in the eastern region of Guatemala; even today, the results of that study continue to provide valuable information about the impact of nutrition supplementation on pregnant women and their infant children, on later schooling and work performance, and on chronic disease in adults. Incaparina became a model for the many fortified products that have followed since, and it remains popular in Guatemala. But malnutrition and stunting still plagued the country, so Ted, who has long worked with Maya communities, set up Mani-Plus as a social enterprise to develop additional products to meet the needs of rural Guatemalan children in the 1,000 days.

A generator that hadn't been used in twenty-five years was now back in action, powering the original blender that had once mixed the nutrients of Incaparina. With additional funding, Ted hoped that the old INCAP factory could produce twenty-five tons of Mani-Plus per month, which could cover about 20,000 children. Walking through the factory with his team, he marveled that they truly were going back to the future.

IN UGANDA, HOWDY continued his walk through the biofortified fields. Everywhere he went, he was greeted by songs and poems and stories of great wonder. An elderly man rushed to Howdy's side to tell him that he used to stumble blindly once the sun went down, but now he could see just fine in the dark. A woman begged him to introduce other fortified crops to her village: "If there are other crop varieties you are hiding, please bring them here," she pleaded. In another village, pregnant women and moms with infants lined up to show off a new generation of biofortified babies. One mom presented her three-year-old son: "I have waited to name him because I heard you were coming," she told her visitors. "He will now be called Howdy."

Howdy, embarrassed by the attention, smiled sheepishly and spoke a gracious, "Thank you."

Finally, a mom who had been waiting at the back of the crowd approached Howdy and thanked him for the orange sweet potatoes and the high-iron beans. Molly Ekwang introduced her son Stephen. He was now one year old, she said, and already talking up a storm. He had walked at eight months. Her five older children, she noted, didn't walk until they were eighteen months old. "Stephen is very bright," she said. He toddled over to Howdy and climbed up onto the visitor's lap. Molly laughed and asked for someone to take a picture, Stephen and Howdy together.

"I want to be able to show it to my child someday," Molly said, "and say to him, 'This is the man who made you smart, the man who gave you a successful future.'"

Howdy smiled, his misty eyes glistening. He was clearly touched by this mother and child, and also challenged. "It's very satisfying to hear this," Howdy told me. "But it also makes me anxious. You can't be satisfied, because we still have much more to do. You want to move faster, introduce more crops, get them to everyone."

chapter eleven

"I WANT HER TO BE A HEALTHY GIRL"

IT WAS DINNERTIME IN CHICAGO. JESSICA FINISHED READING A book to Alitzel—*Spot's Favorite Words*—and together they adjourned to the kitchen of her mother's house. Jessica slid Alitzel into a highchair and gently draped a bib around her daughter's neck. She then opened a cupboard and scanned a shelf laden with jars of baby food. Jessica reached for the pureed sweet potato—creamy and orange, it was one of Alitzel's favorites, just like the real thing was Aron's favorite in Uganda. Jessica twisted the lid and it popped open. That would be the extent of her foraging. She sat beside her daughter and fed her with a spoon.

Alitzel was six months old and had begun eating solid food to complement the formula milk. An hour earlier, she had finished off a bottle of milk with a burp. "Very good," Jessica said with a chuckle. Jessica was now using her WIC coupons to obtain a wide variety of baby-food flavors. The nutrient content was openly printed on the labels. Along with the sweet potato, which contained vitamins A and B6, calcium, iron, potassium, and protein, Alitzel also liked the pureed peas and the peaches.

On many days, a pot of homemade soup warmed on the kitchen stove, and the comforting aroma of simmering vegetables filled the house. Jessica would scoop carrots or beans from the broth and mash them up for her daughter.

"I want her to be a healthy girl," Jessica told me, "just eating healthy things."

IN THE TRANSITION period when breastmilk or formula is no longer sufficient to meet the nutritional requirements of infants, other foods and liquids are gradually introduced into the diet in what is called complementary feeding. This stage generally begins at around four to six months and continues through the second birthday. These eighteen to twenty months can mark a delicate transition; they constitute the largest portion of the 1,000 days, forming the critical period when nutrient deficiencies and illnesses can cause infants to fall behind on growth charts, showing signs of stunting.

The United Nations Children's Fund stressed the importance of complementary feeding in its *Progress for Children* report: "Starting at six months of age, when infants increasingly start to rely on nutrients in other food for their optimal growth and development, the diversity of their diet becomes a key measure of how well they are eating and acts as a proxy for their micronutrient intake." This dietary diversity is elusive for many parents around the world. UNICEF analyzed health data from thirty-eight countries across the poverty-wealth spectrum and found large disparities in diversity of diet by country income as well as by wealth quintile within countries. Only about 20 percent of children aged six to twenty-four months in low-income countries received food from four or more food groups; even in the wealthiest families in those countries, just over one-third of the children met the minimum requirement for diet diversity. In middle- to upper-income countries, about 30 percent of infants and toddlers didn't receive sufficient nutrient diversity.

One of the main reasons for these failures has been the global absence of complementary feeding guidance for parents. Even in the United States, the Dietary Guidelines for Americans have ignored children below the age of two, focusing instead on adults and children older than two, "because of the unique nutritional needs, eating patterns and developmental stages of infants and toddlers from birth to 24 months of age," according to the US Departments of Agriculture and Health and Human Services, the curators of the guidelines. In other words, the diets of infants and toddlers were deemed to be too complicated; there was no consensus on what the best foods were for them to eat and apparently no inclination for the US government to find out. It was only when the 1,000 Days movement began gathering steam and the Farm Bill of 2014 demanded action that the guideline curators began reviewing nutrition evidence for the birth to twenty-four-month period and for pregnant women. That nutrition advice, still being researched and formulated, is scheduled to be included in the 2020 edition of the Dietary Guidelines.

The Farm Bill also authorized $31.5 million in funding to local, state, and national organizations to support programs that help participants in the Supplemental Nutrition Assistance Program (SNAP), or food stamps, purchase more fruits and vegetables. One of the innovations, growing in popularity, was to use this money to match SNAP purchases of fruits and vegetables at farmers markets, effectively doubling the amount of fresh produce recipients could take home. It was a good idea that was taking hold in Chicago's farmers markets. But neither Jessica nor Quintana were capitalizing on it, because there were no farmers markets reasonably close to where they lived. The incentive wasn't enough to override the inconvenience and cost of traveling to the more-distant markets. And at the same time as these incentive programs were being implemented, Congress was cutting back SNAP funding; Jessica's family was receiving $40 less every month than it had been getting. What the government gave with one hand it took back with the other.

THE COMPLEMENTARY FEEDING transition should be a time when infants are exposed to a wide variety of fruits and vegetables. Mounting research indicates that children eating these foods early in life continue to eat them as they grow, reducing their chances of becoming overweight or obese later in childhood or as adults. Instead, infants, particularly those in the United States, are more often exposed to junk-food and fast-food diets.

Thus, we find that French fries have become the most common vegetable consumed by one-year-olds in the United States. By fifteen months of age, at least 18 percent of American children are eating macaroni and cheese, and about 15 percent are eating pizza. Seventeen percent of US infants are consuming sugar-sweetened beverages or desserts on any given day by the time they are nine months old, and this figure quickly rises, reaching 43 percent by twelve months and 81 percent by twenty-four months.

The 2008 Feeding Infants and Toddlers Study (FITS), conducted by the Nestlé Nutrition Institute and analyzed in various journals in recent years, revealed these dietary snapshots. Among Nestlé's vast stable of products are Gerber baby foods. On the day of the survey, researchers found that 16 percent of infants and 27 percent of toddlers didn't consume any fruit, and even more didn't eat any vegetables. The study also recorded this phenomenon:

> In addition to lack of vegetable consumption, the data show a major shift in the consumption of different types of vegetables. Sweet potatoes, carrots and squash were the most frequently consumed vegetables among infants aged 6–8 months. Yet, the consumption of white potatoes and corn, as well as green beans, become more common with age. By the age of 9 months, mashed potatoes were as common as sweet potatoes, and after the first year, it is striking to see French fries surpassed the sweet potato as the most popular vegetable. Moreover, the proportions of children who consumed fried potatoes (French fries) almost doubled those who consumed mashed potatoes or corn by the age of two years.

It was a declining scale of nutrients and healthy eating: from sweet potatoes, carrots, and squash, brimming with vitamins and minerals, to white potatoes laden with carbs, to fried potatoes heavy with oil and salt.

THE CONGRESSIONAL DEMAND in the Farm Bill to come up with guidelines for complementary feeding came just as Alitzel entered that transition. Jessica did the best she could, relying on the things she learned from Patricia, her doula during pregnancy. Namely: Eat your vegetables. Alitzel gained a pound a month as she transitioned to solid foods. She weighed twelve pounds at four months, sixteen pounds at eight months, and eighteen pounds at ten months. At seven months, she fell sick with a fever; she didn't eat for several days. She recovered and resumed eating, but Jessica feared she had lost too much weight. "I worry now she's too skinny," she told me. One of Alitzel's cousins had weighed twenty pounds at six months. "I think that's too big," Jessica said defiantly. "In our culture, a big baby is healthy and a skinny one isn't healthy. But I don't believe that. I think too big brings more problems."

Jessica was bringing home a supply of baby food from the WIC store each month. At eight months, Alitzel still liked sweet potatoes, carrots, and green peas, but she had a new favorite, too (true to the FITS survey): mashed potatoes. Jessica began adding pieces of chicken to the vegetables, and there were more soups. By ten months, Alitzel was turning away from the baby food in the jars and reaching for the food her parents were eating: cereal and oatmeal for breakfast, then chicken, rice, beans, pasta, and eggs during the day. Alitzel was also squirming to escape the high chair, and she began drinking water out of a sippy cup, leaving the bottle behind. Her doctor was pleased with the eighteen pounds at ten months. It was spot-on with the international growth charts, as was Alitzel's height of about twenty-eight inches. Jessica was happy, too, but always vigilant. "It's hard to know what to feed her," she told me. "I hope I'm doing right."

IN INDIA, ANSHIKA wasn't eating much solid food at ten months. Shyamkali tried to coax her youngest daughter into eating a piece of *roti*, flatbread, that had been dipped in milk. Anshika wasn't interested, turning away. She liked crackers, crumbled up. "It's the salt," Shyamkali said. She had given her daughter some sweeter foods, like biscuits, but Anshika spit them out. So she continued with the breastfeeding, which she supplemented with cow's milk mixed with water.

Shyamkali wasn't worried. "The baby has been very healthy. Now and then she has a cold and cough, but we haven't had to take her to the doctor," she told me. Anshika was thin but appeared to have plenty of energy. She was crawling around the veranda and trying to stand by grabbing onto the edge of a *charpoy* and pulling herself up. She had expressive dark eyes and was beginning to speak, calling to her mom and sisters. Shyamkali held Anshika in a standing position while I measured her: twenty-six inches, a couple inches shy of Alitzel at the same age. Shyamkali, who had no education, didn't know the relationship of numbers and was unaware Anshika was nearing the stunted range. Based on her observations, Anshika seemed to be developing much like her older sisters. "I can say she's a very content child," Shyamkali said. "She doesn't cry much. Only when she is hungry."

Food was scarce in the house. The family didn't have a ration card, so there was no way to participate in the government's distribution of subsidized food. Shyamkali's father had once had a card, just for cooking oil, but he had died several years earlier and the card didn't transfer to his family. Shyamkali and her husband, Rajender, had appealed to the village headman many times for a card, and had filled out an application. Shyamkali wasn't hopeful: "He told us, 'When the card is ready, I'll send it to you.' But it has been a year. We haven't heard anything."

The regular distribution of the *panjiri*, the fortified flour distributed to pregnant and breastfeeding moms and to their infants, had also stopped throughout the Shivgarh area. The village health workers, the *anganwadi* women, said they had nothing to distribute; they themselves also hadn't been paid for months by the state government. Rajender was still in pursuit of day jobs, and he had recently been working on a crew that was cleaning out a pond. It was part of the government's guaranteed work program; for twenty days, Rajender dug out mud and carried it away in a bucket balanced on his head. The payment, about $2 a day, was supposed to automatically go to his bank account, but so far nothing had arrived. Shyamkali said he was now working on the wheat harvest, moving from field to field, receiving pay in the form of the wheat itself: the standard one-eighth of whatever he harvested. When one of the older daughters could stay home from school and watch Anshika, Shyamkali also worked in the fields, cutting the wheat with a scythe. Whatever wheat she brought home would be ground into flour and made into *roti*.

Their main vegetables were assorted greens that grew around the village. Dal with lentils, India's staple, was rare, as was any kind of fruit. "If fruit falls from the trees, we'll take it," Shyamkali said. The girls were always on the lookout for mangoes, apples, or guavas. Their cow had begun producing milk a few months earlier; the youngest sisters were first in line for that.

"We eat what we can afford," Shyamkali told me.

This day, it was potatoes and rice, on the boil over a wood fire. Her older daughters liked potatoes. She hoped Anshika would, too.

In the nearby village of Rampur Khas, Sushma was also trying to discover what Sunny liked to eat. At ten months old, he was just a few weeks into eating solid foods. So far, he only seemed to like biscuits—the "G for Genius" brand, high in carbs, sugar, and fat—dipped into milk. Now Sushma was trying a little bit of dal and rice, which she mixed on a tin plate. Sunny, wearing a green "Alvin and the Chipmunks" T-shirt, crawled across the veranda and sat in his mother's lap. She fed him with a spoon. After several bites, Sunny burped. Sushma laughed. "I think you like this," she told him.

She was still breastfeeding Sunny, but increasingly she was also giving him a bottle of infant formula milk. It was the country's most popular brand, Amulspray, with a pink teddy bear on the front of the can. Cow or buffalo milk was too expensive; if she mixed it with water to make it easier to digest, she worried it would be too weak. Sushma had suspected for several months that she wasn't producing enough milk to satisfy her son. She never went to the doctor for a checkup for herself. "I'd feel bad, asking a doctor if I had difficulty producing milk and if Sunny was getting enough to drink," she told me. "He's my child; I should know myself."

She had taken Sunny to see a doctor when he had a fever and runny nose and wouldn't eat. She filled a prescription for medicine, and Sunny improved. I measured him. He was just a bit taller than Anshika, almost twenty-seven inches.

The food they ate came from their own small plot beside the house. Sushma and her husband grew rice, potatoes, tomatoes, squash, and okra. They also cultivated peppermint and mustard when those crops were in season to sell for some household income. And they brought home wheat when they helped others harvest their fields. Sushma's family rarely, if ever, ate fruit, in a country that was second only to China in fruit production.

"No fruits," Sushma said. "I'd really love to buy fruit, but we can't afford it. I'd love to have mangoes. A whole bowl of them!" She laughed a sarcastic laugh, a "Yeah, like that would ever happen" laugh.

They didn't have a ration card for subsidized food either. "What we eat, we grow ourselves," Sushma told me. And as her family grew, she wondered if it would be enough. Already, at some meals, she was stretching the food to satisfy her husband, her seven-year-old son Shiva, and her three-year-old daughter Khushboo. Sushma, of course, ate last. "I don't want to have any more children," she told my translator from the Community Empowerment Lab. "If you have medicine that keeps me from getting pregnant, can you bring it to me?" She looked over at her husband, who was at the edge of their field, out of hearing range. "Please."

IN GUATEMALA, INTERNACIONALES Conejos, the International Rabbits marimba band, was back at it, transitioning themselves from singing about breastfeeding to singing about the importance of complementary feeding, in partnership with Save the Children. "Dale Comiditas" (Give Complementary Foods) was another hit:

> Today I've come again to tell you
> To care for your kids, don't neglect them
> If you already gave them the breast, don't be afraid
> From six to eight months you can start
> to give them porridge, good and thick
> It won't hurt their little belly
> Lots of fruits and veggies
> They won't hurt their little belly
>
> After nine months, you can give them
> Chicken liver, also beef
> After twelve months give them everything
> But never forget, to give them the breast. . . .
>
> And remember at 12 months you can give them goat milk
>
> And don't forget to give them their zucchini, squash, and carrots
> So they can be a good Rabbit.

Some families in Guatemala were even eating rabbits. It was part of Save the Children's effort to introduce more animal protein, a critical ingredient for brain and body growth, into the diets of moms and children for the 1,000 days. In the western highlands, at a center run by nuns, Save the Children was breeding two hundred female rabbits to distribute to families with young children, so they could then breed their own rabbits as a cheap source of meat. The rabbit program followed Save the Children's goat project, which was launched to provide goat milk for the complementary feeding period.

"We can't tell people to drink milk because they don't have many cows in the highlands," Carlos Cardenas, Save the Children's Guatemala director, told me. "But they can raise goats." The idea was to give goats to families with children under three years old. A single goat would produce enough for one glass of milk a day for one child. "The main thing was to get animal protein into their diets," Carlos said.

But before the goats arrived in 2008, Save the Children had to answer an elemental question: What's a goat?

Diego Sarat scratched his head when his wife returned from a community meeting with the exciting news that she had signed up for a new program that would give them a goat. "I didn't even know what a goat was," Diego recalled when I visited his homestead in the village of Media Luna, about an hour's drive from Quetzaltenango. He was a farmer—a corn farmer, of course. "We didn't know how to handle livestock."

That befuddling day in May 2008 turned out to be a turning point for the health of his family. At the time the goat arrived, Diego's youngest child, two-year-old Haroldo, wasn't doing well. He was small, skinny, lethargic. "He was malnourished," his father acknowledged. "But once he started drinking milk every day, we could see him improve."

Now, eight-year-old Haroldo bounded down the hill to greet visitors with high-fives and fist-bumps. His father proudly reported that Haroldo was thriving in both Sunday school and primary school, where he was in the first grade. The impact of the earlier malnutrition was still visible; he was physically stunted. He wasn't much taller than his five-year-old brother, Ariel, who had had the benefit of a daily glass of goat milk since he was a toddler.

Since 2008, more than 1,600 families had received goats (others received chickens for daily eggs), and for many of them the program had grown beyond a single glass of milk. Diego now had seven mature goats producing more than enough milk for his family; he shared the surplus with neighborhood children. He had also constructed goat pens to collect the droppings and urine, which he funneled into big plastic Pepsi bottles (he found those discarded along the road and in rubbish bins) and sold as urea-rich fertilizer. The goats were now milk producers and income generators; Diego used the money to diversify the family's diet and buy vegetables and fruits he couldn't afford before.

Where once there were no goats, a chain of milk production was beginning to stretch across that area of the highlands. Save the Children, with support from Green Mountain Coffee Roasters, was building the Highland Goat Production Center to train hundreds of local farmers in goat-rearing practices. It was a sleek complex that could house up to three hundred goats. Some of the pens were reserved for pairing native goats with other breeds from Mexico and the United States to improve the milk production of their offspring. The center would also be a collection point for the surplus milk of individual farmers in the area. It was gearing up to turn out an array of dairy products, including cheese, yogurt, sweets, and even facial creams.

It was an ambitious program to reduce the poverty of highland families. But Carlos Cardenas urged the farmers to never lose sight of the central purpose: a daily glass of milk to help conquer the malnutrition of their children. Satisfy your family first, and then the market, he would tell them. And, above all else, resist the temptation to eat the goat. A barbeque may provide food for a day. But a living goat would provide a daily glass of milk for years.

"This is all about sustained availability of milk for your children," Carlos told the families. He wanted everyone to be able to answer yes to the question: "Go(a)t milk?"

THE GOATS HADN'T yet arrived in the Palajunoj Valley. But Maria Estella did have a chicken in a coop outside her house. She was saving the chicken to eat on a special occasion; until then, the family would be enjoying the eggs. In the meantime, Maria Estella's two children continued their divergent development. Eleven-month-old Jorge was chubby, with ruddy cheeks; he was crawling and climbing and getting ready to walk. He had begun eating solid foods at six months and hadn't stopped since. Now he was eagerly eating three meals a day—soups, vegetables, fruits, and occasionally meat. And he was still breastfeeding. His sister Yesica, who was almost three, was thin, clinging to her mother, not yet speaking. She first walked at fifteen months. "She doesn't eat much, she doesn't want to," Maria Estella told Susy. When she ate, she preferred chips or other snack foods. Maria Estella said Jorge only cried when he was hungry; Yesica cried more often.

Susy hung her scale from a wire in the little yard beyond the tidy two-room house. Hummingbirds flitted around flowering bushes. It was a pleasant contrast to the filthy, barnyard mess found at many homes in the valley. Maria Estella keenly watched as the black pointer on the scale bounced around and then settled on a number. Jorge weighed in at a bit more than twenty-three pounds, Yesica at twenty-five pounds. He was twenty months younger and almost weighed the same as his sister. Susy stretched out her measuring board. Jorge was twenty-eight inches; Yesica was thirty-two.

Maria Estella told Susy that she prioritized meat when she went shopping, particularly calf liver. She remembered the importance of iron from the classes. "I think meat is necessary for their growth," she said. If meat was too expensive, she bought extra vegetables. She also made an effort to buy soap and detergent to keep the house and clothes clean. She thanked Susy for the nutrition and cleanliness lessons, and for the recipes. For breakfast that day, she had prepared fish soup with potatoes. For dinner, she was planning rice with small pieces of beef.

When Susy weighed Jorge, she told him, gently, "You keep eating. You'll be a strong boy." Then she pleaded with Yesica, "Please, you must eat. Your mother is worried."

Susy turned to Maria Estella. Her tone shifted between encouraging and scolding. "Yesica is too small, she needs to eat more," Susy said. "She needs to grow, her brain needs to develop. She isn't speaking. When she goes to school, she'll be bored and drop out early." Susy suggested mashing up bananas or papayas or squash for Yesica. Cook meat; if she doesn't like it plain, add tomato and onion or a salsa. And don't give her chips and sweets, because that won't help her grow.

It was tough love, a hallmark of Susy's home visits. Gabriela was next up. Her eight-month-old son José wore a green Mickey Mouse sweater and a striped baseball hat. Gabriela said José had been battling an intestinal infection that gave him diarrhea. He also had an eye infection and a sore throat. A doctor in Quetzaltenango gave him an injection and cough syrup. He told Gabriela that her son, who was born premature, was severely underweight, and suggested feeding him the fortified Incaparina drink every day. He also urged her to buy vegetables.

Susy observed Gabriela breastfeeding José. She noticed that Gabriela only used her right breast and suspected that José wasn't getting enough milk. Susy spotted another problem: Gabriela, who was illiterate, wasn't mixing the Incaparina properly. She was diluting it too much, stretching it to last longer, so José wasn't getting the correct dose of nutrients that he needed.

Gabriela confided that they didn't have much money for food. Her husband was struggling to find work, and they lived in her mother's single-room house with a rough dirt floor. Flowers grew in a patch behind the house; Gabriela's mother wouldn't let her turn it into a vegetable garden. An apple tree stood sentry in a corner of the small yard; ripe fruit was still months away. Gabriela was on the verge of tears. "It's frustrating," she told Susy. "We can't buy enough food. You want to eat like you see other people eating." As she spoke, a man selling ice cream off the back of a motorcycle drove slowly down the dirt road, playing the "Do Your Ears Hang Low?" tune to attract attention. For Gabriela, it was a cruel taunt.

Susy did the measuring. José was just fifteen pounds and twenty-five inches. "I can see he's underweight," Gabriela conceded. Susy nodded her head. She typed the numbers into her laptop. They were the standard measurements for a four-month-old, an infant half José's age.

Susy's advice was comforting and stern. "I understand that it's hard because there isn't work or money to buy what you need," Susy said. "But try to make simple things like rice soup. Buy cheaper vegetables so you can get more for what you have. When you have vegetables, use them to the max, use all the parts, don't throw anything away. Your son needs you to keep trying."

We walked up the hill to Dianet's family homestead. The kitchen was busy with preparations for a birthday feast. Slices of pork were marinating in a tomato-pepper-garlic-chili sauce. White potatoes were on the boil. It would all be wrapped up in a palm leaf and served like a tamale. Dianet carried eight-month-old Keytlin in her arms as she helped with the cooking. The baby would eat the potatoes and some sauce. She had begun eating fish and chicken, but hadn't yet tried pork. Dianet feared it would give her stomach problems, and she already had enough of those. Keytlin had been battling a cold and sore throat as well. The local government health center had run out of medicine, so Dianet searched the valley for treatment and increasingly relied on the Primeros Pasos clinic. "It's sad and disappointing. We get no help from the government," she told Susy. Dianet had heard the government's big proclamations about attacking Guatemala's malnutrition crisis, but she saw no evidence of action in the valley. More like retreat, she thought. There were no efforts to create jobs, and there was no food distribution or nutrition education. "They need to take seriously what they say and go out into the communities and see the reality," she said. "Get out of the city and into the rural areas. I don't know if they really don't know, or if they are ignoring it."

Keytlin was crawling on the floor of the living room, playing with a plastic yellow Shrek doll. She often stopped and sat up to observe the visitors with her bright eyes. Dianet was happy with her daughter's mental development; Keytlin was curious, expressive, active. She liked to color and dance and clap to "Dora the Explorer" music. Dianet believed she was close to walking, but she didn't think she had grown much in the past couple of months.

Susy needed to confirm that with her measurement charts, so she and Dianet hoisted Keytlin into the weighing sling. Keytlin smiled good-naturedly. She weighed nearly fourteen pounds, a small improvement, but still low. Next was the measuring board: twenty-four inches, also a slight increase from the previous month but still small. Susy said Keytlin wasn't growing as much as she should be; her chart was heading into stunted territory.

Dianet looked weary. Giving birth had taken its toll on this small woman. She was still breastfeeding, and Susy worried that maybe her milk wasn't sufficient. Was she taking the multivitamins she had gotten from Primeros Pasos? Yes, Dianet said.

"Are you eating enough yourself?" Susy asked. "You have to eat really well to be sure your milk has all the nutrients Keytlin needs."

"Yes," Dianet said, "I'm eating."

It was puzzling. Dianet had always been very attentive at the nutrition classes. The house was clean; there seemed to be enough food, both inside the kitchen and outside in the fields. But mother and daughter weren't thriving. Susy had a nagging feeling: something wasn't right.

PART FOUR | THE SECOND YEAR

chapter twelve

WORRYING

DIANET'S LIFE WAS IN UPHEAVAL. FIVE MONTHS LATER, WHEN next I visited, I found Dianet and Keytlin in an unfinished room in an unfinished house on her in-law's property. They had decided to move there while the house was still being built because it gave them a place of their own—it would be four rooms with a separate kitchen— instead of sharing space in her family's house. Dianet thought it was a good idea for Keytlin to become accustomed to what would be her childhood home. Winter was approaching; the room was cold. Arnold Schwarzenegger, in the movie *Terminator*, spewed mayhem on a small black-and-white television perched on a chair. Keytlin, wrapped in a pink sweater, was on the bed, lying down, holding a tube of skin cream. She had been sick with diarrhea for a couple of days; she also had a nasty diaper rash. For two weeks before that she'd had a cough and slight fever.

"She's lost weight," Dianet reported. Before the series of illnesses, Keytlin had been eating well, trying almost everything the family ate. Dianet was following recipes she had learned in Susy's class: pancakes made with grated carrots; noodles with celery, peppers, and chicken; rice and beans with *pico de gallo*. And she was still breastfeeding. Keytlin had been walking by herself and was beginning to speak. Dianet was happy with her progress. They read books together.

"When Keytlin turns the pages, she licks her fingers first. It's funny. I don't do that," Dianet told Susy. "Maybe she picked it up from someone else. Maybe it's instinctive for her."

Keytlin sat up on the bed and saw herself in a mirror in a "Dora the Explorer" frame inscribed with a Bible verse: "Create in me a clean heart, oh Lord, and renew a right spirit within me." Keytlin played peek-a-boo with her image in the mirror, closing her hands in front of her eyes and then opening them.

"I notice the difference between her and other children her age," Dianet volunteered. The day before, Keytlin had played with a flock of children at a big family wedding party. "One child, four days younger, wasn't speaking yet. He wasn't very active. He fell down when he walked and couldn't get back up by himself." She recounted the comparison with a mother's pride.

Susy hung her weighing scale from a hook on the ceiling. As Keytlin swung in the sling, Dianet watched the needle settle: a little over six kilograms, just a tick above thirteen and a half pounds. According to the measuring board, Keytlin was sixty-three centimeters, a shade over twenty-five inches. Scarlet Samayoa Rios, a new nutritionist at Primeros Pasos, recorded the numbers on the laptop. Keytlin's weight-for-height ratio was normal—for a child several months younger. Keytlin was fourteen months old and falling further behind in physical growth. But her social and cognitive skills seemed to be ahead of other children. Dianet said maybe Keytlin was meant to be small. After all, she herself was just four-foot-five.

Dianet told Susy and Scarlet that money was tight in the house. A lack of rain at crucial times of the season had severely weakened the corn crop. "It's never been this bad before," she said. The drought had also impacted her family's other crops: the broccoli was smaller, the beets paler, the lettuce skimpier. Dianet was now having to buy corn on the market, a rare occurrence for her family. She estimated they consumed about five to seven pounds a day, eating it in some form at all three meals. The corn grown on Guatemala's Pacific Coast was cheapest, costing about $25 for a hundred pounds. But it was also the lowest quality, sometimes riddled with the mold that can lead to aflatoxin poisoning. Dianet reckoned they were spending about $40 a month on corn, dramatically cutting into her food budget.

What were they going without?

"Meat!" Dianet proclaimed. "And vegetables, carrots, and potatoes." All those luscious images on Susy's food charts now seemed so elusive.

On top of the unexpected corn costs, Dianet hadn't been paid in four months. She worked at the local health post, but throughout the highlands those centers had been shut down by a government budget crisis. "The government says they don't have money," Dianet said, rolling her eyes. "Well, we don't either." As the household budget tightened, the construction of the house stalled.

The condition of the house and the failed corn crop were serious worries, but Susy and Scarlet believed there was something else bothering Dianet. She seemed more distracted, less responsive to Keytlin than they had seen during the nutrition classes. They pressed for answers.

Dianet confided that she was worried about her husband: he was trying to emigrate to the United States, where he believed he could find a job and better provide for his family. Throughout the Palajunoj Valley, new construction projects—houses and shops—were popping up; it was almost all fueled by money sent back home from relatives who had begun a new life in the United States. The temptation to make a run north was contagious, like a virus. Three times Dianet's husband had tried, traveling overland through Guatemala and then all the way up through Mexico to the US border. Three times he made it across, only to be rounded up by US authorities and sent back. I had never met him on any of my visits, and now I knew why. He was likely on the move, part of the great wave of migrants from Central America straining to get into the United States in 2014.

On his last attempt, he'd made it to California and had been staying in a house with other migrants. Someone called the US immigration authorities, who swiftly rounded up and deported the Guatemalans. Now, Dianet's husband was pressing her to come with him on another attempt, and to bring Keytlin as well. He knew the routes and was certain that the next time he could succeed if they were all together. He claimed the odds of staying in the United States were better if he had a family with him. The Americans wouldn't send back a family with a small child, he insisted.

Dianet was consumed with fear. Each attempt to get to the United States cost them a minor fortune—a couple of thousand dollars at least for the guides. Lenders offered money at high rates, and their debt was growing. The trip was arduous and extremely dangerous. It required walking, riding on the tops of trains, being crammed into the backs of trucks, and crossing rivers and harsh terrain. They followed the same trails as the drug smugglers, and bandits lay in wait to prey on the migrants. And in the United States, there could be detention and arrest. Each time her husband left, Dianet worried that she would never see him again.

This was no journey for a child, she told her husband, particularly one as young as Keytlin, who was just learning to walk. Dianet doubted that she herself could make it; she felt she still hadn't regained all her strength after giving birth. And she was suspicious of her husband's claim that it was unlikely they would be sent back from the United States. The human smugglers, called coyotes, had spread the rumor that President Obama had changed the law to allow children from Central America to come to the United States, and it was what was driving the stream of humanity—including thousands of unaccompanied children—pressing against the border in Texas, New Mexico, Arizona, and California. Some of them were fleeing drug and gang violence, but many were chasing a better life in America. Dianet's husband was one of them.

The rumors concocted by the coyotes to drum up more business were wrong. The United States hadn't loosened its immigration policy toward Central Americans. Instead, it was working on a program to help the economies of Guatemala, Honduras, and El Salvador so citizens there would be less inclined to leave, thus slowing the immigration wave. It was called the Plan for the Alliance for Prosperity in the Northern Triangle of Central America. President Obama had asked Congress for $1 billion to help those countries improve their security, crack down on corruption, and create jobs and economic opportunities. Vice President Joseph Biden would travel to Guatemala in early 2015 to meet with the leaders of the three countries.

Dianet didn't know what to do if her husband insisted on making an-other run. "Sometimes he convinces me," she told Scarlet. "But then I say, 'No! What if they take Keytlin?'"

Then she would look at Keytlin and think this might be the best chance to secure a better future for her daughter. That was Dianet's dream, af-ter all, that Keytlin eventually go to a land of greater opportunity. Her emotional pendulum would swing back again as she heard more horror stories of the hair-raising journey north from those who had been turned back. "When I think of the three of us going . . . Oh, what would we do?" Dianet said. "They might let me and Keytlin through into America and arrest my husband. I'd be by myself. I don't know English. How would that be better than here?"

The uncertainty, the risk, the cost, and the possibility of disaster, which could include a family separation—it was all an incredible burden that Dianet was carrying. Should she stay or should she go? Susy and Scarlet knew that stress in the home could be just as debilitating for a child's development in the 1,000 days as a lack of nutrition or lousy sani-tation and hygiene. They feared that Keytlin was getting lost in the worry.

JESSICA'S STRESS LEVEL was also escalating in Chicago. She had re-turned to high school, pulling herself away from Alitzel every morning, and at school the pressure mounted as she pushed to make good on her commitment to graduate and go to college. Amid all this, she, too, had moved: first to live with Marco's family about a mile or so away, and then back home to her mother's house with Marco. Jessica was trying to escape what she thought was overbearing advice on how to raise Alitzel, but then had come to accept that she needed family support as she nav-igated motherhood and high school. Her mother's house was just three blocks from school, so Alitzel would always be close.

Jessica was determined not to lose sight of her daughter amid the stress. After the final bell every afternoon, she packed up her books and immediately hurried home to see Alitzel. There would be no sports, no debate club, no Model United Nations competition. "No time for any of that," she said. Marco and Jessica's mother cared for Alitzel during the day; they both worked late shifts at separate restaurants and left for their jobs when Jessica returned from school in the afternoon.

It was difficult for Jessica to walk out the door every morning to head to school. "I miss my baby so much when I'm in school. I tell myself, just a few more hours and I'll be home with her," she told me one afternoon, having just returned home. She spent any free time she had during school working on homework assignments so she wouldn't have much to do at home. The mornings went by fast, but the afternoon classes became an endurance test. Like most other students, Jessica watched the minutes on the clock tick by. But unlike the others, she wasn't anxious to begin an afternoon of freedom; she couldn't wait to race home to see her daughter.

At home, she plopped her backpack on a sofa and hugged Alitzel. They played on the floor, read books, watched kids' shows on television: *Curious George, Peg and Cat, Dora the Explorer*. Over and over they sang the songs from the movie *Frozen*. Jessica prepared dinner, gave Ali a bath, played more, read more. When Ali dozed off, Jessica would return to her books. She tried to finish her homework before Marco returned shortly after 11 p.m., his shift at the restaurant over, but sometimes she would study into the wee hours of the morning.

They had decided not to put Ali in day care. Their schedules worked out so that someone could always be at home with her, and they wanted to save money. Jessica was encouraging Marco either to return to school or to study to take the General Educational Development (GED) exam. But the prep classes were at night, and he didn't want to stop working. Instead, he hinted at having another baby; he wanted to have his children close together in age, and be a young father for them. "You're crazy," Jessica replied. One day, sure, "but not now. Many, many years from now."

Jessica was committed to graduating from school and exploring college options. School was much less fun now than it had been for her in the past; it was more like a job, with the attendant pressures to keep up her grades and do well on the college acceptance tests. And social tensions rose as well. She didn't have much time for her friends, and they drifted away. Their interest in how she was doing during the pregnancy and excitement over her new baby had faded. Before, she had gathered with them at a Buffalo Wild Wings restaurant once a week; they would have celebrated Jessica's seventeenth birthday there. But Jessica decided not to go if she couldn't take her daughter. She and Marco rarely went out alone together. Jessica would scan her friends' updates on Facebook, seeing the posts from various parties. She saw one photo of a friend, also a teen mom, smoking a cigarette; the baby was in the background. "I don't think that's right," Jessica told me.

She heard the talk in the school hallways, how teen pregnancy ruined your life. Jessica turned on one of her friends after a dose of criticism: "You don't understand the struggles. I'm still going to school. You should be happy for me. I'm trying. I go to my classes, study hard, and then go home to my baby."

Reminders of how her life had changed were everywhere in school. Jessica often walked past a large bulletin board encased in glass. It was a display for an organization supporting teen parents called Options for Youth. "Our main focus," it said, "is to encourage our parents throughout Chicago to graduate from high school and continue onto higher education, delay another pregnancy and be the best parent you can be to your child." Other montages in the display were more biting than encouraging. In one, a drawing illustrated goals receding in the distance: "Your Window of Opportunity Shrinks Each Time You Get Pregnant Before You Are Ready." Another featured a picture of a little girl and the caption, "Honestly Mom, chances are he won't stay with you. What happens to me?"

Jessica tried to ignore it all. She felt she was furiously swimming upstream, trying to achieve academic goals in an underachieving school. Her math teacher was a Spanish teacher just filling in. She worried that her math scores on the college entrance tests would hold her back. She had already determined that Ali would go to a Catholic school and avoid public education. When Jessica looked out the windows of her homeroom class on the second floor, staring at the intersection below, she saw derelict buildings on two corners. The White Castle hamburger joint occupied the third. She felt trapped in a no-hope neighborhood.

Her lone refuge was that first period One Goal class. One Goal was a Chicago-based organization helping students in impoverished, underserved areas graduate from high school and go to college. Jessica had joined as a sophomore, before she was pregnant; by her senior year there were still sixteen kids in her group. A favorite history teacher, Vickki Willis-Redus, led the class all three years, exhorting her students to set high expectations for themselves, have a game plan, and be happy with their own choices and actions. She had become Jessica's mentor and inspiration.

Ms. Willis exhorted Jessica to stay in school, persevere, keep up the grades. She taught by example: her own mother had been a young mom, and she told Jessica that although they had struggled, she and her mother had both ended up going to college. They received their diplomas within three days of each other. "This may not be the life you envisioned," she told Jessica, "but it's what you have. Life is what you make of it. You can't use stuff happening as a crutch, as an excuse of why you didn't succeed." She posted a phrase on a bulletin board at the back of the classroom: "Learn from your mistakes, but do not get all your education that way."

She was proud of Jessica. "Becoming a mother made her more committed to graduation," Ms. Willis told me one morning before the students arrived in her classroom. "Her grades have improved since she had the baby. She's embracing the responsibility and wants to be a good model for her daughter."

Jessica arrived and opened her laptop. On the cover she had proudly placed a sticker: MAMA JESS. Senior year had begun. Ms. Willis discussed preparations for college testing. They reviewed financial aid possibilities. They talked about visiting schools and possible majors. Jessica had applied to about a dozen schools. She was now thinking of studying nursing or social work; she figured her onetime ambition of being an architect would require too many years of study. High school graduation was in sight. The only obstacle would be maintaining the necessary 85 percent attendance rate. She had missed a week of classes when Alitzel was sick with a cold, and then she got sick as well. Jessica considered dropping out of the WIC program because she couldn't afford to take time off from school to attend the checkup appointments with Alitzel required to get the food coupons. She agonized over the decision: she was grateful for the WIC assistance, but what could she do?

A series of tweets she blasted out early in her senior year reflected anxiety, pride, and defiance:

I stay up so late to do all my homework and I'm proud to say, I'm on honor roll. #hardworkpaysoff.

Honor roll WITH a baby and a 90% attendance. No excuses, doing for myself and family. To those who said I would drop out, suck it!

My stress level is way high up but that doesn't stop me from being on honor roll, doing all I have to do to keep moving and succeeding.

I could've quit school, but my mother never got that education like I do so why throw it away? That's an opportunity I have that she didn't.

Not only will I make my mother proud in June when I graduate, but I will be the one yelling out "I did it!" I will be the proud one.

Ms. Willis asked her One Goal students to compose statements of affirmation, capturing what they think of themselves. Jessica wrote:

> I take care of myself.
> I am strong.
> I am valued.
> I am powerful.

IN PURE BAISHAN, India, Shyamkali was also trying to project strength. She worried that the well-being of her daughters was being compromised by the desire for a son. She hoped she had finally convinced her husband, Rajender, that their family was large enough.

Rajender had first seen his fifth daughter, Anshika, more than a month after her birth. He was immediately captivated by her; he said her expressive dark eyes commanded his love. It was then that he realized his lot in life was to have daughters.

"I have wanted a son, but in the process I've had five girls," Rajender told me with a laugh when I first met him. "I now know that whatever has to be given is given by God. If God says it is to be a girl then that is how it is. God won't give you a buffalo if you are meant to have a cow. It is my place in life to have girls."

He was a friendly man with a big smile beneath a pencil-thin mustache. He was wiry and short—barely five feet. His name was tattooed in English script—RAJENDER—on his right forearm. He couldn't read it, for he spoke no English; in fact, he hardly read any Hindi words, for he had very little education. He had gotten the tattoo years earlier, as a souvenir from the time he first worked in Punjab state. He had once been a gardener at a park; he even still had the undergarments that he was given on his first day of employment. He didn't know what kind of tattoo to get, so the artist engraved his name. It had since become his stamp of pride; among his friends and neighbors in the Hindi-speaking rural villages, it was an English word that only he could read.

It was obvious he was also proud of his girls: Pooja, Sashi, Tulsi, Shivani, and Anshika. He gathered them, and Shyamkali, around him as he sat on the floor of their veranda. He held Anshika by her hands and helped her take a few steps. "Look!" he said. "*Meri Rani.*" My Queen.

He beamed. "She is very friendly. She goes to anyone. She hardly ever cries."

Rajender declared that his daughters would all have an education—something neither he nor Shyamkali had. He hoped he would be able to send each to school for twelve years. The four oldest girls were already in school, but some compromises had to be made. Pooja had been held back so she and Sashi, though two years apart, could be in the same class; they shared the lessons and homework when one of them had to stay home from school to look after Anshika while their parents worked.

"Because I have five children, it will be expensive. They will all have to go to government schools," Rajender said. He calculated the costs, perhaps $2 or $3 a month for all of them combined, for textbooks, supplies, and the standard uniform. It might double when they reach high school. "It's a lot of money for us, because we are so poor."

It would mean many sacrifices. Already, for lack of money, they had delayed two traditional rituals for Anshika, customs deemed important for a child's physical and spiritual development: the first cutting of hair at several months by a barber and a priest, and later the massaging of the body with oil to strengthen bones and help the child walk. They went without malaria bed nets; instead, Shyamkali fashioned nets out of old saris and bamboo poles. And rather than repair their well, which had filled with mud and all manner of insects, they would go from neighbor to neighbor, begging for permission to fetch water from their wells.

Rajender was a hard worker, sometimes doing two jobs a day to provide for his family. Though sometimes he worked under the government's guaranteed work program, he didn't always get paid. But he did get money from another government program to improve his house, as did others in the village who fell below a certain poverty level. Rajender had completed the room where Shyamkali had been in confinement with Anshika, and he had also closed in the courtyard, finishing the walls and ceiling. He added a smaller third room: not a toilet, but a little space to store grain for family consumption and straw for his cow. Now he thought about making that room into a bedroom for himself; it would remove him from his wife, and any temptations that might lead to another child. Rajender laughed mightily at this plan. Shyamkali, who had been contemplating getting some method of birth control, blushed and pulled the edge of her sari over her face.

Rajender knew his wife wasn't to blame for having girls. He had heard about the responsibility of his chromosomes. And he confessed that he had been foolish to listen to all those who had been insisting that he must have a son. Accepting the prodding of the people of the village, the local busybodies, and giving in to their nagging could be ruinous. He had heard a parable that really made him think: A father and son were walking through town with a mule. One of the villagers said: "Look at those two idiots. They have a mule and yet they walk." Hearing that, both father and son jumped on the mule and rode together.

They passed another group of villagers. One said, "Look at these two selfish guys. They make such hard work for the mule to carry them both." So the son got off and walked beside his father riding the mule.

They proceeded on and passed another group of villagers. One said, "Look at that father, he makes his son walk." So they switched. The father now walked beside his son riding the mule.

They passed another group of villagers. One said, "Look at that son, he makes his father walk."

Rajender summed up the moral of the story. "You can never satisfy the crowd," he told me. "If you listen to them, you'll be ruined."

So, I asked, will he try again for a boy?

"No, that's okay," Rajender said with a shake of his head. "No, this is enough."

A big smile spread across Shyamkali's face.

It wouldn't last. Soon her face would be creased with even deeper lines of worry. As time would tell, even as they spoke with me on their veranda, Shyamkali was already pregnant again.

chapter thirteen

WALKING, TALKING

Esther's son, Rodgers, was a ceaseless crawler, curiously patrolling the ground between the family huts and a small vegetable garden. He was fourteen months old. Esther had thought he would be walking by now, but his development had been slowed by a bout of malaria as he turned one. The family faithfully used bed nets inside the house at night, but the malaria threat was constant, particularly at dawn and dusk when the mosquitoes swarmed most aggressively. Feverish and listless, Rodgers stopped eating solid foods for a couple of weeks. It seemed his only comfort was when he breastfed, though Esther was weakened by her own battle with malaria. Together, they recovered on a regimen of antimalarial drugs.

Rodgers was now eating more than before the malaria; Esther mashed up the high-iron beans and orange sweet potatoes, as well as cabbage and cassava and other foods that grew in their fields. Along with her milk, Esther had introduced her son to homemade passion-fruit juice.

As I talked with Esther and Tonny under the canopy of a broad shade tree, Rodgers played with a group of cousins and neighbor children who were all a bit older than him. He watched them walk, and crawled after them. "He's about to get up and walk himself, you can see that," Tonny said. "I'd say one month from now he'll be walking."

It was as if Rodgers understood and took his father's prediction as a challenge, for just a few minutes later, at the end of a summer day, he pushed off the back of one of his cousins and stood up. Rodgers wobbled and steadied himself. He was a determined figure in a red sleeveless shirt and oversized blue shorts that came down nearly to his ankles. His tongue poked out of his mouth. Then he took his first steps. Three of them, over a patch of dirt. He fell on his backside, and picked himself up. A few steps more and then another fall, this time into a green patch of kale. His parents laughed and clapped. "Rodgers, you have healthy tastes," Esther said.

Her face lit up as she watched her son. The first steps are a big milestone for children everywhere. But in rural Africa, walking is more than a developmental marker. It brings independence for child and mother. Several times a day Esther would walk a mile to the communal well, balancing jerricans on her head and Rodgers on her back. When she planted, weeded, or harvested, there he was, too, on her back. Now, as Rodgers's walking improved, he could toddle beside her, or walk in the company of other children. It was one less physical load for an African mother to bear.

Brenda also experienced an easing of her chores once her son began walking. Aron had set off on his own at about thirteen months, and never stopped exploring. His parents marveled at how he grabbed and examined everything he could. "He's good with his hands," his father, Dennis, told me. "Maybe he'll be a builder."

Harriet's daughter, Apio, began walking before her first birthday, just after she, too, had recovered from malaria. The strain of the disease that infected Apio was more severe than the one that had afflicted Rodgers; she had needed a quinine injection along with the tablets. Her recovery, followed by her first steps, was a big relief for Harriet, who continued to suffer dizziness and headaches during times of exertion and stress. She noticed that her pain was particularly bad during the time of school exams, when her three older children would come home asking for money to cover the test fees. It was a double whammy: the stress of scraping together the money, and, if there wasn't enough at hand, the hard labor of breaking rocks for several days to earn more.

Harriet had walked for an hour through the fields to the Ongica clinic for a checkup with midwife Susan Ejang. Susan monitored her blood pressure; it was still alarmingly high. She begged Harriet not to work so hard, to get more rest. Susan prescribed some hypertension medicine and apologized that the clinic's supply had run out. At a pharmacy, Harriet was dismayed to learn that the medicine cost 1,000 shillings (about 40 cents) per tablet. She only had enough money for eight tablets; the prescription called for thirty. To afford the medicine, she would have to do more work in the quarry, which only increased her suffering. Harriet bought the eight and finally accepted Susan's plea to stop pounding rocks. Maybe then, she thought, she wouldn't need the pills.

But without that work, the family would have less income, so Harriet focused on stretching the food supplies. A drought had reduced the bean crop and was threatening to diminish the corn yield; Esther and Brenda also complained of harvests that were only half as much as they expected. Harriet was relying on the orange sweet potatoes as their bulwark against hunger, for the potatoes could survive drought better than the other crops. Harriet had planted them nearby, all around her house. By properly managing the vines, she could produce two harvests in a year.

As we spoke, Harriet sat in the shade of her cooking hut, slicing up newly harvested sweet potatoes. It was the best way to store them, she explained, as they would last for months as dried chips. Another hardy crop covered the ground between the huts; Harriet had spread out pods of pigeon peas like a bushy carpet to dry in the sun. A cauldron of sweet potatoes was on the boil over a wood fire, as was a pot of the peas. It would be the family's lunch and dinner.

Apio sat on the ground beside her mother. A half-dozen chickens pecked at the drying peas with impunity, betraying no fear that they might end up in a pot themselves. "We never eat meat," Harriet told me. The family had become vegetarians, but not by choice: "We can't afford it." The chickens were too precious to eat. Their eggs, which could be hatched or sold, made them productive assets. The chickens were also the family's savings account; if money was needed for medicine for the children, they could sell a chicken or two. That was how they could afford

Apio's malaria treatment. And, Harriet calculated, the chickens could also be her last resort if she needed more tablets for her high blood pressure.

One thing they couldn't afford, Harriet told me, was another child. Her husband, Moses, worried about her health and the risk of another pregnancy, and they both knew it would only get more difficult to provide for their family as Apio grew. "We agreed," Harriet told me; she would review contraception possibilities with midwife Susan. Apio, whose name meant "the first," should be the last.

In India, Shyamkali was once again fervently praying for a boy. So, too, of course, was her husband, Rajender. He had accepted that his lot in life was to have girls, but now Shyamkali's unexpected pregnancy presented one more chance to maybe slip in a son. He sought additional work and tried to stay closer to home, particularly during the harvest seasons, so he could at least return with food every evening. With Anshika now eating solid food, he needed to put more on the table. One day, while walking home from work, he was hit by a motorcycle, which ran over his right foot and ankle. For one month, Rajender hobbled around in a cast, but he kept working as a gardener.

When the time came for the birth, again in the early morning hours, Shyamkali went to the same little clinic, this time accompanied by her husband. Rajender stayed outside, in the dark, and waited for word.

He dozed off, and then awoke with a start. There was great commotion in the clinic. A baby cried. "It's a girl," he heard. Was he dreaming? he wondered. He ran into the clinic and found confirmation of his fate: he was indeed meant to be a father to girls. He was now six for six.

"You got emotional. You cried," Rajender said to Shyamkali as they told me about the birth.

"You're lying. You were the one who was crying," Shyamkali replied. "Why would I cry? I had five daughters and now I had a sixth. I didn't cry when the others were born. Why would I cry for this one? There's nothing to be gained by crying. It's not going to change my destiny. I am proud and grateful to have six girls. I know they will always stand by me."

Rajender looked at me with a smile. "I was fine," he insisted. "I had to complete the streak of having so many girls."

The baby, named Avantika after a long-ago princess, was sleeping on a reed mat on the floor of their house. Anshika was twenty months old when the baby was born. Now that she was walking and talking, she was even more endearing to her father than I had observed on previous visits. Rajender doted on her. "Anshika is very fond of me, as I am of her," he told me. "We are close. When she sees me, she comes running to me. I feel very special to have her. And now Avantika. Of course, I'm attached to all of my daughters." He didn't know how much harder he could work to provide for his family. But he would try. "It is what I must do," he told me.

And again Rajender vowed: this child was the last. "That's it. I've been greedy for a son, but no more."

Shyamkali wouldn't rely solely on her husband's word this time, or on chance. The monsoon season was again approaching. Temperatures were rising. As Shyamkali regained her strength after delivering Avantika, she had talked with the community health worker about contraception options; she wanted something permanent, foolproof. Could she have a tubal ligation? she asked. She learned it was possible at the Shivgarh hospital. "When the temperature cools after the rains," Shyamkali told me, "I will go and have an operation."

IN THE NEARBY village of Barjor Khera, Sanju also had a new baby, a daughter named Jhanvi. She was born before Adarsh was even one year old. Now, as Adarsh approached his second birthday, Sanju clearly saw the importance of child spacing. She had stopped breastfeeding Adarsh early, about two months after he was born. Her milk production had been decreasing, but she would have weaned him early in any case, for local custom dictated that a mother stop breastfeeding when she becomes pregnant again. Sanju feared that Adarsh had missed out on something in his development. He was a sweet boy with a mop of curly black hair who seemed cursed with recurring diarrhea and fevers. He was noticeably bowlegged, and he didn't walk until he was about eighteen months old. He rarely spoke—"he only says Mama, he calls everyone Mama," Sanju told me—and he largely kept to himself while his cousins played. Jhanvi, who was still exclusively breastfeeding at ten months, seemed to be developing faster than her brother. "She's brighter than him. She's more alert," Sanju observed.

Sanju had noticed the same thing when comparing Adarsh with Priyanshi, the daughter of her sister-in-law Seema. Priyanshi was just two weeks older than Adarsh, but developmentally she appeared to be many months ahead. Priyanshi had bright eyes and a ready smile, and she laughed and ran about the veranda. On a sweltering hot day, she worked the pump at the well in front of the house, drawing water for herself and other children to play in and cool down.

On the dirt road just beyond the well, a street vendor ambled by, pushing a cart piled high with watermelons. I asked Sanju if her family grew watermelons on their land. "No," replied her husband, Anil. "If you grow vegetables or fruits, you have to be vigilant through the night, every night. People will steal the crops." So year after year they planted the traditional standbys—rice, wheat, and mint—forsaking the nutrients and diversified diets that would have come with a field of fruit or vegetables. Since everyone grew those staple crops, there was no inclination to steal them.

Illness continued to plague the household, both kids and adults. Seema herself was sick with a stomach pain that she hadn't been able to shake for the past month. She had put off going to the doctor to spare the expense, but finally she relented. The doctor said she was suffering from an intestinal virus. He ordered her to rest, so Seema spent most days lying on a *charpoy* in the shade. The doctor also suggested that the family practice better hygiene.

That was the motivation the husbands of Seema and Sanju needed to finish constructing the outhouse that had stood as a symbol of unfulfilled government promises for a couple of years. They completed the brick walls, bought thatching for the roof and a curtain for the doorway, and dug a hole more than a meter deep. They had saved up money for the task; it all cost the equivalent of about $20. Anil told me that the children were frequently shooed away by landowners when they went into the fields to poop. "The children are having difficulty finding a place to go," he said. Now, they could go at home, in peace, and in private.

IN GUATEMALA, MARIA Estella's son, Jorge, was on the move. He was running after chickens and cats and climbing up stairs and over furniture. And he was growing. At eighteen months, he weighed more than his sister, Yesica Marisol, who had just turned three years old. Maria Estella was trying to serve meat at least once a week; the chicken coop was now empty.

Jorge's grandmother, Candelaria, stopped by to watch Scarlet, the Primeros Pasos nutritionist, do the weighing and measuring. Candelaria marveled at Jorge's development. She herself had given birth to eight children; two of them had died within a week of coming into the world. She now had thirteen grandchildren, and all of them had so far survived. Even with all that childrearing experience, she said, she had learned new things from Maria Estella and her Primeros Pasos class: recipes and cooking skills, hygiene tips, nutrition principles.

Suddenly, the song "Happy" by Pharrell Williams echoed through the neighborhood. It was blaring from a loudspeaker mounted on a truck, and was followed by an excitable pitch from a traveling salesman for a wonder drug, a "cure-all for any ailment." Maria Estella and Candelaria laughed at the spectacle. They knew there was no such cure-all, for what they had learned during Maria Estella's 1,000 days journey was that many things were necessary for good health: vitamins and nutrients, a diversified diet, and proper hygiene.

Maria Estella, Scarlet, and the moms of the Primeros Pasos nutrition program had been making some noise of their own on the streets of the Palajunoj Valley. They had marched together, fifty women strong, in a parade during World Breastfeeding Week that was featured on the national news. The women carried balloons and banners and shouted slogans: "Breastmilk helps your children to grow healthy and strong"; "Let's make breastfeeding while working possible."

That last slogan was meant to be a message to the government to live up to its promises to support women and children in the 1,000 days. Since the introduction of the Zero Hunger Pact, government services in the valley had been in retreat. Health posts were closing. Vaccines were vanishing. When Dianet took her daughter, Keytlin, to the local health post for the series of vaccines due when a child is one year old, she was told the medicine cupboards were bare. She went to the hospital in Quetzaltenango and learned that it, too, was out of the vaccines. She took her search to private hospitals, and finally, at eighteen months, Keytlin had all her shots.

"How can they not have vaccines?" Dianet asked. She had been a steadfast skeptic of the Zero Hunger Pact and government promises. "It's the government's fault. They say they bought the vaccines, but then they didn't distribute them around the country. Now there's another election. They say there will be change, but there won't be any. There never is."

The impact on children and moms from the breakdown of public health services was escalating. Doctors at the Quetzaltenango hospital said they were once again seeing cases of whooping cough and mumps, two diseases making a comeback in the absence of the vaccines. And they said resources to combat the illnesses had been slashed. Under the Zero Hunger Pact, "we've gotten nothing, except more malnourished kids," said Sonia Barrios, the head of the hospital's nutritional recuperation unit.

Dr. Jorge Gramajo, overall chief of the nutrition department, said the hospital's budget had been slashed by 80 percent, resulting in shortages of drugs and medical supplies. His nascent research into just what micronutrients were missing from the Guatemalan diet and what was holding back children's growth—he suspected it was a lack of zinc, iron, and vitamin D, in particular—was threatened by meager funding. He blamed the ongoing presidential election campaign, which had all the candidates reaching into the trough for public money. The first place to be raided—it happened every four years, he said—was the federal health budget. Also, the outgoing government—the one celebrated for its commitment to the 1,000 days—was embroiled in a scandal of bribery, fraud, and pillaging of government coffers that left far less money for public services, especially health care. It had gotten so bad that the public hospital in Quetzaltenango—the place people came when they couldn't afford private care—was now having to charge patients for medical materials and services that had previously been offered for free, and patients were refusing treatment because they couldn't pay. Dr. Gramajo pointed to a recurring tragedy: parents of children with hydrocephalus, an abnormal accumulation of cerebrospinal fluid in the brain, were being asked to pay for both the draining tubes and the surgical procedure to insert them.

A treatment once performed at minimal expense to the parents could now cost them upward of $500. Dr. Gramajo said the lack of funding forced parents to choose between purchasing the tubing and letting their children die.

"I've heard parents say they have other kids at home and they wouldn't be able to feed them if they paid for the procedure. They say it is cheaper to bury their child." His face twisted with anger. "People here in the highlands work for maybe $150 a month, and yet in Guatemala City they take more for themselves. This makes you furious. You want to take them by the neck . . . "

The Zero Hunger Pact, so hailed around the world, held up as a model for the 1,000 days, was being strangled by negligence, inefficiency, and corruption. Before Keytlin's second birthday, both Guatemala's president and vice president, who had promised to do so much for the children of Guatemala in the glossy Zero Hunger magazine, would be forced to resign under corruption charges.

Griselda's daughter, Sucely, was one of the children caught up in the disintegration of the health-care system. For more than a year, Griselda and Sucely had ridden the bus regularly to the Quetzaltenango hospital seeking treatment for a clubfoot. They tried physical therapy and corrective shoes, but nothing worked (the shoes didn't fit properly). Griselda was now told that Sucely needed surgery if she was ever to walk, but the hospital required the parents to cover some expenses. The family was struggling to scrape together the money. So, at eighteen months, Sucely was still crawling—over the floors and the soil where the chickens, goats, sheep, dogs, and horses roamed and pooped. If she was ever to rise above the filth, to conquer the parasites and debilitating bouts of diarrhea, she needed to stand and walk.

IN CHICAGO, PUBLIC services were also coming under budget pressure. But Jessica and Quintana were taking full advantage of one program that was a key element of the Healthy Chicago initiative and that was becoming more popular in the city: home visits with new moms and their children. During home visits, child development specialists affiliated with social service agencies in the city showed parents how to turn everyday activities into opportunities to speak to their children, expand their vocabularies, and develop their brains. The home visits featured singing, reading, and playing—activities I rarely observed in the homes in Uganda, India, and Guatemala. In those homes, there were few, if any, books or toys—though the children were often in the presence of other kids their age or older.

"What's the first thing we do?" Celeste Bowen asked as she walked into Quintana's split-level rowhouse, a new section of public housing stretching along railroad tracks. Celeste, from Ounce of Prevention's Healthy Parents and Babies home visitation team, stopped by once a week.

"We wash our hands," Quintana answered. So she and ShaLawn were off to the bathroom, singing, "Wash, wash, wash, we wash our hands," to the tune of the Beach Boys' "Barbara Ann." They scrubbed under a faucet, using plenty of soap, then returned to the living room singing, "Shake it off," like Taylor Swift.

The singing continued. "Time for the 'Hello' song," Celeste cheerily announced. Together, they all sang: "Hello, hello, hello and how are you? I'm fine, I'm fine, and I hope that you are, too. Shake hands, shake hands, with the one that's next to you. Shake hands, shake hands, and say 'How do you do?'" ShaLawn shook hands with her mother and Celeste. Then she climbed up on the sofa.

"This is painting day," Celeste said. The night before, in preparation, she had made orange and purple paint by mixing water and flour and food coloring. Now she spread out drawing paper on the wooden floor of Quintana's living room and the three of them commenced finger painting. ShaLawn quickly was doing circles and squiggles and handprints.

"All babies like making a mess," Celeste said.

Quintana admired the progress of her daughter, who had been born so small. "Celeste reminds me that I am ShaLawn's first teacher," Quintana told me. "It's really important that we have this time to play and sing. Otherwise, it can slip." Quintana was expecting her third child. An ultrasound indicated this one would be a boy, whom she would name Maurice. ShaLawn and her older brother, Alex, often played together; he liked reading to her, especially Dr. Seuss books. Quintana believed ShaLawn was helped by trying to keep up with Alex; she had been quick to crawl and then walk and climb stairs. Now Quintana envisioned

ShaLawn similarly helping her younger brother. By eighteen months, ShaLawn would be beginning to speak in full sentences. "You're a bright girl," Quintana whispered in her ear as the painting continued. "I know," ShaLawn said.

Jessica also cherished her weekly home visits, in her case with Lorena Sanchez of Metropolitan Family Services. Jessica had graduated from high school in a traditional pomp and circumstance ceremony. "I did it!" she triumphantly proclaimed to her family afterward, as she clutched both her diploma and Alitzel. Though she was still committed to going to college, Jessica had decided to wait a semester before enrolling. She wanted to spend time with her daughter and just be a mom unencumbered by a student's schedule. And it would give her and Marco a chance to save up some money for school.

Lorena's visits provided structure and purpose to the time Jessica spent playing with Alitzel. The living room was full of children's books, simple musical instruments, like a toy piano, and balls and dolls. Lorena stressed the importance of conversation during playtime, the "serve and return" rhythm of any dialogue that stimulated the brain.

"It's important to work on communication skills, repeat words, develop socialization skills," Lorena explained to Jessica. Alitzel was often a moving target as she dashed between the living room and kitchen. She was supremely curious; she had discovered how to turn on Jessica's iPad and activate the apps for kids' television shows. Alitzel turned the pages of the alphabet book, eager to learn what comes after A, what comes after B.

Lorena opened her bag and out spilled a set of plastic farm animals: a pig, a cow, a lamb, a horse. "Cow says moooo. Which one is the cow?" Lorena asked.

Alitzel picked up the cow and repeated "Moooo."

"Pig says oink. Which one is the pig?"

"Oink, oink," repeated Alitzel as she reached for the pig.

Lorena, Jessica, and Alitzel read an Elmo book. "How many stars twinkle in the sky? Elmo counts five. 1, 2, 3, 4, 5!"

Lorena also continued to talk with Jessica about good nutrition for herself and Alitzel. "Do you think she's too skinny?" Jessica asked. "She's perfectly fine," Lorena said. "We always think chubby babies are healthier babies, but no, that's not the case. As long as they're eating from all basic food groups."

The home visits were also a time to assess development skills. Over time, Jessica and Lorena noticed that Alitzel had a lazy eye—the left eye wasn't focusing all the time. Lorena helped set up an eye examination, and Ali was fitted with glasses in hopes of an early correction. Lorena also noticed that while Alitzel's vocabulary was growing, and she clearly understood conversation, her verbal responses were inconsistent. So she recommended that Jessica take advantage of early intervention speech therapy, a service offered by several social work agencies in the city. Jessica was taken aback, for she and Ali had long been reading together, practicing the alphabet, singing songs. And Marco, too, was active with reading and singing. But then Jessica thought perhaps Alitzel could interact better with others—she had always attributed any reticence to shyness, and the extra attention at therapy might help her overcome it. Jessica had enjoyed her experiences with the doula and home visitation programs and found them to be invaluable in guiding her through the 1,000 days, so she was open to trying another service that could benefit her daughter. Perhaps it would help prepare Alitzel for school. Jessica believed it would also be a good learning experience for her. She was now thinking of a career as a social worker. Every day she was gaining experience from her own life; she had become a big believer in the importance of early intervention.

EIGHT MILES EAST across the South Side, in an ivy-covered oasis of gothic architecture and higher learning, Dr. Dana Suskind was putting the finishing touches on a pilot project demonstrating the importance of early language in building a child's brain. Dr. Suskind is a professor of surgery and pediatrics at the University of Chicago Medicine and a leading specialist in cochlear implantation. While she gave her young patients the ability to hear, she found that their ability to achieve optimally later in life depended on their early language environment—the quantity and quality of vocabulary the child heard in the home. It was this connection between the ability to hear and the power of language in childhood brain development that had led her to establish an initiative called Thirty

Million Words. Her work built upon a milestone study conducted twenty years earlier by child development researchers Betty Hart and Todd Risley, who found that some children heard 30 million fewer words by their fourth birthdays than others. Their research revealed that the children who heard more words were better prepared when they entered school. When followed into the third grade, these children were found to have bigger vocabularies, to be stronger readers, and to perform better on tests. This disparity in learning has been called "the achievement gap."

While the Hart and Risley study found that children in lower socioeconomic homes generally heard far less language than children in wealthier homes, they also discovered that demographics didn't have to be a limiting factor. A healthy language environment—the quantity of words, the types of words, and how they are spoken to a child—could overcome income and social inequalities. In her Thirty Million Words initiative, Dr. Suskind has set out to convince parents and caregivers, whether rich or poor, that they have the ability with their language to help build their child's brain. Her mission, as a daughter of a nutritionist, is to popularize the power of parent talk and the notion that words are nutrients for the brain.

"It all comes down to words," she told me one spring day in her office. "We can all talk to our kids. It doesn't cost anything."

While this may seem like another obvious piece of advice for the 1,000 days—like eating your vegetables and washing your hands—Dr. Suskind has found that quality talking in homes today is as lacking as balanced diets and good hygiene. So her Thirty Million Words team produced a short video that combines science, animation, and real footage of parent-child interactions to explain the importance of creating a healthy language environment. It centers on three Ts: Tune In, Talk More, Take Turns. Dr. Suskind hopes that the video, initially tested in two Chicago hospitals, will become part of newborn hearing screenings; it would be shown to all parents at the same time their babies undergo an initial hearing test shortly after birth. This is some of the advice parents will hear:

When people think about hearing, they think about the ears, but hearing is all about the brain. It's the brain that hears. The ears just let in sound. For your baby to learn, her brain must be exposed to language.

Some people think a child's intelligence is all about their genes, how much education their parents have, or what their parents' job is. What it really comes down to is how and how much their parents talk and interact with them.

Every word you say strengthens your baby's brain. Every snuggle you share strengthens his brain. Every diaper you change strengthens his brain. Just by talking, just by caring, just by responding, you build your baby's brain. Your baby will use these same connections to think and talk for the rest of his life.

Tune In: Respond to everything your baby communicates. Some parents worry about responding immediately every time she cries. There's no such thing as responding too quickly or too often to your newborn. When your baby cries, all she knows is she feels stress. When you tune in and respond right away, her stress is replaced with feelings of comfort. This creates connections in her brain and creates a special bond between the two of you. The baby is better able to learn, trust, make friends later in life.

Talk More: Think of your baby's brain as a piggy bank. Every word you say is another coin in his bank. The more you talk, the richer her brain gets. The more you put in now, the richer he'll be later. Your day is full of opportunities to talk more if you talk about what you're do-ing as you do it. Don't just change your baby's diaper, don't just wipe the baby's face, don't just do it, talk your baby through it.

Take Turns: Have a conversation. Start with good old-fashioned cuddling. When your baby makes eye contact, it's his way of taking a turn. When you meet his gaze, you're responding. This back-and-forth eye contact is building your baby's brain, just like a real conversation.

Babies aren't born smart. They're made smart. They're made smart by their parents.

PARENTS AS AGENTS of change: That was Vishwajeet Kumar's core mes-sage in the efforts of the Community Empowerment Lab to reduce in-fant mortality in Shivgarh, India. He had been successful on that front, but a nagging doubt hovered over his work: more children were surviving, yes, but were they thriving?

To answer that question, he set up a program, supported by the Saving Brains project of Grand Challenges Canada, to test the children born during the first years of the Community Empowerment Lab interventions. They were now seven to nine years old. Vishwajeet refurbished the second floor of an old palace in Shivgarh. The Community Empowerment Lab, known in the villages as Saksham (Empowerment), constructed little booths for the intelligence testing as well as a lab to measure nutritional status through blood testing. Those administering the intelligence tests used electronic notebooks programmed with standardized tests for memory, language, problem solving, and mental dexterity. Many times I saw the children sitting in bamboo chairs in a foyer while waiting to be tested. Some of them looked to be just four or five years old. But Community Empowerment Lab staff assured me that they were indeed eight or nine.

One of the children they tested was Meenu, Kiran's sister-in-law, who had been born more than a month premature. She had survived, her mother believed, thanks to the kangaroo-care techniques that Saksham had introduced. Meenu was ten years old when I met her, and in third grade in Rampur Khas. She was small, barely four feet tall, with short, cropped hair and an eager smile. She remembered hopping on one leg for the testers, giving a blood sample, having her eyes tested, and playing computer games with shapes and numbers. She got nervous when she was told one game was a race against time—so nervous, she said, that she lost her place midway through the exam. When the testing was over, Meenu was told she was slow in the timed test and that she needed glasses. Her eyes watered as she followed images on the iPad. The testers also said she was too thin.

Meenu told me she didn't much like the tests and felt she didn't do well. She said she preferred learning songs and poems. To prove it, she stood straight, as if at attention, and recited her favorite poem in Hindi:

> Queen of birds, queen of birds,
> You wake up early in the morning,
> Nobody knows what you sing.

Do you also go to study?
Or to work?
You return before evening
Bringing seeds for your children.
You sing choo-choo.

After rigorously testing hundreds of children, the Saksham team found no appreciable improvement in the intelligence of the sample group—those whose mothers had participated in their program—compared to children elsewhere. As Grand Challenges reported:

> No correlation was found between the healthy birth intervention and child development metrics at seven to nine years. Authors suggest benefits of the intervention that successfully reduced neonatal mortality were lost over time due to high prevalence of multiple risk factors. There was no test difference in general intelligences between village clusters, suggesting that while the intervention successfully reduced deaths at birth by altering the environment within the home, overall improvement in human capital may be more dependent on the overall state of development and infrastructure of the community level.

In other words, saving lives was well and good, but there is no improvement in the quality of those lives if the children grow up in communities of hunger and poor sanitation with little access to health care and education and lack parental stimulation.

When the findings were in, Vishwajeet had an epiphany.

"For almost ten years of my life, I did only survival because I was convinced that saving lives was most important. Then when we started looking at the neural development of the children, I discovered a huge opportunity was lost," he told me. "What was I doing? We were preoccupied with children surviving. I didn't layer in the thriving part. To see nine-year-old children who couldn't solve simple problems, or write the alphabet in Hindi, it comes as a bolt."

A new task commanded his attention. Vishwajeet would call it One Thousand Dreams—a combination of child survival work and the promotion of neural development. He needed to go back to his original inspiration as a doctor and take advantage of the potential to effect change at the source of the problem. The Community Empowerment Lab would now examine the impact of caste and gender discrimination, of societal violence, and of hygiene and sanitation on malnutrition and child development. "Every child has a right to dream!" Vishwajeet told me, nearly leaping out of his chair. "Our job as scientists is to bring information to their doorstep that will allow them to reach their potential."

In One Thousand Dreams, surviving would just be a milestone. Thriving would be the goal.

chapter fourteen

TURNING TWO

O N THE DAY OF HIS SECOND BIRTHDAY, RODGERS WAS UP EARLY with his mother. Under the rising sun, they walked to the family's fields together, and by 7:30 they were digging in the dirt. Esther was on her knees, forming orange sweet-potato mounds. Rodgers was at her side, holding the vines.

It had rained overnight, a good omen for a birthday. Rodgers would be celebrated, at least on this day, as the birthday boy who brought rain and relief to a drought that had strangled many of the crops. As they picked their way along the narrow pathways between the fields, Esther and Rodgers were greeted by many of their neighbors, smallholder farmers all, who were also out early to take advantage of the moisture and work the soil.

Esther wore the same orange HarvestPlus shirt she had been wearing when we had first met, though now the orange was fading. Rodgers wore a teal and purple sweater with the buzzing hornet logo of the Charlotte Hornets National Basketball Association team, an incongruous look that had come from the United States in a bundle of used clothing. Esther, attracted to the logo, had bought the sweater in a local outdoor market.

There would be no grand birthday party; even without the rain, Esther hadn't been planning one. They couldn't afford it, and it wasn't really a tradition in rural Uganda; birthdays came and went without much notice. But Esther and Tonny were thankful that their son was healthy and growing—he was close to thirty-five inches tall, which was on track with the international growth norm for a two-year-old boy. Esther was buoyed all day in the field with the thought that Rodgers had beaten the odds, surviving malaria and diarrhea and avoiding stunting.

ARON AND APIO were thriving as well. Aron, who had given his mother, Brenda, such a fright when he had come down with dysentery, was thirty-four inches tall on his second birthday. And Apio, born so small but surviving when her sister did not, reached thirty-two inches as her second birthday neared. (Anything shorter than thirty inches at two years of age would be in the stunted category.) The girls in Chicago were similarly robust. Alitzel was thirty-six inches on her second birthday, and ShaLawn was already close to thirty-two inches at eighteen months.

The children were generally shorter in India and Guatemala, where the mix of malnutrition and bad water and sanitation was the most virulent. In India, Anshika and Sunny were each a shade under thirty inches as they turned two, and cousins Priyanshi and Adarsh were each thirty-one inches as they approached that age. In Guatemala, Keytlin and Sucely were each about twenty-nine inches, José was thirty, and Jorge, the tallest, stood at over thirty-three inches.

The tape measure indicated that Keytlin was stunted physically, but she seemed more advanced than the others in her walking, talking, and sociability. At a gathering with nutritionist Scarlet and other families in the Primeros Pasos program, Keytlin was climbing steps and running in the yard more nimbly than any of the other children. She was pestering the other children to play with her, and she was speaking far more than them. She asked her mother, Dianet, when she could go to school. Dianet had a supply of books and pencils and crayons around the house. Now she told Keytlin, "You have to wait until you are six. Then you will have even more books and pencils." Later, Keytlin asked for a birthday cake. "Chocolate," she insisted.

I asked Dr. Dana Suskind at the University of Chicago Medicine about this paradox of physical stunting and cognitive acuity in the first 1,000 days of life. Dr. Suskind, who stands just a few inches taller than five feet herself, said that while being short at two years of age could reflect stunted development and indicate that something had interfered with growth in the 1,000 days, it didn't necessarily dictate that a child would also be cognitively stunted (although all too often they were). Keytlin may have been lacking the nutrients necessary for physical growth, but not for mental development; the repeated diarrhea may have taken a great physical toll. And the language environment— the nutrients of words—may have been better for Keytlin than for the other children; books, rare in most other homes in the valley, were relatively plentiful in her home. The extent of mental stunting in the 1,000 days would only become evident later, beginning with school performance. Dr. Suskind concurred with many other development specialists that the long-term toll of physical stunting on education and future job performance was generally less debilitating than the impact of cognitive stunting.

Keytlin and her mother were still in the Palajunoj Valley as her second birthday neared. Her father had a premonition that something bad would happen should he attempt to migrate to the United States again, so for the moment he was staying put. Beyond the cake requested by Keytlin, and a meal of favorite foods, including chicken, rice, and tamalitos, Dianet said there wouldn't be much of a party. They didn't have the money to do anything special.

Griselda hung a Happy Birthday banner for Sucely in their home, but the celebration was also muted. The day after Sucely's birthday, Griselda was getting her daughter ready to finally have surgery on her clubfoot. The ability to walk unencumbered would be the best present of all.

IN PURE BAISHAN, India, Rajender came home early from his morning shift of work to be with Anshika on her second birthday. No party was planned; they couldn't afford that. Rajender's presence would be his present. "I miss my girls so much when I'm at work," he told me. "But I must work for them."

He was working twelve hours a day carrying coal to a brickmaking kiln. It was a horrible, dangerous job; a task from hell. With temperatures soaring past 100 degrees every day, the sun of a clear sky beating down, heat rising from the barren ground, it was like he was firing up the devil's furnace. His assignment was to shovel coal shards into two metal baskets hanging from opposite ends of a wooden yoke. Once the baskets were full, he squatted deeply and lifted the yoke onto his shoulders. Slowly straightening like a weightlifter—the burden surpassed one hundred pounds—Rajender scrambled up an incline to a plateau topped with a smokestack. Continuing his momentum, he jogged fifty yards to the smokestack, dropped the yoke, and emptied each basket into a bin. He then picked up the yoke, turned, and hustled back down the incline and over to the coal pile again. All day long, he performed this agonizing shuttle. His lungs filled with black coal dust and the dry brown dust of the plateau. For all this, he was paid about $2 a day.

Rajender wore thin sandals, ragged pants, and a tattered black T-shirt with a stylized drawing of a guy skateboarding between skyscrapers. It said, in English: "I prefer dangerous freedom over peaceful slavery." He had bought it when he worked in Delhi. Rajender didn't understand the words, or the irony. He was indeed a slave to his growing family's well-being. That much he did know.

"I'll do what I have to do. You can see how hard I work; there is no way out of that," Rajender told me as he again loaded up his yoke at the kiln. "It's difficult, because I now have seven with my wife to support." He had a nasty, hacking cough. He spoke morosely, fatefully. "As long as I am alive, I will take care of them. When I die, my responsibility will be over. But before then, I must do what I can."

He worried about his girls' future. "Since I don't have much money to provide education, I don't have big ambitions. I'd like to give each of my daughters a sewing machine, so they can work in the clothes business. They must be prepared. If anything happens to me, they'll have to provide for themselves."

Back home after the morning shift, Rajender washed up and changed
into clean clothes. Then he joined his family on the veranda. His daughters gathered around him. Shyamkali held the littlest one. Rajender
pulled Anshika in tight for a birthday hug. She wore her finest dress,
emerald green with silver and purple embroidery. Shyamkali had rubbed
coal around Anshika's eyes, making them appear bigger and darker.

"You can see she is healthy, sturdy," her father said. What he couldn't
see, for he had no perspective beyond his community, was that she was
small for her age by international standards. Here, she didn't look out
of proportion at all; she looked to be of normal size. Rajender himself
was barely over five feet tall. Anshika's next oldest sister, seven-year-
old Shivani, hadn't yet reached three feet. Ten-year-old Tulsi was just
past four feet. Pooja, the oldest at fourteen, was an inch taller than her
mother, so that was progress.

It was a birthday, so Rajender made jokes. He teased his girls, imagin-
ing their wedding days. There were six in the future, which meant there
were six dowries to be paid. "I will place an upper limit on the dowry
that I can pay, so the boys will have to agree if they want to marry my
girls," he said playfully. "Boys around here have trouble finding a mate,
there are more boys than girls. They marry even if the woman is fee-
ble." He winked at his daughters. "But my girls are healthy, and strong.
I hope they will be educated. And they are beautiful. The boys, they
will agree."

As Anshika turned two, so did the Y Chromosome Campaign, which
had been launched on the day of her birth by Poonam Muttreja of India's
Population Fund. The centerpiece of the campaign was the production
of a TV and radio drama called *I, a Woman, Can Achieve Anything*. It
featured the life of a young woman doctor in Mumbai; the scripts were
written to influence social norms and behaviors on sex-selection, child
marriage, the age of first pregnancy, spacing between pregnancies, quality
of health care, domestic violence, nutrition, mental health, and hygiene.
The weekly episodes were followed by call-in shows and We Can Do
Anything discussions. Visions of great achievements took flight in the
viewers and listeners.

After one episode, a high school girl named Pragya called in from Bihar,
a state bordering Uttar Pradesh, and one equally poor and malnourished.

She was caught up in the empowering spirit of the show. "I am a daughter of this nation and am proud of this nation," she said. "I promise that I will be president of the country one day. And when I am president, I will ensure that no girl in this country is victimized or oppressed."

THE ONLY BIG birthday celebration was in Chicago. On the day she turned two, Alitzel was baking cupcakes with her mother. The next day, the cupcakes were front and center on a table in the banquet hall of a Mexican seafood restaurant. Behind the table was a montage of Ariel, the little mermaid from the Disney movie, and highlights celebrating Alitzel: "I like dolls, I like to run, I am outgoing, I am very silly. Love to read with Mommy. I love drawing. Favorite show: Mother Goose Club, Elmo and Mickey. Favorite movie: Tinkerbell, Lilo and Stitch, Smurfs. ABCs and Twinkle Twinkle Little Star are my favorite songs."

The birthday girl was wearing a green and blue tutu with a matching green bow in her black hair. She was also wearing her new glasses: sleek black frames with a red strap in the back to hold them in place. "She likes them," Jessica said.

It was a big family gathering, with plenty of food: chicken, rice, green salad, assorted vegetables, pizza, chips, and a big cake. There were grandparents, uncles, aunts, cousins, friends. For Jessica and Marco, it was a celebration of both their daughter's birthday and the 1,000 days that preceded it.

"It's been a roller coaster, from being a student to mom and back again every day. I honestly can't believe that we actually did it," Jessica told me. "Alitzel is two, I went to school and graduated with honors, and came home to being a mom. I'm proud of myself for what I have accomplished, being a young mom and having her."

She watched Alitzel playing with her cousins. "I think back to those countless nights I was awake doing my homework, and doing all my work before the deadlines, to not leave anything behind or turn in anything late. That pushed me when I saw her sleep and I was up almost to two in the morning doing my homework. That was my motivation."

Now Alitzel is her motivation to resume her studies: Jessica planned to enroll at St. Augustine College in Chicago and begin working toward a four-year degree in social work. She sees herself in her daughter. "Al-itzel likes to really explore. She's really independent. She likes to do everything herself." Her speech would come along, Jessica believed. She could already see the emergence of some of the dream characteristics she spelled out in her diary back when she was pregnant: amenable, lustrous, inspirational, zany, loving.

At the end of her 1,000 days, Jessica's vision for her daughter hadn't wavered. "I see her having a great future."

EPILOGUE

A S THE CHILDREN TURNED TWO IN THE SUMMER AND FALL OF 2015, Scaling Up Nutrition and the 1,000 Days movement turned five. Of the fifty-five countries that had joined SUN, twenty of them, including Uganda, were implementing national nutrition plans with specific budgets, and seventeen were succeeding in reducing stunting at a 2 percent annual rate. Civil society alliances, involving about 2,000 organizations, had formed in thirty-three countries. Donor spending commitments on nutrition as a percentage of development aid increased to 4 percent from 1 percent.

But for SUN, as for most of the families, celebration was muted by the knowledge that more challenges and perilous years loomed on the horizon. SUN and the 1,000 Days movement set aside any accolades and focused on achieving a roster of ambitious global nutrition targets set by the World Health Assembly for 2025: reduce the number of stunted children under five by 40 percent; reduce low birth weight by 30 percent; increase breastfeeding in the first six months to at least 50 percent; reduce anemia in women of reproductive age by 50 percent; and hold the line on childhood overweight and obesity.

To achieve success on these grand global goals, the development community has the experiences of the women and children during their 1,000-day journeys as a guide. We have seen, most crucially, that for children truly to thrive they need simultaneous advances across multiple development fronts. While these families live in communities facing myriad challenges every day, the world's development programmers and their funders have for decades mostly cloistered themselves in silos where efforts were concentrated on single issues. Successes have been achieved over the years, yes. But every mother and father and mother-in-law we encountered knew both instinctively and explicitly that it's not just about better nutrition or cleaner water or a new toilet or a bed net or breakthrough vaccines alone. It's about how they all join up together, at the same time, to promote better child development as a whole.

Brenda wept when Aron's improved nutrition through the new crops was undermined by a few swallows of bad water. Maria Estella despaired that her heightened knowledge of how to care for Jorge could be eroded by rising prices and the ongoing neglect of her government. Shyamkali saw her ability to provide for her girls compromised by cultural pressures and fundamental inequalities in her home and society. Jessica worried about raising Alitzel in the shadow of random violence.

With their new focus on the 1,000 days, the theoreticians and practitioners are catching up with the moms. As the children of our narrative were turning two, the nations of the world assembled in New York to replace the expiring Millennium Development Goals, which largely aimed at achieving a series of single-issue wins, with the Sustainable Development Goals (SDGs), which promote a more holistic view of development. The seventeen SDGs—among them: eradicate poverty, end hunger, improve nutrition, provide clean water and sanitation for all, ensure healthy lives and lifelong learning, achieve gender equality—are linked with a recognition that success in achieving one of them depends on the success of achieving them all. Optimal early childhood development is the overarching target. "The Sustainable Development Goals," UN Secretary-General Ban Ki-moon said at the launch in September 2015, "recognize that early childhood development can help drive the transformation we hope to achieve over the next 15 years." UNICEF added, "These new SDGs recognize that children are agents of change when they channel their infinite potential to create a better world."

The secretary-general also introduced a new Global Strategy for the UN's Every Woman Every Child initiative under the slogan "Survive, Thrive, Transform." The initial focus on ending preventable deaths of mothers and infants is now seen as just a starting point in fostering environments where moms and children can thrive. The new strategy, Ban Ki-moon proclaimed, "aims to transform societies so that women, children and adolescents everywhere can realize their rights to the highest attainable standards of health and well-being. This, in turn, will deliver enormous social, demographic and economic benefits."

At the same time, the Sackler Institute for Nutrition Science at the New York Academy of Sciences published a series of studies in 2015 that marshaled the scientific evidence. *Every Child's Potential: A Call to Action* outlines the impact of integrating effective interventions on nutrition and child development into one global effort: "Integration can simultaneously address multiple, related barriers to children's development, including poor nutrition, impoverished family circumstances, parents' poor mental health, and lack of opportunities for early learning. Experiences show that combining efforts can result in a more efficient use of resources. Integration is an approach that helps us set priorities and focus health, education and other community services."

Where there has been progress, such integration has been key. In the series of *Global Nutrition Reports* released since 2014, Lawrence Haddad of the International Food Policy Research Institute noted a number of common, simultaneous successes that significantly reduced child stunting rates in Bangladesh, Tanzania, Brazil, and the Indian state of Maharashtra: broad economic growth, household poverty reduction, parental education, better sanitation coverage, access to improved health care throughout the 1,000 days, increased investment in nutrition, women's empowerment, and sustained government commitment. Brazil's accomplishments—sharp drops in extreme poverty, malnutrition, and infant mortality in just one generation—will be highlighted during the Rio Summer Olympics in 2016 and the accompanying Nutrition for Growth summit.

The potential of this multidimensional approach has been confirmed by the study in eastern Guatemala that began five decades ago and continues to produce insights into the importance of the 1,000 days. Aryeh Stein and Reynaldo Martorell of Emory University, two of the project's researchers, have noted that the initial nutrition intervention was crucial for improvements in child development, but that the steep drop in stunting and malnutrition over the years in the study villages was aided by a number of other improvements: the spread of electricity; a cleaner water supply; better sanitation, with running water to wash hands and flush toilets; and increased infrastructure investments that lifted the area's economy. That matrix of development still hasn't arrived in the country's neglected western highlands, where the child malnutrition rates remain over 70 percent.

The importance of integrated development for improving the first 1,000 days of life is also clear from recent innovations. In addition to the programs featured in these pages, two other projects stand out from my reporting: one called "Suaahara" (which means "Good Nutrition" in Nepali) in the Himalayan foothills of Nepal, implemented by the Nepalese government and local development agencies along with Save the Children, Helen Keller International, and the Johns Hopkins Bloomberg School of Public Health, Center for Communication Programs; and Resiliency Through Wealth, Agriculture and Nutrition in the Karamoja region of eastern Uganda, implemented by Concern Worldwide with the support of the United States Agency for International Development and nongovernmental organizations such as ACDI/VOCA and Welthungerhilfe. Both projects mobilize entire communities to improve child development and train mothers to lead the introduction of new practices on the multiple fronts of nutrition, agriculture, water, sanitation, hygiene, child care, and family planning.

A host of other efforts both large and small are taking place around the world. In Guatemala, young architect Alejandro Biguria has designed Casita de los Mil Días, the 1,000 Days House, which he hopes to see constructed in every village. The compact casitas would serve as centers for both health care and public education. There's a room for maternal and infant care, a handwashing station for sanitation training, scales and measuring boards for charting a baby's growth, an ecological stove that demonstrates how to contain the smoke from wood fires, solar panels on the roof, and open-space classrooms for lessons on nutrition and hygiene.

In Jamaica, the University of West Indies, supported by the Saving Brains project of Grand Challenges Canada, is developing its Reach Up Early Childhood Parenting program, an international web-based platform that provides access to Jamaica's home visitation program for the benefit of new moms and their infants. Governments and social service agencies in low-income countries could use the Jamaican model to train workers and implement their own parent-child stimulation and nurturing programs. In Chicago, Ounce of Prevention's Diana Rauner, who is also First Lady of Illinois, has been developing a "universal newborn support" program that would provide at least one home visit to every baby born in the state.

In India, a social enterprise called Digital Green is expanding its community video project beyond its original agriculture and nutrition themes to promote messages about the 1,000 days, especially on maternal and infant health behaviors. The videos feature villagers speaking in local dialects and are shown via simple projectors in community centers or classrooms. I attended one viewing in a village near Shivgarh, where the video was projected on a white plastic sheet hanging on a wall beneath a portrait of Mahatma Gandhi and posters of green vegetables.

Elsewhere in India, organizations like The Hunger Project and the Rajiv Gandhi Charitable Trust have been empowering women through self-help groups. The women come together to access financial resources, gain representation in local governing bodies, and demand participation in the government's food-distribution and health-care programs. One group I visited had gained control of the midday meal program at the local primary school after rising in protest over the quality of food served to their children.

Despite this escalating momentum, a certain disquiet hovered over the 1,000 days and SUN's five-year anniversary gatherings: Had the movement taken root? Could the momentum be maintained, or would it be another development fad? Sustained success, SUN officials determined, now depends on two critical issues: firm, long-term government commitments, and growing financial investment in nutrition and the multi-front approach.

As we have seen in the four countries on our journey, government commitments can be fickle. In some places, progress is being made, while in others, setbacks and obstacles still hinder the work that could be done:

- Uganda has been aggressively implementing its nutrition action plan, placing optimal child development at the center of its drive to become a middle-income country in coming decades. With the help of a World Bank grant, the government is moving to take the orange sweet potatoes and high-iron beans, as well as any other biofortified crops introduced in Africa, to all districts of the country.

- In Chicago, the mayor has assembled representatives from throughout city departments and local communities to develop Healthy Chicago 2.0, a four-year plan to eliminate health inequities in the city, beginning with early child development, so all residents can "attain their potential." It focuses on what the mayor called "opportunity deserts" and calls for action on multiple fronts at the same time: access to health care and human services; chronic disease prevention and control; community development; education; maternal, infant, child, and adolescent health; mental health and substance use; violence and injury prevention. Many of the goals aim for a successful 1,000 days: expanding home visitation and early intervention programs, ensuring access to prenatal care, promoting breastfeeding for the first six months. Although there still were no certified Baby-Friendly Initiative hospitals in the city as this book neared publication, a few, including Mercy, where Quintana gave birth, were closing in on certification. On a national scale, the SNAP and WIC programs, essential for a successful 1,000 days in so many families, were under renewed threat from federal budget cuts. To stave off a decrease in funding, some program advocates argued for greater nutritional benefits and education; SNAP and WIC needed to be seen as "nutrition safety net" programs that went beyond aid to individuals and families by safeguarding the health and security of the entire nation.

- India celebrated its space mission for reaching the orbit of Mars in less than one year, but after more than two years of delays and political bickering, the much-ballyhooed National Food Security Act had yet to take off. The government "is bleeding it with a thousand cuts, both fiscal and otherwise," wrote Biraj Patnaik, the principal adviser to the commissioners of the Supreme Court on the right to food law. Writing in India's *The Hindu*, a daily newspaper, he noted that the states have delayed identifying families who would be covered under the act and thereby eligible to receive more monthly food rations at heavily subsidized prices; instead, the participation rolls in some places were shrinking. Also, the new national budget slashed the funding of some of the key programs under the act: the Integrated Child Development Services program suffered a 50 percent cut, while the midday meal budget was whacked by about one-third. The Shivgarh families had yet to receive any of the promised benefits.

- In Guatemala, the government that had promised to deliver the country from its wretched malnutrition was in ruins—and some leaders were even in jail. A former television comedian who said nothing about continuing the Zero Hunger Pact was elected president in 2015. If the fight against malnutrition is to continue, it will be up to the powerful business community— once also so vocal in support of the pact—to man the ramparts. Architect Alejandro Biguria was counting on civil society to continue to press for action. He had been a leader of the Wake Up Guatemala campaign that initially sparked outrage at the country's malnutrition. Many of those same protesters returned to the streets clamoring for the corrupt government to resign. Now Alejandro believes that those voices are emboldened to continue to press for social reforms. "We have to push and make people understand we need to continue with the fight against malnutrition," he told me. "It's not just a political commitment but a moral commitment to the country as well. We have to invest in the 1,000 days. It's our future."

While donor investments in nutrition globally may have quadrupled over the past five years—billions were pledged from public and private sources at the first Nutrition for Growth global summit in 2013—SUN calculated that another quadrupling was needed to reach the World Health Assembly targets and optimize child development around the world. In June 2015, at the European Development Days conference in Brussels, the Bill & Melinda Gates Foundation announced that it would more than double its nutrition investments, spending $776 million on nutrition over the next six years to "help all women and children survive and thrive."

"Nutrition is an investment in our collective future, in the potential of individuals, communities and nations," Melinda Gates told the assembled leaders of Europe. She then urged them to elevate the health and nutrition of women and children to a top priority of their development spending. Their next chance to step up would come at the Rio Olympics nutrition summit.

The private sector was slowly beginning to step up investments in the 1,000 days as knowledge of the economic consequences of stunting spread; businesses rely on healthy and robust consumers, a condition that begins with a healthy 1,000 days. But the SUN business network was treading carefully with overtures to the private sector, for many of the companies that could most influence child development—food and beverage enterprises—were profiting greatly from the global advances of their snack foods and soda pop.

Above all, moving forward, those involved in SUN and the 1,000 Days movement knew they needed to expand the movement's hold on the world's conscience. Few made this connection better than Carolyn Miles, president and CEO of Save the Children USA. In Save the Children's *Surviving the First Day* report, she wrote:

Every night, millions of mothers around the world lean over their sleeping newborns and pray that they will be safe, happy and healthy. It's what we all want for our child. And it's certainly not too much to ask. When a child is placed into his mother's arms for the first time, that woman's life is changed forever. The moment is brief and precious. We must seize the opportunity to invest in this most basic, most enduring partnership—between a mother and her child—if we are to change forever the course of history.

As their 1,000 days came to an end, the moms of Shivgarh, Ongica, Chuicavioc, and Chicago looked upon their children and wondered how they would navigate the next years. Their dreams began in the 1,000 days but they had no end date. Seeing their children through school would be a challenge, as would feeding them with nutritious foods. Their toddlers would all too soon be teenagers. For the girls, the adolescent years would be particularly critical. Some in the SUN movement were looking to expand the time frame to better prepare adolescent girls for their 1,000-day journeys with their own children: Marc Van Ameringen, the executive director of the Global Alliance for Improved Nutrition, spoke of the "3,000 Days," including the years before conception. Uganda has begun distributing iron and folic-acid supplements to adolescent girls. Reducing the birthrate among teens is a key goal of Healthy Chicago 2.0. In India, more 1,000-day journeys commence each day than anywhere else, and many of them begin for the moms in adolescence. According to the Population Foundation of India and UNICEF, almost half of all Indian girls are married by the age of eighteen, and about one in every three are pregnant by the time they leave their teenage years.

In Shivgarh, as Shyamkali and Rajender gathered their six daughters on Anshika's second birthday, their wish—like that of parents all over the world—was that their children would all thrive. For as they grow, it will now be their challenge to finally break the generational cycle of malnutrition, stunting, and inequality.

ACKNOWLEDGMENTS

To all the families in India, Uganda, Guatemala, and Chicago featured in these pages, my supreme gratitude. These families—especially the moms—repeatedly and graciously welcomed me into their homes throughout the 1,000 days and good-naturedly endured my many, many questions. I hope their stories will be as inspiring to you as they have been to me.

A long journey through time and place such as this required a stout supply line of narrative sustenance, wisdom, and encouragement. Thank you to those who opened doors and gave me guidance on the road:

In India: Vishwajeet and Aarti Kumar, Bhoopesh Tripathi, and their colleagues at the Community Empowerment Lab in Shivgarh, and Purnima Menon, Hideko Piplani, Emily Bielecki, Swati Kapur, Digital Green, The Hunger Project, and the Rajiv Gandhi Charitable Trust.

In Uganda: Agnes Kabaikya, Simpson Biryabaho, Grace Akullu, Morris Ogwal, Solomon Okino, and their World Vision colleagues; Anna-Marie Ball, Sylvia Magezi, and the HarvestPlus team; and Mary O'Neill and Concern Worldwide.

In Guatemala: Brent Savoie, Jamie de Guzman Pet, Megan Peyton, Susy Menchu, Scarlet Samayoa, and their colleagues at Primeros Pasos; Carlos Cardenas and his team at Save the Children–Guatemala; Carolina Siu and Paul Melgar at the Institute of Nutrition of Central America and Panama; and Ted Fischer, Miguel Cuj, Henry Schmick, and Alejandro Biguria.

In Chicago: Diana Rauner, Tony Raden, Claire Dunham, Portia Kennel, Diana McClarien, Patricia Ceja Muhsen, Celeste Bowen, and their colleagues at the Ounce of Prevention Fund and Educare; Lorena Sanchez at Metropolitan Family Services; and Angel Gutierrez at Catholic Charities.

All along the way: The Pulitzer Center on Crisis Reporting, especially Jon and Peter Sawyer, Nathalie Applewhite, and Tom Hundley; the Bill & Melinda Gates Foundation, notably Shelly Sundberg; the John and Editha Kapoor Charitable Foundation; Kelly and Jim McShane; and other supporters of the Chicago Council on Global Affairs. Also Chicago Council colleagues present and past, including Ivo Daalder, Marshall Bouton, Lisa Moon, Louise Iverson, Sung Lee, CaSandra Carter, Meagan Keefe, Isabel DoCampo, Elizabeth Marquardt, Elisa Quinlan, Dawn Miller, Bob Cordes, Niamh King, Tria Raimundo, Natashur Brown, Marcus Glassman, Sara McElmurry, Carolyn Chelius, Rebecca Davidson, Andre Nickow, Kelsey Bailey, and Drew D'Alelio.

For the hours of conversation and stacks of reports and documents, many thanks to Lucy Sullivan, Adrianna Logalbo, Andrea Beegle, Jennifer Rigg, Mannik Sakayan, Yesenia Garcia, Rebecca Olson, Manuel Claros, Tom Arnold, Patrick Webb, Jeffrey Griffiths, Shibani Ghosh, Robert Black, John Hoddinott, Lawrence Haddad, Marie Ruel, Shawn Baker, Karlee Silver, Howdy Bouis, Yassir Islam, Asma Lateef, Marc Van Ameringen, Bonnie McClafferty, Greg Garrett, Florencia Vasta, Klaus Kraemer, John Oldfield, Jordan Teague, Sangita Vyas, Harsh Mander, Alvaro Castillo, Juan Carlos Paiz, Reynaldo Martorell, Aryeh Stein, Dara Burke, Winfred Ongom, Dana Suskind, Mari Gallagher, Naideen Galek, Carolyn Miles, Eileen Burke, Holly Frew, Laura Blank, Nabeeha Kazi, Andrea Jimenez, Tanuja Rastogi, Kate Maehr, Bob Dolgan, John Coonrad, Scott Bleggi, Allan Jury, Todd Post, Rebecca Middleton, Dan Silverstein, and David Lambert.

This is my third collaboration with PublicAffairs in telling the story of hunger in the twenty-first century. My abiding thanks to publisher Clive Priddle, my editor Lisa Kaufman and her keen narrative vision, managing editor Melissa Raymond, production editor Shena Redmond, copyeditor Katherine Streckfus, marketing director Lindsay Fradkoff, and publicity manager Chris Juby. Laurie Liss, my agent, encouraged the storytelling and the global journey. And Charles and Alex Karelis provided a desk and a collegial redoubt at the Writers Room DC.

From beginning to end, this has been a family project: My wife, Anne, with me every step of the way, has been my trusty photographer, my first reader, and my better eyes and ears on the reporting trail; our daughter, Aishling, organized my research at the outset and introduced me to Primeros Pasos through her work at GlobeMed; and our son, Brian, raised my storytelling game for the new media landscape. For all this, and much more, thank you.

NOTE ON SOURCES

THE NARRATIVES OF the mothers and children and their families, and those working with them, are from my own reporting. The passages on the science of the 1,000 days and the medical, economic, and social impacts are based on my interviews with sources named in the text and from the following resources:

REPORTS AND ARTICLES

Alive & Thrive: FHI 360: Elizabeth Prado and Kathryn Dewey, *Insight: Nutrition and Brain Development in Early Life*, 2012.

American Society of Tropical Medicine and Hygiene: Francis M. Ngure et al., "Formative Research on Hygiene Behaviors and Geophagy Among Infants and Young Children and Implications of Exposure to Fecal Bacteria," *American Journal of Tropical Medicine and Hygiene* 89, no. 4 (2013): 709–716.

Barker, David: "The Barker Theory: New Insights into Ending Chronic Disease," 2006.

Bread for the World: *2016 Hunger Report. The Nourishing Effect: Ending Hunger, Improving Health, Reducing Inequality.*

Center for Social Inclusion: *Removing Barriers to Breastfeeding: A Structural Race Analysis of First Food,* 2015.

The Chicago Council on Global Affairs: *Healthy Food for a Healthy World: Leveraging Agriculture and Food to Improve Global Nutrition,* 2015; *Feeding an Urban World: A Call to Action,* 2013.

Chicago Tribune: Crime in Chicagoland, "Chicago Homicides," http://crime.chicagotribune.com/chicago/homicides.

City of Chicago: *A Recipe for Healthy Places: Addressing the Intersection of Food and Obesity in Chicago,* 2013.

Copenhagen Consensus Center: Copenhagen Consensus papers, 2004, 2008, 2012; John F. Hoddinott, Mark W. Rosegrant, and Maximo Torero, "Investments to Reduce Hunger and Undernutrition," Challenge Paper on Hunger and Malnutrition, 2012.

Global Alliance for Improved Nutrition: *Cultivating Nutritious Food Systems,* 2014; *Fortifying Our Future,* 2015.

Government of Guatemala: *El Plan Del Pacto Hambre Cero,* 2012.

Government of Uganda and UNICEF: *Situation Analysis of Children in Uganda,* 2015.

Government of Uttar Pradesh, India: *State Nutrition Mission: Vision,* 2014.

Institute of Nutrition of Central America and Panama: Manuel Ramirez-Zea, Paul Melgar, and Juan A. Rivera, "INCAP Oriente Longitudinal Study: 40 Years of History and Legacy," *Journal of Nutrition* 140, no. 2 (2010): 397–401, and various other reports on the INCAP Longitudinal Study.

International Food Policy Research Institute: *2013 Global Food Policy Report; Global Nutrition Report 2014; Global Nutrition Report 2015.*

The Lancet: Every Newborn series, 2014; Maternal and Child Nutrition series, 2013; Maternal and Child Undernutrition series, 2008.

Mari Gallagher Research and Consulting Group: *Examining the Impact of Food Deserts on Public Health in Chicago,* 2006.

McKinsey Global Institute: *Overcoming Obesity: An Initial Economic Analysis,* 2014.

Nestlé Nutrition Institute: Feeding Infants and Toddlers Study (FITS), 2008; J. M. Saavedra, D. Deming, A. Dattilo, and K. Reidy, "Lessons from the Feeding Infants and Toddlers Study in North America: What Children Eat, and Implications for Obesity Prevention, *Annals of Nutrition and Metabolism* 62, Supplement 3 (2013): 27–36.

ONE Campaign: "Poverty Is Sexist: Why Girls and Women Must Be at the Heart of the Fight to End Extreme Poverty," 2015.

Research Institute for Compassionate Economics: *Sanitation Quality, Use, Access and Trends (SQUAT)*, Research Brief, 2014–2015.

The Sackler Institute for Nutrition Science at the New York Academy of Sciences: *Fulfilling Every Child's Potential Through Integrated Nutrition and Early Childhood Development Interventions: A Call to Action and Policy Brief*, 2015.

Save the Children: *The Lottery of Birth: Giving All Children an Equal Chance to Survive*, 2015; *Ending Newborn Deaths: Ensuring Every Baby Survives*, 2014; *Superfood for Babies: How Overcoming Barriers to Breastfeeding Will Save Children's Lives*, 2013; *Surviving the First Day: State of the World's Mothers 2013*; *Food for Thought: Tackling Child Nutrition to Unlock Potential and Boost Prosperity*, 2013; *Nutrition in the First 1,000 Days: State of the World's Mothers 2012*.

Thomson Reuters StreetEvents: Mead Johnson Nutrition, Consumer Analyst Group of New York Conference, 2014; Mead Johnson Nutrition, Consumer Analyst Group of New York Conference, 2015.

United Nations Children's Fund (UNICEF): *Progress for Children: Beyond Averages—Learning from the MDGs*, 2015; *Improving Child Nutrition: The Achievable Imperative for Global Progress*, 2013.

US Centers for Disease Control and Prevention: *Breastfeeding Report Card: United States 2013*; *Breastfeeding Report Card: United States 2014*.

US Department of Health and Human Services: *The Surgeon General's Call to Action to Support Breastfeeding*, 2011.

World Bank: *Repositioning Nutrition as Central to Development: A Strategy for Large-Scale Action*, 2006; Dean Spears, *How Much International Variation in Child Height Can Sanitation Explain?*, 2013.

World Health Organization: *Country Implementation of the International Code of Marketing of Breast-Milk Substitutes: Status Report 2011*.

World Health Organization and UNICEF: *Water, Sanitation and Hygiene in Health Care Facilities*, 2015; *Twenty-Five Years Progress on Sanitation and Drinking Water: 2015 Update and MDG Assessment*.

BOOKS

Fischer, Edward F., and Peter Benson. *Broccoli & Desire: Global Connections and Maya Struggles in Postwar Guatemala*. Stanford, CA: Stanford University Press, 2006.

Mander, Harsh. *Ash in the Belly: India's Unfinished Battle Against Hunger*. New Delhi: Penguin Books New Delhi, 2012.

Murkoff, Heidi. *What to Expect: Eating Well When You're Expecting*. New York: Workman, 2005.

Suskind, Dana. *Thirty Million Words: Building a Child's Brain*. New York: Dutton, 2015.

LYRICS

"Dale Pecho" and "Dale Comidita": Anibal Coro, composer, and Internacionales Conejos, performers.

"Hot Cheetos & Takis": Y.N.RichKids, artists, and Beats and Rhymes, program.

Rwanda High-Iron Bean song: various Rwandan artists, including King James, Miss Jojo, Riderman, Tom Close, and Urban Boyz. See "Afro-Pop Music Video on Healthy Eating," www.youtube.com/watch?v=fo6449Rd3I0. Courtesy of HarvestPlus.

OTHER RESEARCH MATERIAL on the 1,000 days can be found at my website, www.outrageandinspire.org, and also at the 1,000 Days movement website, http://thousanddays.org.

INDEX

ROGER THUROW is a Senior Fellow for Global Agriculture and Food Policy at the Chicago Council on Global Affairs. He was a reporter at the *Wall Street Journal* for thirty years, twenty of them as a foreign correspondent. He is, with Scott Kilman, the author of *Enough: Why the World's Poorest Starve in an Age of Plenty*, which won the Harry Chapin Why Hunger book award and was a finalist for the Dayton Literary Peace Prize and for the New York Public Library Helen Bernstein Book Award; and the author of *The Last Hunger Season: A Year in an African Farm Community on the Brink of Change*. He is a 2009 recipient of the Action Against Hunger Humanitarian Award. He lives in Washington, DC.

PublicAffairs is a publishing house founded in 1997. It is a tribute to the standards, values, and flair of three persons who have served as mentors to countless reporters, writers, editors, and book people of all kinds, including me.

I. F. STONE, proprietor of *I. F. Stone's Weekly*, combined a commitment to the First Amendment with entrepreneurial zeal and reporting skill and became one of the great independent journalists in American history. At the age of eighty, Izzy published *The Trial of Socrates*, which was a national bestseller. He wrote the book after he taught himself ancient Greek.

BENJAMIN C. BRADLEE was for nearly thirty years the charismatic editorial leader of *The Washington Post*. It was Ben who gave the *Post* the range and courage to pursue such historic issues as Watergate. He supported his reporters with a tenacity that made them fearless and it is no accident that so many became authors of influential, best-selling books.

ROBERT L. BERNSTEIN, the chief executive of Random House for more than a quarter century, guided one of the nation's premier publishing houses. Bob was personally responsible for many books of political dissent and argument that challenged tyranny around the globe. He is also the founder and longtime chair of Human Rights Watch, one of the most respected human rights organizations in the world.

•   •   •

For fifty years, the banner of Public Affairs Press was carried by its owner Morris B. Schnapper, who published Gandhi, Nasser, Toynbee, Truman, and about 1,500 other authors. In 1983, Schnapper was described by *The Washington Post* as "a redoubtable gadfly." His legacy will endure in the books to come.

Peter Osnos, *Founder and Editor-at-Large*